KU-529-669

ACADEMIC
ENCOUNTERS

LIFE IN SOCIETY

Property of
Effective Learning Services
Queen Margaret University

ACADEMIC ENCOUNTERS

The *Academic Encounters* series uses authentic materials and a sustained content approach to teach students the academic skills they need to take college courses in English. There are two books in the series for each content focus: an *Academic Encounters* title and an *Academic Listening Encounters* title. As the series continues to grow, books at different levels and with different content area concentrations will be added. Please consult your catalog or contact your local sales representative for a current list of available titles.

Titles in the *Academic Encounters* series at publication:

Content Focus and Level	Components	*Academic Encounters*	*Academic Listening Encounters*
HUMAN BEHAVIOR High Intermediate to Low Advanced	Student's Book Teacher's Manual Audio Cassettes Audio CDs	ISBN 0 521 47658 5 ISBN 0 521 47660 7	ISBN 0 521 57821 3 ISBN 0 521 57820 5 ISBN 0 521 57819 1 ISBN 0 521 78357 7
LIFE IN SOCIETY Intermediate to High Intermediate	Student's Book Teacher's Manual Audio Cassettes Audio CDs	ISBN 0 521 66616 3 ISBN 0 521 66613 9	forthcoming forthcoming forthcoming forthcoming

ACADEMIC
ENCOUNTERS
LIFE IN SOCIETY

Reading
Study Skills
Writing

Kristine Brown
& Susan Hood

Intermediate to High Intermediate

PUBLISHED BY THE PRESS SYNDICATE OF THE UNIVERSITY OF CAMBRIDGE
The Pitt Building, Trumpington Street, Cambridge, United Kingdom

CAMBRIDGE UNIVERSITY PRESS
The Edinburgh Building, Cambridge CB2 2RU, UK
40 West 20th Street, New York, NY 10011-4211, USA
477 Williamstown Road, Port Melbourne, VIC 3207, Australia
Ruiz de Alarcón 13, 28014 Madrid, Spain
Dock House, The Waterfront, Cape Town 8001, South Africa

http://www.cambridge.org

© Cambridge University Press 2002

This book is in copyright. Subject to statutory exception
and to the provisions of relevant collective licensing agreements,
no reproduction of any part may take place without
the written permission of Cambridge University Press.

First published 2002

Printed in United States of America
Typeset in New Aster and Frutiger

A catalog record for this book is available from the British Library

Library of Congress Cataloging in Publication data
Brown, Kristine
    Academic encounters: reading, study skills, and writing / Kristine Brown & Susan Hood.
    p. cm.
    ISBN 0-521-66616-3
    1. English language – Textbooks for foreign speakers. 2. English language – Rhetoric –
    Problems, exercises, etc. 3. Academic writing –Problems, exercises, etc. 4. Study Skills –
    Problems, exercises, etc. 5. College readers. I. Hood, Susan II. Title

    PE1128 .B727 2002
    428.2'4 – dc21   2002024639

Book design: Adventure House, NYC
Art direction, production management, and layout services: GTS Graphics, Los Angeles, CA
Cover illustration: Private Collection/Diana Ong/Superstock
Illustrations: Charlene Potts and Randy Lyhaus

See credits on page 237, which is an extension of this copyright page.

Unit 1 Belonging to a Group 1

Chapter 4 | Gender Issues Today

Authors' Acknowledgments

We would like to thank Cambridge staff both in the U.K. and in the U.S. for their support in development and publication of this book. The original concept for a sociology-based text aimed at building academic reading and writing skills was supported by Jeanne McCarten in the U.K. Jeanne recognized from the early chapters how well it would fit with *Academic Encounters: Human Behavior*, the psychology-based text by Bernard Seal. And so commenced a happy partnership with Bernard and the New York office in the production of another text in the *Academic Encounters* series. We would especially like to thank Bernard for his early guidance and of course for providing an excellent model in *Academic Encounters: Human Behavior*, and Jane Mairs for her constant guard over the project. We are also grateful to Mary Vaughn for her continued support, and to Nada Gordon and Kathleen Ossip for editing and research work along the way, and to Donna Lee Braunstein for her meticulous work in checking all references and seeking out permissions. We reserve special thanks for Kathleen O'Reilly whose energy and enthusiasm for the book have been so greatly appreciated in the later stages.

There are of course numerous others who have helped us in various ways, at different times and in different places. These include colleagues who have provided sounding boards for our ideas and who have piloted sections of the book and given us feedback. We would especially like to thank Rod Gardner at the University of New South Wales, and Gail Forey, Sima Sengupta, and Carol McLennan at the Hong Kong Polytechnic University. We also thank students in the Masters in TESOL program at UNSW and in the Masters in English Language Teaching at the Hong Kong Polytechnic University for many stimulating discussions and practical ideas.

Our on-going interest in reading pedagogy was fueled many years ago as colleagues in literacy programs in the Adult Migrant English Service in Australia, and we would like to acknowledge here the debt we owe to the many outstanding teachers we were able to work and write with in that institution.

On a personal front we are indebted to our close friends, partners, and children for their constant support and encouragement – so special thanks to Nicky Solomon, Jim Martin, and Phoebe, Hamish and Conal, and to John, William, Hannah, and Hamish McLean.

Kristine Brown
Susan Hood

Introduction

To The Instructor

ABOUT THIS BOOK

Academic Encounters: Life in Society is a reading, study skills, and writing text based on material taken from sociology textbooks used in North American community colleges and universities. The student who will benefit most from this course will be at the intermediate to high-intermediate level. This student may well be encountering academic text in English for the first time. However, the readings are short enough and the tasks sufficiently well scaffolded to allow a student at this level to access the texts successfully.

ABOUT THE ACADEMIC ENCOUNTERS SERIES

This content-based series is for non-native speakers of English preparing to study in English at the community college or university level and for native speakers of English who need to improve their academic skills for further study. The series consists of *Academic Encounters* books that help students improve their reading, study skills, and writing, and *Academic Listening Encounters* books that help students improve their listening, note-taking, and discussion skills. Each reading book corresponds in theme to a listening book, and each pair of theme-linked books focuses on an academic subject commonly taught in North American universities and community colleges. For example, *Academic Encounters: Life in Society* and *Academic Listening Encounters: Life in Society* both focus on sociology, and *Academic Encounters: Human Behavior* and *Academic Listening Encounters: Human Behavior* both focus on psychology and human communications. A reading book and a listening book with the same content focus may be used together to teach a complete four-skills course in English for Academic Purposes.

ACADEMIC ENCOUNTERS READING, STUDY SKILLS, AND WRITING BOOKS
The approach

In the *Academic Encounters* Reading, Study Skills, and Writing books, students are presented with authentic samples of academic text. The material has been abridged and occasionally reorganized, but on the sentence level, little of the language has been changed. Students study these texts to develop their reading and study skills. The high-interest content of the texts also provides stimulus for student writing assignments.

The content

The fact that each book has a unified thematic content throughout has several advantages. First, it gives the students a realistic sense of studying a course in college, in which each week's assignments are related to and build on each other. Second, as language and concepts recur, the students begin to feel that the readings are getting easier, building their confidence as readers of academic text. Finally, after studying an *Academic Encounters* book, some students may feel that they have enough background in the content focus area to actually take a course in that subject (e.g., sociology) to fulfill part of their general education requirements.

The skills

The main goal of the *Academic Encounters* Reading, Study Skills, and Writing books is to give students the skills and the confidence to approach a piece of academic text, read it efficiently and critically, and extract the main ideas and key details. But the goal of academic reading is not just to retrieve information. It is also important for a student to be able to display that knowledge in a test-taking situation. For this reason, students are taught highlighting, note taking, and test-preparation skills. An additional goal is the development of students' academic writing. Writing, reading, and study skills are developed in tasks that accompany each reading and that appear in two separate sections: "Preparing to Read" and "After You Read."

The format

Each Reading, Study Skills, and Writing book consists of five units on different aspects of the book's content focus. Units are divided into two chapters, with four readings in each chapter. Each reading is one to four pages long.

Preparing to Read

Each reading is preceded by a one-page section of prereading tasks called "Preparing to Read." Prereading is heavily emphasized since it is regarded as a crucial step in the reading process. Some of the prereading activities teach students how to quickly get a good overall idea of the content. Students learn to skim for main ideas and to survey the text for headings, graphic material, and terms in boldface, all of which can provide important content clues. Another type of prereading task has students think about the topic of the reading, predict its content, and recall their prior knowledge and personal experiences to help them assimilate the new information they are about to encounter in the reading.

After You Read

Each reading is followed by a variety of postreading tasks in a section called "After You Read." Some of these tasks ask students to demonstrate their understanding of the text, either by answering reading comprehension questions or by doing an activity such as drawing a graph or performing a roleplay. Other tasks ask students to reflect on the content and deepen their understanding of the text by personalizing the information. Some tasks ask students to analyze the structure of the text, looking for main ideas, supporting details, and authorial commentary. There are language tasks which focus on vocabulary or on some of the salient grammatical features of the text. Students learn how to highlight a text, take notes in the margins and in a notebook, and practice test-taking skills. The rich variety of tasks and task types allows students to experiment with different study-skill strategies and to discover their learning-style preferences.

Writing

There are plentiful and varied opportunities in Reading, Study Skills, and Writing books for students to practice their writing skills. Students write essays, text summaries, and journal entries, as well as short answers to test questions. At the same time, as students continually read and analyze academic English, they begin to acquire insight into its organization and style, and their own writing begins to develop a more academic tone.

Task pages and text pages

Task pages are clearly differentiated from text pages by a colored vertical bar that runs along the outside edge of the page. The task pages contain the activities that students are asked to do either before or after reading the text. Tasks and texts never occur on the same page, and the text pages have been designed to look like authentic college textbook pages. This helps to create a sense for students that they are actually reading from an academic textbook. The readings and tasks have been carefully laid out so that each new reading begins on a right-hand page, opposite a one-page "Preparing to Read" section. These design features make the book easy to use.

Task commentary boxes

When a task type occurs for the first time in the book, it is headed by a colored commentary box that explains what skill is being practiced and why it is important. When the task occurs again later in the book, it may be accompanied by another commentary box, either as a reminder or to present new information about the skill. At the back of the book, there is an alphabetized index of all the tasks. Page references in boldface indicate tasks that are headed by commentary boxes.

Opportunities for student interaction

Many of the tasks in *Academic Encounters* are divided into steps. Some of these steps are to be done by the student working alone, others by students in pairs or in small groups, still others by the teacher with the whole class. To make the book as lively as possible, student interaction has been built into most activities. Thus, although the books focus on reading, study skills, and writing, speaking activities abound. Students discuss the content of the texts before and after reading them; they often work collaboratively to solve task problems; they perform role play activities, and they frequently compare answers in pairs or small groups.

Order of units

The units do not have to be taught in the order in which they appear in the book, although this order is recommended. To a certain extent, tasks do build upon each other so that, for example, a note-taking task later in the book may draw upon information that has been offered in an earlier unit. Teachers who want to teach the units out of order, however, may do so. They can use the task index at the back of the book to see what information has been presented in earlier units and build that information into their lessons. In terms of reading topics, also, the order of units is regarded as optimal, although teachers may use them out of order if they wish.

Course length

Each of the five units of a Reading, Study Skills, and Writing book contains a unit preview section and eight readings, and represents approximately 16-20 hours of classroom material. An *Academic Encounters* book could thus be a suitable course book for a 64- to 80-hour course (when a teacher selects four of the five units) or an 80- to 100-hour course (when all the units are used). The course can, however, be made shorter or longer. To shorten the course, teachers might choose not to do every task in the book and to assign some tasks and texts as homework, rather than do them in class. To lengthen the course, teachers might choose to supplement the book with some content-related material from their own files and to spend more time developing students' writing skills.

To The Student

Welcome to *Academic Encounters: Life in Society*. In this book, you will encounter readings that have been taken from sociology textbooks used in regular North American university or community college courses. *Academic Encounters: Life in Society* will teach you how to become a more efficient and competent reader of such texts and provide you with the study skills that you will need to be successful in an American college classroom.

Texts that appear in college textbooks are different from other types of texts that you may have read in English. They are organized differently and are written in a distinctive style. Since a great deal of effort has gone into making the texts in *Life in Society* look and read exactly as they might in an academic textbook, by studying this book you will have an excellent opportunity to become familiar with the special features and style of academic text.

The approach in *Academic Encounters* may be different from what you are used to. First, you are asked to try to master the subject matter, as if you were studying in a regular university course. Then, after having studied the texts and having read them critically, you are taught the skills that would allow you to retrieve the information you have learned in a test-taking situation. For example, you are taught highlighting, note taking, and test-preparation skills.

Although the primary emphasis in the book is on reading and study skills, there are also opportunities to study the language of the texts. It is particularly important as you get ready to study in an English-speaking university that you broaden your vocabulary, and many of the activities are designed to help you do so. Sometimes, too, the focus of instruction is on a grammatical structure that occurs commonly in academic text.

There are also plentiful opportunities in *Life in Society* for you to practice your academic writing skills. You will find that by continually reading and studying academic English your own academic writing will improve. As you become more and more familiar with academic texts, how they are organized, and the language in which they are written, you will find yourself naturally beginning to adopt a more academic writing style of your own.

The topics in this book all come from the academic discipline of sociology. One effect of studying subject matter that comes only from one field is that you will build up a lot of new knowledge in this area. After using this book, you may feel that you have had enough background information in the subject matter to go on and take an introductory course in sociology to fulfill part of your general education requirements. Or, perhaps you will have gained the knowledge and confidence to do so at some future date.

Finally, we hope that you find this book to be not only useful, but enjoyable. The topics have all been chosen for their high interest, and you will have many opportunities to discuss them with your classmates. It is important to remember in all your studies that the most successful learning takes place when you enjoy what you are studying and find it interesting.

ACADEMIC ENCOUNTERS

LIFE IN SOCIETY

Belonging to a Group

In this unit we look at the different ways in which human beings are part of larger groups. In Chapter 1, we focus on families – the different types of families and households that can be found in U.S. society, and their importance in developing our social skills and behaviors. In Chapter 2, we look beyond the family. First, we examine the role of culture in general, and then we look at one very influential group within most cultures: the peer group. We also look at an example of collective or group behavior – the behavior of people when they are part of a crowd.

Previewing the unit

Before reading a unit (or chapter) of a textbook, it is a good idea to preview the contents page and think about the topics that will be covered. This will give you an overview of how the unit is organized and what it is going to be about.

Read the contents page for Unit 1 and do the following activities.

Chapter 1: Marriage, Family, and the Home

1 The first two sections of Chapter 1 look at different types of families and households. Work with a partner and explain what each of the following terms probably means:

- two-career families
- single-parent families
- stepfamilies
- living together (cohabitation)
- communal living
- child-free marriages

2 Sections 3 and 4 of this chapter focus on how children learn to take their part in society. Write down 5–10 things that are considered to be good behavior for children in your country (for example, saying "thank you" when they are given something). Then discuss the following question with your classmates:

How do people in your country generally try to teach these behaviors?

Chapter 2: The Power of the Group

1 In Chapter 2 we look at what influences people's social behavior. Look at these pictures and discuss the following question with your classmates:

How likely are you to see people doing these things in your country?

2 In this chapter, we learn that people belong to many different social groups besides their families. Make a list of the different social groups to which you belong (for example, sports team, school, neighborhood).

Unit
Contents

Preparing to read

THINKING ABOUT THE TOPIC

> Thinking about the topic before you read can make a text easier to understand.

Discuss the following with your classmates:

> Is the family group in the photograph above typical of families in your country? Why or why not? If not, what is typical?

EXAMINING GRAPHIC MATERIAL

> Before reading a text, it is helpful to look at any graphs, tables (sometimes called charts), or diagrams. This will give you an idea of the content of the text.

Look at the graphs in this text (Figures 1.1 to 1.3) and read the words that explain them. Which graph is about

_____ **a** single-parent families?

_____ **b** never-married women with children?

_____ **c** married women who work?

Now read

Now read the text "The Family Today." When you finish, turn to the tasks on page 7.

Marriage, Family, and the Home

1 THE FAMILY TODAY

The traditional image of the average family in the United States shows Mom taking care of her two kids and a house in the suburbs while Dad drives off to work. In fact, such a family is relatively rare today, both in the United States and in many other countries. Meanwhile, new forms of the family unit have become increasingly common.

Two-career families

Where a family does consist of husband, wife, and children, it is less and less common for the wife to stay at home. Recently in the United States, there has been a tremendous increase in the numbers of married women who work outside the home – from 32 percent in 1960 to 62 percent in 1998 (see Figure 1.1).

The employment of married women has increased family income significantly, but research indicates that this economic gain does not necessarily bring happiness. Where husbands fully support their wives' employment by doing their share of cleaning and child care, the couples are usually happy in their marriages (Cooper et al. 1986). Where husbands expect their wives to do all the housework as well as their jobs, there is frequently conflict (Skinner 1980).

1

2

3

two-career families
families where both parents work

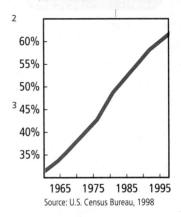

Source: U.S. Census Bureau, 1998

Figure 1.1 Percentage of married women in the workforce.

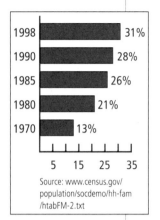

Figure 1.2 Percentage of single-parent families.

stepfamilies

families where one of the parents is not the biological parent of at least one of the children in the household

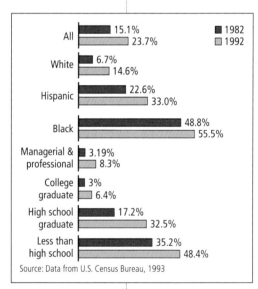

Figure 1.3 Percentage of never-married women aged 18 to 44 who have children.

Single-parent families

With increased divorce, there has been a huge rise in the number of children growing up in households with just one parent. From 1970 to 1998, the proportion of single-parent families in the United States more than doubled – increasing from 13 to 31 percent (U.S. Census Bureau 1998). A large majority (82 percent) of such families are headed by women. It has been estimated that more than half of all children born today live for some time with only their mothers before they reach age 18 (Strong and DeVault 1992; U.S. Census Bureau 1998).

Most of these families live below or near the poverty level. Compared with two-parent families, female-headed families are more likely to experience unemployment, lack of social support, problems at school, and so on. These problems do not result from the absence of a father but from factors that can also affect two-parent families, for example, low income and poor living conditions.

Another factor in the rise of single-parent families is the increase in the number of never-married women having children. In 1982, 15.1 percent of never-married women between 18 and 44 had children. In 1992, the figure was 23.7 percent.

Stepfamilies

Because of the high rates of divorce and remarriage, stepfamilies have also become quite common. They number some 7.3 million and account for 16 percent of all married couples with children under age 18. Because women usually win custody (that is, care and guardianship) of children in divorce cases, most stepfamilies consist of mothers, their biological children, and stepfathers.

The happiness of stepfamilies depends largely on how well the stepfather gets along with the children. It can be difficult to be a stepfather. Stepfathers are likely to have problems with discipline. If a stepfather tells his 12-year-old stepson that he should not watch an R-rated movie, he may reply: "My dad lets me watch them. Besides, it's Mom's television set" (Nordheimer 1990).

Conflicts are most likely with teenagers. Teenagers are trying hard to break free of adult control. They may accept parental discipline only out of love and respect, which they may not have for their stepfathers. During an argument, teenagers are likely to shout at their stepfathers: "You're not my real father!" While most families are relatively free of serious problems, conflict with stepchildren is one of the main reasons that second marriages fail at a higher rate than first marriages (Nordheimer 1990; Strong and DeVault 1992).

After you read

Task 1 READING FOR THE MAIN IDEA

> Understanding the main idea of the whole text is an important reading skill in college. Two strategies that will help you identify the main idea of a text are:
>
> - reading the introductory paragraph of the text
> - paying attention to the headings used to organize the text

Re-read the introductory paragraph (par. 1) and headings of "The Family Today." Read sentences **a–d** below. Then choose the sentence that best states the main idea of the text.

a In the United States, the number of traditional family units is decreasing and new forms of family units are becoming more common.

b In the United States, traditional families do not have the problems that other types of family units do.

c Stepfamilies are increasingly common in the United States, but are likely to have many problems.

d Two-career families, single-parent families, and stepfamilies are the main types of family units in the United States.

Task 2 BUILDING VOCABULARY: DEALING WITH UNKNOWN WORDS

> It is important to develop strategies for dealing with difficult or unfamiliar vocabulary in the texts you read. Strategies you might use are:
>
> - finding the definition within the text
> - looking at the context (that is, the words and sentences that come before and after the unknown word) for clues to the word's meaning
> - using knowledge of a related word

1 Find these words in the text. Decide which strategies to use for each word, and write a brief definition next to each one.

Word	Definition
significantly (par. 3)	*a lot*
conflict (par. 3)	
households (par. 4)	
poverty (par. 6)	
custody (par. 8)	
discipline (par. 9)	

2 Discuss the meanings of the words with your classmates. Compare the different strategies you used.

Task 3 LANGUAGE FOCUS: WRITING ABOUT CHANGES

College textbooks often include texts (like this one) about changes over a period of time. Some common ways to describe changes over time are shown in the tables below:

has become/became	less (and less) somewhat relatively fairly increasingly more (and more) quite	common frequent rare unusual

there has been a / there was a	tremendous huge significant	increase decrease rise	in

(has) increased (has) decreased has gone up (or down) / went up (or down)	greatly significantly a little by a small / large amount

(has) almost (has) more than	halved doubled tripled

1 Find examples of some of these language patterns in the text.

2 Use the language patterns to write two to three sentences about each of the graphs in the text. Do not copy sentences from the text. Compare your sentences with a partner.

The percentage of married women in the workforce almost doubled between 1960 and 1998. (Figure 1.1)

Task 4 READING ACTIVELY

> When you read you should be doing more than simply taking in the words on the page. To understand a text well and to remember what you have read, you need to read actively – that is, constantly think and ask questions about what you are reading.

1 Re-read these paragraphs from the text, and read the questions in the thought bubbles. Discuss the answers to the questions with your classmates.

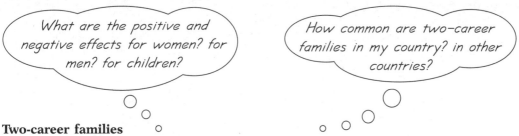

Two-career families

Where a family does consist of husband, wife, and children, it is less and less common for the wife to stay at home. Recently in the United States, there has been a tremendous increase in the number of married women who work outside the home – from 32 percent in 1960 to 62 percent in 1998.

The employment of married women has increased family income significantly, but research indicates that this economic gain does not necessarily bring happiness. Where husbands fully support their wives' employment by doing their share of cleaning and child care, the couples are usually happy in their marriages (Cooper et al. 1986). Where husbands expect their wives to do all the housework as well as their jobs, there is frequently conflict (Skinner 1980).

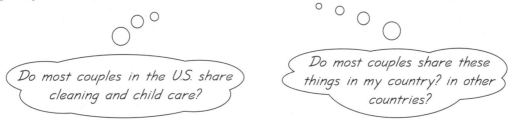

2 Choose one other part of the text to re-read, for example:

- Single-parent families
- Never-married women who are having children
- Stepfamilies

Discuss the following questions with your classmates:

1 Are these family groups becoming more common in your country?
2 What do you think about these changes in family groups (in the United States or your own country)?

Preparing to read

The text "Alternative Lifestyles" examines many different ways of life that can be found in the United States. Discuss the following questions with your classmates:

1 How acceptable are these ways of life in your country?

- a man and a woman living together without getting married
- a man or a woman living alone and never getting married
- a group of people living together who are not related, but who share interests and beliefs
- people marrying two or three times during their lifetime

2 How common do you think these living arrangements are in the United States?

SKIMMING

Skimming a text before you read it will make the text easier to understand. Skimming means looking quickly over a text to get an idea of what it is about and of how it is organized. You should not read every word. Instead, you should look at headings, pictures, graphs, and highlighted words. It is also a good idea to read the introduction and the first sentence of each paragraph.

1 Give yourself one minute to skim the text "Alternative Lifestyles." Without looking back, write down the headings you saw.

2 Give yourself another minute to skim the text. Without looking back, write down some key words you remember.

3 Re-read the introduction to the text (par. 1) and then check (✔) the statement that best describes how the introduction relates to the text.

_____ **a** It gives an example of something explained in the text.

_____ **b** It links the reader's own experiences to the text.

_____ **c** It asks questions that will be answered by the text.

_____ **d** It tells you how the text will be organized.

Now read

Now read the text "Alternative Lifestyles." When you finish, turn to the tasks on page 13.

2 ALTERNATIVE LIFESTYLES

Joe and Anna are both in their mid-twenties. They met and fell in love [1] two years ago and soon after decided to live together. They have thought about getting married but have no plans to do this just yet. They think they would like to have children one day, but want to be sure they get along well as a couple before taking this big step.

Living together

Many couples in the United States today, like Joe and Anna, choose to [2] live together without marrying. In the past, very few couples lived together without a formal wedding ceremony or marriage license. Today, **cohabitation** occurs in all sectors of U.S. society – college students, young working adults, middle-aged couples, and even people in their sixties and seventies. In 1970, the number of unmarried couples living together was only slightly over half a million. By 1998, it had soared to over 4 million (U.S. Census Bureau 1999). A similar trend has occurred in many countries.

cohabitation
when an unmarried couple
live together as if married

These days there is very little social disapproval of living together, [3] and courts increasingly protect couples' rights as if they were legally married (Lewin 1982; Bumpass and Sweet 1989; Steinhauer 1995). Nevertheless, it is still quite rare for couples to live together permanently without marrying. For most couples, living together is a temporary arrangement that leads to marriage after two or three years.

Living together is just one example of the many alternative lifestyles [4] found in the United States and other parts of the world today. Others include staying single, and living with a large group of other adults and their families.

Staying single

Over the last twenty years, there has been a huge increase in the number [5] of people who remain single. In 1998, about 25 percent of all U.S. households were single-person households. In other countries, similar statistics can be seen. In Australia, for example, approximately one in twelve people lives alone, and this number is expected to double over the next twenty years. Most people who live alone are young adults who postpone marriage into their late twenties, but some are in their thirties and forties. One reason they often give for staying single is that they have not met the right person. Others say that marriage involves too much commitment and responsibility, or that they prefer the single lifestyle.

There are two important sociological reasons for the increase in sin- [6] glehood. First, the social pressure to get married has declined. Second, the opportunity for singles to have a good life has expanded. This is especially true for women. As educational and employment opportunities for women increase, marriage is no longer the only path to economic security, emotional support, social respectability, and meaningful work.

Communal living

7

Sometimes a group of people who are not related, but who share similar ideals and interests, decide to live together as one unit or community. In these types of communities, sometimes called **communes,** the members share their possessions and their skills in order to be independent of mainstream society. Many, for example, grow all their own food and educate their children in their own small schools. It is difficult to estimate how many communes exist in the United States or other countries around the world, but the Fellowship for Intentional Communities estimates there are thousands. More than 600 of these are registered members of their organization. While these vary in type and size, all are based on a principle of cooperation among members.

8

The concept of communal living is now being applied to some city housing projects. In **cohousing,** buildings are designed so that residents can really live as part of a community while keeping their own personal space. In one project in Sacramento, California, residents have their own private areas but share a garden, a dining room, a children's playroom, a laundry, and lounge. They take turns cooking three common meals a week, and in many ways behave like one big family – sharing their possessions and helping each other out when needed (Harrison 1999).

communes

where a group of people who share similar ideals, beliefs, and interests live together as one community

cohousing

housing projects where buildings are designed to encourage social contact while preserving private space

Members of a commune cook together.

Monogamy, polygamy, and serial monogamy

There are two major types of marriages: monogamy and polygamy. In *monogamy,* one wife and one husband have an exclusive sexual relationship. In *polygamy,* a person has more than one spouse, (usually the husband has more than one wife). Monogamy is the only legal type of marriage in the United States and most other nations. Polygamy is still legal in some parts of the world, especially Africa and the Middle East, although it is declining in both regions.

Some people have only one husband or wife at a time, but marry, divorce, and remarry a number of times. This is sometimes called *serial monogamy.* The famous actress, Elizabeth Taylor, who has had seven husbands, is an example of a serial monogamist.

Elizabeth Taylor is seen here with her 7th husband.

After you read

Task 1 READING BOXED TEXTS

Many academic textbooks include boxed texts. Their purpose varies.
They can do the following:

- give an interesting example of an idea in the main text
- describe a research study
- give some detailed statistics
- give a definition or definitions
- ask you to apply ideas to your own life

Whatever the purpose, these boxed texts usually contain high-interest
material that will add to your understanding of the main text.

1 Read the boxed section at the end of this text again.

2 Discuss its purpose with a small group. Does it match one of the purposes
mentioned above?

Task 2 BUILDING VOCABULARY: USING KNOWLEDGE OF RELATED WORDS

One way to figure out the meaning of an unknown word is to look for
its relationship with other words in the same word family. Even if you
cannot figure out the exact meaning, your understanding can be
enough to allow you to read on. For example, in paragraph 2 of the
text, you can get an idea of the meaning of the word *sector* by recognizing that it is related to the word *section*.

1 Look at the phrases from the text below. Write down at least one other word you
know that is related to the underlined word.

in order to be <u>independent</u>	*depend*
<u>formal</u> wedding ceremony	
there are two important <u>sociological</u> reasons	
share similar <u>ideals</u>	
of <u>mainstream</u> society	
is sometimes called <u>serial</u> monogamy	

2 Try to figure out the meanings of the underlined words. Use your dictionary to
check your answers.

Task 3 NOTE TAKING

> When you take notes, it is important not to write down everything. You should only write down the main points and important details or examples. You should also try to abbreviate (shorten) words (for example, incr = increase).

1 Look at these notes taken from the subsection "Living together."

Living together
- great incr in last 20 years
- all sectors of soc
- 1970, 1/2 m
- 1994, 4 m
- reasons for incr – soc approval & protect'n of couple's rights as if married

2 Complete these notes taken from the subsection "Staying single."

Staying single

- huge incr in last 20 yrs
- 1998, _____ lived alone – _____ of all households
- most _____
- reasons given – _____

  _____
- 2 sociological reasons – 1) _____, 2) opps for singles to have good life incr'd esp for women

3 Use the note-taking models in steps 1 and 2 above to write your own notes for the subsection "Communal living."

Task 4 TEST TAKING: PREPARING FOR A SHORT-ANSWER QUIZ

> One of the best ways to prepare for a short-answer quiz is to make up some questions that you think you will be asked. Short-answer quizzes usually include three types of questions.
>
> - Type 1: questions about the data (that is, the information and ideas in the text) – *who, what, when, where,* and *how* questions.
> - Type 2: questions that ask you to look more closely at the data – to find relationships between different parts of the data, to compare and contrast, to analyze, and so on.
> - Type 3: questions that ask you to think critically about what you have read – to evaluate or assess the data, and to justify your answer.

1 Work with a partner. Answer the following questions about the "Living together" subsection of the text:

1 What is the meaning of *cohabitation*?
2 Why are more people living together these days without marrying?
3 Do you think that marriage will soon be a thing of the past? Why or why not?

2 With your partner, read each question again and decide if it is Type 1, 2, or 3.

3 You and your partner each write two or three questions about the rest of the text (any type).

4 Exchange your questions with your partner, and answer each other's questions orally.

5 In step 1 you were asked if you think that marriage will soon be a thing of the past. Discuss your opinion with the class, using evidence from the text and from your own experience to justify your answer.

6 Discuss your opinions on any other Type 3 questions that your classmates wrote in step 3.

Preparing to read

> Trying to predict what information will be in a text before you read is a good habit. It can motivate you to read the text and help you start thinking about some of the language that you might find there. You can often predict the general content of a text by looking at its title and headings.

The title of the text on the next page is "How We Learn to Behave," and the headings are:

Rewards and punishments
Modeling
Differences across cultures

Without looking at the text, discuss with a partner the type of information you expect to find there. Then, skim the text to check your predictions.

PERSONALIZING THE TOPIC

> Thinking about your personal connection to a topic can help you take in new information about the topic. You should do this while you are reading as well as before you read.

Before reading the text "How We Learn to Behave," discuss with a small group what you would do if you were the parent in each of the situations below.

1 Your 5-year-old child hits another child without reason while playing. You have never seen him/her do this before.
2 Every night, your 4-year-old child refuses to go to bed.
3 Your 10-year-old child offers to help you clean up the house.
4 Your oldest child, a 16-year-old, has started smoking. You smoke, but do not want your children to smoke.
5 You want your 14-year-old to take care of your younger children when you are at work, but he/she complains, "It's not my job."

Now read

Now read the text "How We Learn to Behave." When you finish, turn to the tasks on page 19.

Many behaviors are learned in families.

3 HOW WE LEARN TO BEHAVE

- A woman turns off her cell phone as she enters a movie theater.
- A driver eats a candy bar and puts the paper wrapper in the ashtray.
- A couple decides to have a baby.

1

Being polite, neat, and family-oriented are characteristics of the well-socialized American. **Socialization** is the process of learning how to behave in the society we live in. For societies to exist, there must be some organized way of teaching the members what is expected of them and how they are to behave. Through socialization, the infant develops into a person like one of those described above.

2

socialization

the process of learning what to expect and how to behave in the society the individual lives in

Every society tries to socialize its members. The task is performed by several groups and institutions (called *socializing agents*). The family, the school, and the peer group (that is, people of the same age) are the most important socializing agents. Of these, the family is the most important, especially during the first few years of life. A review of various studies of families has concluded that warm, supportive, moderately strict family environments usually produce happy and well-behaved children; and that cold, rigid, and overly strict families tend to cause youngsters to become rebellious, resentful, and insecure (Gecas 1981).

3

How, then, do families and other socializing agents teach children how to behave? Two important ways are by sanctions (rewards and punishments) and by modeling.

4

Rewards and punishments

Sanctions are consequences following a behavior that influence whether the behavior will be repeated. *Positive sanctions* mean that the behavior is followed by something that is a reward. If a child asks a parent "May I have some gum please?" and the parent gives the child some gum, the child learns that saying "please" at the end of a request results in getting

5

what he asked for. *Negative sanctions* (also known as punishments) mean that something bad happens after a behavior occurs. When a child says "Gimme some gum" and the parent says "No gum until you learn to ask politely" and does not give the child the gum, the child learns that it is not a good idea to speak this way because he does not get what he wants.

Modeling

Modeling refers to learning by watching the behavior of others – especially parents – and copying that behavior. Modeling influences both positive and negative behavior. For example, children who are respectful to elderly people have probably seen their parents do things such as helping older people onto trains and buses. On the other hand, children whose parents are alcoholics are more likely than other children to become alcoholics themselves. 6

Differences across cultures

It is easy to assume that every culture socializes children in the same way. Studies of other cultures, however, show that children are socialized differently depending on the culture they are brought up in. 7

A study of 6- to 11-year-old children in six farming communities in the United States, Kenya, Okinawa, northern India, the Philippines, and Mexico is a good example of these studies. Beatrice and John Whiting (1975) found a big difference between the types of household chores that children were expected to do in these cultures. More importantly, they found that parental expectations about work around the house were an important part of children's socialization. Where children were expected to take care of other younger children and do chores that helped the whole household (as in the Kenyan and Mexican communities studied), they quickly learned to be responsible and caring toward others. In communities like the one studied in the United States, where children were only expected to do chores such as cleaning their rooms and picking up toys, they were less likely to develop these traits at an early age. Of course, not every family in a particular culture socializes their children in exactly the same way – and this would be true of expectations about household chores also. Nevertheless, many cross-cultural differences in socialization have been identified by researchers. 8

Other evidence of these differences in socialization practices comes from a study of how traditional Vietnamese and Chinese socialize their children (Dillard 1987). In these families, the needs of the group are seen as more important than the needs of the individual, and so children learn that their first responsibility is to their parents rather than to themselves. For example, many children work hard at school so that their parents will be proud of them. 9

After you read

Task 1 LANGUAGE FOCUS: DEFINING

> Textbooks contain many definitions of words or expressions that have a special meaning within the field of study. These words or expressions are sometimes called *technical terms*. Understanding the structure of these definitions will make it easier to recognize them in texts and help you learn to define the terms you use in writing assignments.

1 Read the following examples from "How We Learn to Behave." Circle the term being defined and underline the words that link the term and its meaning.

1 (Socialization) is the process of learning how to behave in the society we live in.

2 Sanctions are consequences following a behavior that influence whether the behavior will be repeated.

3 Positive sanctions mean that the behavior is followed by something that is a reward.

4 Negative sanctions (also known as punishments) mean that something bad happens after a behavior occurs.

5 Modeling refers to learning by watching the behavior of others – especially parents – and copying that behavior.

2 Work with a partner. Discuss the meanings of these words from the text and write a one-sentence definition for each using some of the patterns in the sentences above.

socializing agents (par. 3)
peer group (par. 3)
household chores (par. 8)
cross-cultural differences (par. 8)

Task 2 BUILDING VOCABULARY: LEARNING WORDS RELATED TO THE TOPIC

> It is usually easier to remember words if we learn them as part of a group of related words. So it is a good idea to spend some time after you read a text finding words that you can group together for learning.

1 These words from the text describe different kinds of behavior: *polite, neat, well-behaved, rebellious, resentful, respectful, responsible, caring.*

Work with a partner. Write the words in the chart that follows to show which kinds of behavior are likely to lead to a positive sanction (a reward) and which to a negative sanction (a punishment). Use the context of the word in the text and a dictionary if necessary.

Positive sanction	Negative sanction
polite	*rebellious*

2 Add these other kinds of behavior to the chart: *kind, rude, cheerful, aggressive, obedient, disobedient, selfish, cruel.*

Task 3 SUMMARIZING

> Summarizing is an essential study skill. It means reducing a whole text to a few sentences. A good summary shows that you have understood what the text is about and what the most important points are. When you write a summary for your own purposes, you can freely use as many words from the text as you like. However, when you summarize in an essay, you should use your own words as much as possible.

The paragraph below summarizes the text "How We Learn to Behave." Fill in the missing words by looking back at the text.

Socialization is the ____*process*____ of learning how to behave in the society we live in. The job of socialization is performed by several groups called _____ _____. The family, the school, and the peer group are the most important socializing agents, and of these three, the _____ is the most important, especially in the early years. Two important ways that families and other socializing agents teach children to behave are _____ _____ and _____ _____. Sanctions are the _____ that follow a particular behavior and influence whether or not the behavior will be _____. Sanctions can be positive (_____) or negative (punishments). Modeling is learning by _____ the behavior of others – especially parents – and copying that behavior. Children are socialized differently depending on the _____ they are brought up in.

Task 4 APPLYING WHAT YOU READ

> Finding ways to apply new knowledge is a good way to deepen your understanding of new subject matter.

1 Read the following letters to a magazine advice column and discuss with the class what you would advise the parent to do.

- Would you advise a positive sanction?
- Would you advise a negative sanction?
- Do you think some behavior modeling might help, or do you have some other idea?

Letter 1

My 8-year-old son has never been in any trouble before, but just recently he has been getting into big trouble for swearing at school. I'm not sure what to do. My husband and I don't swear very much around the house, but of course, like many people, we do sometimes. My son is usually quite well-behaved, but he does not seem to take any notice of what I say about this. What should I do?

Letter 2

My 6-year-old daughter has been coming home with small toys that do not belong to her. When I ask her about them, she says that another child gave them to her. But it happens so much that I just cannot believe her. I feel I should punish her in some way, but I'm not sure if it would work and if it could even make the problem worse. What should I do?

Letter 3

My youngest child of four, a 3-year-old boy, has a terrible habit of throwing things at people who visit the house. Because people usually laugh at him when he does this, he thinks his behavior is amusing and keeps doing it. Of course, people usually try to be polite and laugh, but eventually they get upset. It is very embarrassing and I really don't know what to do. Can you help me?

2 Choose one letter and write a short letter of advice in reply.

Preparing to read

THINKING ABOUT THE TOPIC

1 Experts disagree about which is more important in determining the way we are –
what we inherit from our parents or what we learn from our social environment.
From the list below, which do you think you inherited from your parents, and
which do you think you learned from your social environment? Check (✔) the
appropriate column.

	Inherited from parents	Learned from the social environment
Temperament (for example, how easily you get angry, how calm you stay under stress)		
Personality (for example, how outspoken you are, how affectionate you are, your sense of humor)		
Health and fitness		
Mental ability or intelligence		
Sports ability		
Social skills (for example, how easily you get along with new people you meet)		
Attitudes about money and finance		
Attitudes about study and/or work		

2 Discuss your answers and your reasons with a small group. Give examples to
support your answers.

3 Now quickly skim the text and tell another student what you think the text is
about.

Now read

Now read the text "The Importance of the Social Environment." When you finish, turn
to the tasks on page 25.

4 THE IMPORTANCE OF THE SOCIAL ENVIRONMENT

The nature-nurture debate

The roles of *nature* (what we inherit) and of *nurture* (what we learn) in making us what we are have long been debated. In the seventeenth century it was generally believed that people became what they were taught to be. By the second half of the nineteenth century, a quite different view was popular. Instead of looking to nurture – what people are taught – to explain human behavior, many social scientists looked to nature – what people inherit from their parents. Opinion on the question has gone back and forth ever since.

Obviously we do inherit something of what makes us who we are. But what? Physical traits such as skin color are clearly inherited, but people also appear to inherit temperament – a natural tendency to behave and react in a certain way. For example, some people are naturally active, nervous, or easily annoyed. Others, brought up in a similar environment, tend to be the opposite – passive, calm, and rarely upset. The role of heredity in determining our **intelligence** and **aptitude** is less clear, and the debate is far from over.

What is clear is that, although nature may limit what we *can* achieve, socialization plays a very large role in determining what we *do* achieve. That is, whatever potential ability we inherit from our parents may be enhanced or restricted through socialization. Case studies of children who have not been cared for, and of children who have been stimulated to achieve at a high level, are evidence of the importance of social or environmental learning.

Children who are not cared for

Since the fourteenth century there have been more than fifty recorded cases of feral children. **Feral** children have supposedly been brought up by animals in the wild. One of the most famous is "the wild boy of Aveyron." In 1797, this boy was captured by hunters in the woods of southern France. He was about 11 years old and completely naked. The

1 The social environment is important in determining what an individual achieves.

2

intelligence
| the capacity for mental or intellectual achievement

3

aptitude
| the capacity for developing a skill

4

feral
| existing in a wild state

"wild boy" ran on his arms and legs, could not speak, and liked uncooked food. He could not do most of the simple things that younger children can usually do (Malson 1972; Lane 1976). He was obviously deprived of socialization.

There have been similar stories of social deprivation this century. Anna, for example, was born in 1932 in Pennsylvania to a young unwed mother. The father was outraged by the birth and did not want to have anything to do with the child. The mother tried to give Anna away but could not, so she hid her in the attic and gave her just enough food to keep her alive. Anna was neither touched nor talked to, neither washed nor bathed. When she was found in 1938 at the age of 6, Anna could not talk or walk. She could do nothing but lie quietly on the floor, her eyes and face expressionless.

Children who receive little attention in orphanages suffer similar harmful effects. In 1945, researcher Rene Spitz reported on an orphanage where 18-month-old infants were left lying on their backs in tiny rooms most of the day without any human contact. Within a year, all had become physically, mentally, emotionally, and socially impaired. Two years later, more than a third of the children had died. Those who had survived could not speak, walk, dress themselves, or use a spoon (Spitz 1945).

Child geniuses

While the lack of normal socialization can destroy minds, specialized socialization can create geniuses. A young woman named Edith finished grammar school in four years, skipped high school, and went straight to college. She graduated from college at age 15 and obtained her doctorate before she was 18. Was she born a genius? We do not know. However, as soon as she stopped playing with dolls, her father filled her days with reading, mathematics, classical music, and intellectual discussions and debates. When she felt like playing, her father told her to play chess. This very special attention to her academic development is likely to have contributed significantly to her achievements (Hoult 1979). Another example is Adragon Eastwood DeMello who graduated with a degree in mathematics at age 11. When he was a few months old, his father gave up his career as a science writer to educate him (Radford 1990).

Many parents of geniuses have deliberately given their children very stimulating environments. In his study of Einstein, Picasso, Gandhi, and other world-famous geniuses in various fields, Howard Gardner (1993) found that they were all born into families that valued learning and achievement with at least one loving adult who especially encouraged their ability.

After you read

Task 1 VISUALIZING PARTS OF THE TEXT

When you read a text, it can be helpful to imagine a picture of what is being described. Visualizing the information will help you understand and remember what you read.

Match these pictures to people described in the text.

1

2

3

4

Task 2 BUILDING VOCABULARY: USING CONTEXT CLUES

Although there may be many words in a text that you do not know, you do not want to continually stop and look up words in the dictionary. It is often possible to get a general idea of the meaning of the word or phrase by looking at its context. This means looking at the words and sentences that come before and after the word or phrase.

1 Find words in the text that match the definitions below.

1 features or characteristics (par. 2)   _traits_

2 not active (par. 2)   _____

3 encouraged to grow and develop (par. 3)

4 angered and upset (par. 5)

5 home for children with no parents (par. 6)

6 weakened or damaged (par. 6)

7 continued to live after a bad experience (par. 6)

8 bypassed (par. 7)

2 Compare your answers in a small group. Discuss which clues helped you.

Task 3 READING FOR MAIN IDEAS

Understanding main ideas is an important task when reading a college
text. Part of this skill is being able to quickly identify the topic of a
paragraph. Another part is being able to see what the whole text is
about – in other words, the point that the writer is trying to make.

1 Look back at the text quickly and write the number of the paragraph that deals
with each of the following topics.

1 the importance of social learning   paragraph ___3___

2 a twentieth-century example of one child's
social deprivation   paragraph _____

3 changes in opinion about nature and nurture   paragraph _____

4 institutional deprivation   paragraph _____

5 how special socialization can create young geniuses   paragraph _____

6 what we inherit   paragraph _____

7 world-famous geniuses   paragraph _____

8 feral children   paragraph _____

2 Now choose the sentence below that best expresses the main idea of the *whole*
text.

a There has been much debate over the centuries about the role of nature and
nurture in making us into the individuals we are.

b There is general agreement that we inherit physical and temperamental traits
but less agreement about how much we inherit intelligence and aptitude.

c Socialization plays an important role in determining what we achieve in life and
case studies of deprived children and of child geniuses are evidence of this.

d Studies of child deprivation show that social learning is extremely significant in
determining what we achieve in life.

Task 4 CITING STUDIES IN YOUR WRITING

In an essay or an examination answer, you may want to cite (refer to) a study that you have read about. To do so you should include the following:

1 research topic
2 name(s) of researcher(s)
3 year (usually the year of publication of the research)
4 the research finding

To cite a study in your writing you can use this sentence pattern:
In a study of 1, 2 (3) found that 4.

1 Study this example from the last paragraph of the text:

In his study of [Einstein, Picasso, Gandhi, and other world-famous geniuses in various
fields,] [Howard Gardner] [(1993)] found [that they were all born into families that valued learning and achievement with at least one loving adult who especially encouraged
their ability.]

2 Now read paragraph 6 again and write a sentence using this pattern to cite the research of Rene Spitz.

3 Look back at the texts in sections 1, 2, or 3 of this chapter and write sentences about two or three pieces of research cited there.

CHAPTER 1 WRITING ASSIGNMENT

Choose one of the following topics as your chapter writing assignment.

1 Describe the traditional family unit in your country, and also any newer types of family units that have become more common in the past few decades.
2 Imagine you have a friend who is coming to the United States to study, and you are writing a letter to him/her about ways of life in the United States. Write two or three paragraphs to include in your letter that describe some types of U.S. households he or she might find unusual or interesting.
3 Think back to your own childhood. What behaviors did your parents think were most important to teach you? How did they teach them?
4 What evidence can you see from your own life of the influence of heredity and environment? You could write about yourself or others. Think about physical features, temperament, intellectual ability, and aptitude (for example, in sports).

Preparing to read

THINKING ABOUT THE TOPIC

1 In the text "The Influence of Culture" you will read about social norms (or rules). These norms define what is acceptable behavior in a society or group.

Use the rating scale of 1–4 below to indicate how acceptable the following behaviors are in your country. Check (✓) one box for each behavior.

1 = completely acceptable
2 = sometimes acceptable
3 = usually unacceptable
4 = completely unacceptable

Behavior	1	2	3	4
Remaining seated in a crowded bus while an elderly person stands				
Eating with your fingers				
Wearing shorts in the main street of your town or city				
Kissing a boyfriend or girlfriend in public				
Taking too much change in a store and saying nothing				
Hitting children when they misbehave				
Swearing in public				
Wearing shoes inside the house				
Taking a dog into a restaurant or café				
Accepting a gift when you have nothing to give in return				

2 If there are students from different countries in your class, move around the class and talk to other students until you find at least one country that is different from your own for several behaviors. If you all come from the same country, discuss how people's attitudes vary depending on their age or the specific context.

3 Discuss the following question with your classmates:

What happens in your country if you violate or break the rules for one of these behaviors?

Now read

Now read the text "The Influence of Culture." When you finish, turn to the tasks on page 32.

The Power of the Group

① THE INFLUENCE OF CULTURE

Imagine that you are alone with a person that you love and who loves you. You are holding his or her face in your hands as you look into his or her eyes. Slowly you move your lips toward your partner's, and the two of you share a passionate kiss.

You probably think of kissing and the feelings that go with it as natural. To a sociologist, kissing and many other common behaviors are *cultural* rather than *natural*. We are not born with the knowledge of how to kiss and what it means to kiss. Instead, we learn this as part of our culture.

The meaning of culture

Culture is a very powerful force in our lives. It determines many of the experiences we have and the meanings we give to them. But what exactly is culture? To the sociologist, culture is everything that we are socialized to do, think, use, and make. Much of what humans think

> **culture**
> everything humans are socialized to do, think, use, and make

society

a collection of individuals sharing a common culture and living in the same geographical territory

and do is learned from the **society** they live in. Because humans live in groups and communicate with each other, they pass on what they know and believe to their children and to each other.

They pass on, for example, ideas about what they believe is important or not important in life, what they see as normal and abnormal behavior, and what they believe to be right and wrong. All these ideas form the culture of the particular society they live in, and guide the behavior of the members of that society.

Values

Values are socially shared ideas about what we consider to be good, desirable, or important in life. We show what we value by how we live our lives. For example, if we value money we are likely to spend a lot of time thinking or worrying about it, and looking for ways to get more. If many people in a society value money, this will be reflected in the amount of attention that the society gives to it (for example, in its newspapers). The values of a society form the basis of its rules, or norms.

Norms

Norms define what is socially acceptable or unacceptable behavior in particular social situations. When we violate or go against social norms, there may be some kind of negative consequence. That is, there may be a penalty or punishment to discourage us from acting this way again. Most of us are not even aware of many behaviors as social norms. We think they are natural. Kissing is a good example. We usually know what is acceptable and what is not about who we kiss, how we kiss, and when and where. (See the boxed text on page 31 for some interesting examples.) Many norms are not very serious at all. These are sometimes called *folkways*. Folkways are customs that members of a group are expected to follow to show courtesy to others. For example, saying "excuse me" when you burp is an American folkway. Thanking someone if they say you have done a job well is another. If we violate these weak norms, nobody will punish us. They might think we are peculiar or impolite, but that is all.

Norms vary greatly from one society to another throughout the world. Consider, for example, the wide variety of ways that members of different cultures perform daily activities such as eating and dressing. Clothing rules vary from wearing nothing except perhaps some jewelry, to covering the body completely from head to toe. Very strong norms that prohibit or forbid a certain activity are called *taboos*. Certain foods, for example, are taboo in some societies – pork in Jewish and Muslim communities, beef in Hindu communities.

Norms also change considerably over time. In the seventeenth century, in the United States and Europe, people were not allowed to kiss in public. A man caught kissing was likely to have been put in stocks and ridiculed publicly. Today, it is not at all unusual to see lovers kissing in public.

Norms change. At one time, kissing in public was a crime.

You are violating the law if you exceed the speed limit or drive while under the influence of alcohol.

Mores and laws

Mores are social norms that provide the standards of moral behavior for a group or society. They can carry a severe penalty for violation. Sometimes these penalties are informal rather than legal. For example, although there are no laws against middle-aged men dating adolescent girls (assuming the relationship is nonsexual), there are mores in our culture against this behavior. If a man did this, he could expect to get a strong negative reaction from other people. Most mores, however, are formalized in writing and enforced by the government. That is, there are *laws* to make people uphold them. In the United States and many other countries, for example, there are laws that allow the state to take children away from their parents if their parents do not care for them properly. There are also laws in many countries that very strongly encourage people to drive safely by specifying penalties for driving while drunk.

Kissing customs

- In many European countries, it is the custom to give multiple kisses when you greet someone. But it pays to be careful, because the customs vary. In Spain, Austria, and Scandinavia, two kisses is the custom. In the Netherlands it is three. In France, it depends where you are – in Paris, four kisses is the norm, in Brittany, it is three, and in other parts it is two. In Belgium, it can be very tricky – it is one kiss for someone your own age, and three for someone at least ten years older.
- A kiss on both cheeks is a traditional greeting between Arabic men, and Middle Eastern heads of state are often seen kissing and embracing each other on TV news bulletins.
- In the Middle Ages, knights kissed before doing battle, just as boxers touch gloves today before they begin the fight.
- The practice of putting an X at the bottom of a personal letter came from the Middle Ages. People who could not read or write would draw an X instead of writing their names on contracts. They would then kiss the contract to show they were sincere. Eventually the X came to be a sign for a kiss.

After you read

Task 1 UNDERSTANDING KEY TERMS IN THE TEXT

Your understanding of the texts you read depends in part on your understanding of key terms. Pay careful attention to the explanations of these terms and any examples used in the text to help you understand them.

Find explanations and examples of the following terms in the text to complete the chart (using note form).

Term	Explanation	Examples
Values	*Socially shared ideas about what is good*	*"Excuse me" – after burping* *"Thank you" – after job well done*
Norms		
Folkways		
Taboos		
Mores		*Kissing – what is acceptable and what is not*

Task 2 WRITING EXPANDED DEFINITIONS

When you write a definition, it can be a great help to your reader if you expand it by giving one or two examples.

1 | If you were asked to write an expanded definition of "culture," you might say:

Culture is everything we are socialized to do, think, use, and make. Kissing, for example, is a cultural rather than a natural behavior. We kiss in a way that we have learned from others in our cultural group.

Study this expanded definition. It begins by defining the term, but then adds some information about kissing, a culturally learned behavior.

2 | Look back at the text and at the notes you completed for Task 1 and write a one-sentence definition of one of the key terms (for example, *values, norms, mores*).

3 | Now add two examples of the term to help a reader understand it. Don't use the examples in the text. Use examples from your own experience of U.S. society or of society in your own country.

Task 3 READING BOXED TEXTS

> Boxed texts often contain interesting information to accompany the more academic main reading.

Read the boxed text about kissing and discuss with other students:

What are the "rules" about kissing in your country? In other words, how, when, and where do people kiss? Are these rules changing?

Task 4 APPLYING WHAT YOU READ

Even the classroom in which you are studying is an example of a culture with its own acceptable norms and rules of behavior. To discover how each culture has its own rules, do the following activity:

1 | Work in small groups to brainstorm a list of four or five behaviors that are acceptable inside your classroom and a list of four or five behaviors that are unacceptable. Use your list to draft a set of six important rules that includes acceptable and unacceptable behaviors.

2 | Meet as a whole class. Combine the draft rules from each group and decide on a final list of no more than six rules. As far as possible, everyone should agree on the final list.

3 | Write the rules on a large sheet of paper and place them on the wall.

Preparing to read

PERSONALIZING THE TOPIC

1 Work with two or three other students. Think back to when you were 14 or 15 years old and discuss:

1 What did you like to wear?
2 What type of music did you like?
3 Who were your favorite singers, TV and film stars, and sports stars?
4 What did you do in your free time?
5 What did your parents think about your interests and fashions?

2 Still working in the same groups, discuss teenagers now:

1 What clothes do they like to wear?
2 What type of music do they like?
3 Who are the popular singers, TV and film stars, sports stars, etc?
4 What are some popular activities?
5 What do you think about these teenage interests and fashions?

PREVIEWING ART IN THE TEXT

Looking at the photographs or other art in a text and reading the captions (the words that explain visual materials) is a good way to get an overview of the content.

1 Look at the photographs in the text "Peer Group Pressure" and read the captions. Write a sentence to describe what you think the text will be about.

2 Compare your sentence with others in the class. Return to your sentence after you have read the text to see whose sentence was the most accurate.

Now read

Now read the text "Peer Group Pressure." When you finish, turn to the tasks on page 36.

2 PEER GROUP PRESSURE

As children grow older, they become increasingly involved with their peer group, a group whose members are about the same age and have similar interests. The peer group – along with the family and the school – is one of the three main socializing agents. However, the peer group is very different from the family and the school. Whereas parents and teachers have more power than children and students, the peer group is made up of equals.

Members of a peer group have similar interests.

The adolescent peer group teaches its members several important things. First, it teaches them to be independent from adult authorities. Sometimes this can mean that a peer group can teach its members to go against authorities and adults – to ignore home and school rules and even to break the law. Most teenagers, though, rebel only by making fun of older people in a harmless way (Elkin and Handel 1988; Corsaro and Eder 1990). Second, it teaches social skills – how to get along with other people. Third, the peer group teaches its members the values of friendship among equals.

Peer groups often develop distinctive **subcultures** with their own values, language, music, dress, and heroes. Adolescents, in particular, tend to believe in the same things as their friends, talk the same way, dress the same way, listen to the same music, and like and dislike the same TV stars and other celebrities. There may be a considerable difference between these interests, behaviors, and values and those of their parents and teachers.

subcultures

a part of the larger culture but different from it in some values, norms, and behaviors

Adolescent peer groups frequently differ from parents and teachers in what they value. Whereas parents and teachers tend to place great importance on school achievement, peer groups are likely to think that popularity, social leadership, and athletic achievement are more important (Corsaro and Rizzo 1988). These differences do not necessarily mean that parents and teenagers will fight and argue. In fact, most youngsters are friendly with their mothers and fathers. They simply engage in different types of activities – work and task activities with parents but play and recreation with peers. They are inclined to seek advice from parents on financial, educational, career, and other serious matters. With their peers they are more likely to discuss social activities such as which boy or girl to date and what clubs to join (Sebald 1986).

Some peer groups develop distinctive subcultures.

Peer group members look to each other for approval instead of relying on their own personal beliefs. Doing what everyone else is doing is more important than being independent and individual. Early adolescents are most willing to accept this conformity and so they are most deeply involved with peer groups. As young people grow into middle and late adolescence, their involvement with peers gradually declines because of their growing independence. When they reach the final year of high school, they tend more to adopt adult values, such as wanting to get good grades and good jobs (Steinberg 1994; Larson 1994).

After you read

Task 1 SHORT-ANSWER QUIZZES: MAKING USE OF YOUR OWN EXPERIENCE

> Your everyday experiences can sometimes be useful when taking a short-answer quiz. These experiences can help you remember important information and ideas from the text.

1 Work with a partner. Without looking back at the text, discuss the answers to the following questions. Use what you remember from the text and your own experiences.

1 Name one important thing the adolescent peer group teaches young people.
2 Name three ways in which adolescents show membership of their peer group.
3 Name two topics that adolescents are likely to discuss with their parents.
4 Name two things that they are likely to discuss with their peers.
5 Adolescents like to behave in the same way as their peers. Do you think this becomes more or less important in the late teen years. Why?

2 Now look back at the text and check your answers.

Task 2 VARYING YOUR LANGUAGE

> Textbook writers often have to refer many times to one thing (for example, an idea, an event, a group of people) in the same chapter or reading. To avoid repeating the same words over and over, they often choose different words to express the same idea. When you write, you, too, should try to vary the way you express your ideas.

1 Find and list all the words and phrases in the text with a similar meaning to:

• young people   • adults   • be likely to

2 Imagine you are writing an essay about the following social groups:

• people who are over 65   • children under 5
• babies   • people in paid employment (people who work)

Make a list of the different words or expressions you could use to refer to each of these groups.

3 Choose two groups of people from step 2 and write three or four sentences about each group. Vary the way you refer to the group using words from your list. For example, if you choose *people who are over 65*, two of your sentences might be:

Older people tend to spend less of their money on clothes.
Discounts for public transportation are available to senior citizens.

Task 3 LANGUAGE FOCUS: WRITING ABOUT DIFFERENCES

1 Study the four different sentence structures that the writer of this text used to write about the differences between the peer group and other socializing agents:

  1 *X is different from Y (in _____)*
    However, the peer group is very different from the family and the school.
    (par. 1)

  2 *Whereas X does _____, Y does _____*
    Whereas parents and teachers have more power than children and students, the peer group is made up of equals. (par. 1)

  3 *There is a difference between X and Y*
    There may be a considerable difference between these interests, behaviors, and values and those of their parents and teachers. (par. 3)

  4 *X differ(s) from Y (in _____)*
    Adolescent peer groups frequently differ from parents and teachers in what they value. (par. 4)

2 Read the paragraph below that describes one difference between adolescents and adults. Find examples of the four sentence structures in the paragraph and circle them.

Adolescents and adults are different in many ways. Teenagers differ from adults, for example, in the way they handle finances. Teenagers are likely to spend all their money as soon as they receive it, whereas most adults try to save some of their money for future expenses. There is also a difference in what adults and adolescents spend their money on. Young people tend to spend their money on the things they want – music, movies, going out – whereas older people are more likely to spend it on the things they need – clothes, food, housing.

3 Write a paragraph describing another area of difference between adolescents and adults (for example, clothes, friendships, interests). Use the sentence patterns above and vary the way you refer to the two groups.

Preparing to read

THINKING ABOUT THE TOPIC

Look at the news photos and captions below and discuss these questions with your classmates:

   1 What is similar about the scenes in these photographs?
   2 What is different?
   3 Have you ever been in situations like these?

Passers-by stop to watch a street performer juggle basketballs.

The World Trade Organization conference drew bitter protests.

A protester is carried away by police during a demonstration against police brutality in Los Angeles.

SKIMMING: READING FIRST SENTENCES

> Reading the first sentence of each paragraph is a good way of getting an overview of what a text is about. The first sentence of a paragraph is often its topic sentence: the sentence that summarizes the content of the whole paragraph.

Read the first sentence of each paragraph in the text. Then work with a partner to find the paragraphs that do the following things. Write the paragraph numbers next to the things they do.

   ___ **a** defines the term "collective behavior"
   ___ **b** explains some different types of crowds
   ___ **c** asks you to think about your own "crowd" experiences
   ___ **d** explains some common characteristics of crowds
   ___ **e** defines the term "crowd"
   ___ **f** gives some theories to explain why crowds act the way they do

Now read

Now read the text "Crowds." When you finish, turn to the tasks on page 41.

3 CROWDS

Have you ever had an experience like one of these?   1

- You are at a football game, when some people in the crowd stand
  up and wave their arms in the air. Another group of people does
  the same thing. Before you know it, you are standing up and doing
  it, too. Finally, the whole stadium is involved in the action and the
  excitement of the "wave."
- You are walking along the street on your way to work or school
  when you see a crowd gathered on the corner. Although you are in a
  hurry, you walk toward it. You discover that the crowd is watching a
  man selling a wide assortment of gold and silver watches. He is a
  good salesman and, even though the watches are not cheap, many
  people are lining up to buy them. Within minutes, you are joining
  the line yourself, even though you have no real need for a watch.

Crowds are one example of what sociologists call *collective behav-*   2
ior. Collective behavior is social behavior that is relatively unorganized,
spontaneous, and unpredictable. It contrasts with *institutional behav-*
ior, which occurs in a well-organized, rather predictable way. Institutional behavior is frequent and regular. Every weekday, masses of people hurry to work. On every campus, groups of students walk to classes.
These predictable patterns are controlled by social norms and are
essential for social order. We could not survive without them. Collective behavior, however, is unpredictable and operates outside these
norms. Fashion, public opinion, social movements, and revolutions are
other examples of collective behavior.

So what exactly is a crowd? A crowd is a group of people temporarily   3
doing something while physically close to one another. They may be
gathered on a street corner watching a salesman or at a football

Rock concert crowds are good examples of collective behavior.

This crowd of people waiting for a train is a perfect example of institutional behavior.

stadium watching a game (as in the two examples at the beginning of this text). They may be on a street, throwing things at police, or they may be at a rock concert or a religious meeting.

Nearly all crowds share a few traits. Turner and Killian (1987) have described five crowd characteristics. In the first place, the individuals in the crowd do not share clear expectations about how to behave and about what will happen. They also tend to feel that something must be done right away to solve a common problem. Another characteristic is that a feeling, attitude, or idea spreads very quickly among crowd members. Crowd members also tend to go along with the actions of others without thinking too much about them. Finally, people in a crowd tend to say and do things they would not normally say and do.

But not all crowds are the same. Sociologist Herbert Blumer (1978) has identified four types of crowds: casual, conventional, acting, and expressive. The *casual* crowd is the most loosely organized. It emerges spontaneously. The street salesman incident is an example of a casual crowd. In contrast, the *conventional* crowd occurs in a planned manner. The football crowd may be acting spontaneously when they do the "wave," but they are, in fact, an example of a conventional crowd. Whereas the conventional crowd gathers to observe some activity, the *acting* crowd is involved in an activity in which the members are concentrating on one particular goal. Rioters and revolutionary crowds are examples. The *expressive* crowd, on the other hand, has no goal. Its members throw themselves into an activity, expressing their emotions. One example is people at a rock concert.

One theory to explain why crowds seem to act together is the *emergent-norm theory* (Turner and Killian 1987). This theory says that members of a crowd develop a new norm or rule to guide their behavior in a particular situation. Although not everyone might agree about what to do, there is great social pressure to behave like other members of the crowd. For example, not everyone in the football crowd feels comfortable about taking part in the wave but they feel that they have to do it. Sometimes, people may be in crowds where quite dangerous or antisocial behavior becomes the norm – fighting, pushing or throwing stones, for example. Again, not every person in these crowds is likely to think these behaviors are a good idea.

A quite different theory is Le Bon's *social contagion theory*. French social psychologist Gustave Le Bon (1841–1931) believed that the large number of people in a crowd allows our primitive, "animal" side to come out. His theory was that we normally hide this primitive side behind the "mask" of civilized behavior. When we are in a crowd, the large numbers give us a different kind of mask. In a crowd we are faceless and nameless, and this allows us to be emotional and irrational in a way that we cannot be in our normal civilized lives. We are then very easily affected by the emotion and action of others in the crowd.

After you read

Task 1   APPLYING WHAT YOU READ

> Finding ways to apply new knowledge is a good way to deepen your understanding of new subject matter.

1 Use Herbert Blumer's system of crowd classification (casual, conventional, acting, and expressive) to identify which type of crowd is exemplified by each of the following:

1 people watching a street musician _____

2 people watching a movie _____

3 people marching together to protest against a government action _____

4 people waiting at the airport to catch sight of a famous film star _____

5 people watching a burning building _____

6 people at a carnival or other large outdoor celebration _____

7 a street gang looking for a fight _____

8 employees picketing a workplace that has dismissed them _____

2 Discuss your classifications with your classmates. Give your reasons.

3 Think of one crowd situation you have been in. Then complete the checklist below based on the five crowd characteristics described by Turner and Killian.

	Yes	No	Not sure
Did you or other members of the crowd seem uncertain about how to behave and about what would happen?			
Did you or other members of the crowd feel that something had to be done right away to solve a common problem?			
Did a feeling, attitude, or idea spread very quickly among crowd members?			
Did you or other members of the crowd go along easily with the actions of others?			
Did members of the crowd say and do things they might not normally say and do? Did you?			

4 Discuss your checklist with a partner. Begin by describing the crowd scene – where and when it occurred and who was involved.

5 Discuss the following question with your classmates:

Which of the two theories given in the text – emergent-norm or social contagion – do you think offers a better explanation of crowd behavior? Give examples from your experience to support your view.

Task 2 LANGUAGE FOCUS: TOPIC SENTENCES

In most paragraphs there is a topic sentence that summarizes the content of the whole paragraph. The topic sentence is often, but not always, the first sentence.

1 Look back at the first sentence of each paragraph in the text. Discuss with a partner whether or not each sentence is a topic sentence. Give your reasons.

2 The topic sentences of the following paragraphs are missing. Read each paragraph and choose the correct sentence (**a**, **b**, or **c** below) to write in the blank.

  a You are continually moving between crowds.
  b Street actions occur spontaneously when two or more people gather to witness a common event.
  c Another type of crowd is the *blocked* crowd.

1 _____

_____

This could be, for example, a street fight, a car accident, or an arrest. What happens after people stop to watch depends on the nature of the event, the time available to the group members to stay and watch, and the excitement of the event (for example, the person being arrested fights the arresting police officer).

2 _____

_____

In these types of crowds, the members are prevented from achieving their goal. One example is being stopped on a highway because of road repairs. Members share a common feeling. They are irritated and want to get to where they are going. The members may complain to each other about the delay, but otherwise they do not interact much at all.

3 _____

_____

On your way to school, you may have walked or driven in a casual crowd. This weekend you may see a movie and be part of a conventional crowd. Or you may attend an end-of-the-week party and become a member of an expressive crowd. However, you may forgo the parties and just go about the business of life – grocery shopping, for example. If there is a particularly long line at the checkout, you will be in a blocked crowd. It is unlikely that you will be involved in an action crowd unless you are protesting some event in your community.

Task 3 BUILDING VOCABULARY:
USING GRAMMAR TO WORK OUT UNKNOWN WORDS

An important part of figuring out the meaning of a new word is recognizing it as a noun, a verb, an adjective, an adverb, or another part of speech. This can help you narrow down possible meanings for the new word and understand any context clues.

1 Work with a partner. Find these words in the text and decide whether they are nouns, verbs, adjectives, or adverbs. Then try to guess what they mean.

Word	Part of speech	Possible meaning
assortment (par. 1)	*noun*	*variety*
relatively (par. 2)		
spontaneous (par. 2)		
masses (par. 2)		
temporarily (par. 3)		
traits (par. 4)		
emerges (par. 5)		
rioters (par. 5)		
primitive (par. 7)		
irrational (par. 7)		

2 Compare your answers with another pair of students.

Preparing to read

PERSONALIZING THE TOPIC

1 Below are five situations that most people would find frightening. Rank them in order of how frightening you would find them. (Put 1 for the most frightening situation, and 5 for the least frightening.)

___ **a** You are locked inside a large building with a few other people after a power failure that has affected all telephone and power lines.

___ **b** You are alone at home and hear on the radio that a hurricane is approaching your area.

___ **c** You are in a crowded elevator in a tall skyscraper when it gets stuck and the lights go out.

___ **d** You are shopping in a large shopping mall when an announcement is made that you must leave the building because of a fire.

___ **e** You are in a crowded football stadium when an announcement is made that a bomb has been found.

2 Compare your answers in a small group. Tell the others which situations you would find the most frightening and why.

3 Discuss the rankings with the class:

1 Was there one situation that most people rated the most frightening? the least frightening?

2 Was there one factor that people found more frightening than others?

Now read

Now read the text "Panic!" When you finish, turn to the tasks on page 47.

4 PANIC!

On a December afternoon in 1903, a fire broke out in Chicago's Iroquois Theater. According to an eyewitness:

> Somebody had yelled "Fire!" . . . The horror in the theater was beyond all description. . . . There were not enough fire-escape ladders, and many people fell or jumped to death on the street below. But it was inside the house that the greatest loss of life occurred, especially on the stairways. (Schultz 1964)

The theater did not burn down. Firefighters arrived quickly after the alarm and put out the flames so fast that no more than the seat coverings were burned. However, 602 people died, and many more were injured. Panic, not the fire itself, caused the tragedy.

A similar disaster occurred on a July morning in 1990 in the holy city of Mecca, Saudi Arabia. Thousands of Muslim pilgrims were walking through a 600-yard-long tunnel when the lights accidentally went out. Panic started a stampede of people pushing their way through the tunnel and 1,426 people were killed.

The people in the Iroquois Theater and the Mecca tunnel behaved as people often do when faced with unexpected and dangerous situations such as fires, earthquakes, and floods: they panicked. Panic is one of the more extreme types of collective behavior. It is a useless response to a serious threat or danger. It generally involves flight, but it is a special kind of flight. In many situations, flight is a rational response: it is perfectly sensible to run away from a burning house or an approaching car. In panic behavior, however, the flight is irrational and unhelpful. It follows a loss of self-control, and it increases, rather than reduces, danger to oneself and others.

Just because there is a crowd and a threat does not mean that there will be a panic. There are several conditions that can lead to the development of a panic. First, the people must really believe that there is a serious danger. Second, there must be intense fear of the danger. This fear is made worse if the people involved think they will be trapped or unable to escape. Third, there must be some individuals who have a natural tendency to panic. Typically, these are people whose desire to save themselves makes them ignore the fate of others and of the dangerous consequences of their panic. Fourth, the people in the crowd must increase each other's terror by their words and actions. Finally, there must be a lack of cooperation among people. 5

Panic sometimes takes the form of *mass hysteria*. This is when numerous people engage in wild or frenzied activity without checking the source of their fear. One famous case occurred in 1938 when Orson Welles' radio play *War of the Worlds* was broadcast. People heard an announcement that creatures from the planet Mars had invaded Earth, and even before the broadcast had ended, at least a million of the 6 million listeners had panicked. Many prayed, cried, or ran from their homes, frantic to escape death from the Martians. Some hid in cellars beneath their homes. Young men tried to rescue girlfriends. Parents woke their sleeping children. People telephoned friends to say goodbye. Not everyone panicked, though. Some people found the broadcast just too fantastic to believe. Some recognized that the broadcast was probably a dramatic performance or looked up radio program guides to check what it was they were listening to. 6

After you read

Task 1 SCANNING

Scanning is looking quickly through a text to find a specific word or
piece of information. When you scan, you do not read every word. Your
eyes pass over the text, stopping only when you find the word or information you are looking for. You will often need to do this when studying for a test, when preparing to write an assignment, or when select-
ing books in a library.

Scan the text quickly to find:

1 a definition of "panic"
2 two of the conditions needed for panic to develop in a crowd
3 a definition of "mass hysteria"

Task 2 UNDERSTANDING COMPLEX SENTENCES

Textbooks often contain complex sentences. To read efficiently, you
need to learn to see the structure of these sentences quickly. One part
of this skill is seeing which words belong together as a meaningful
group or *sense unit*. A sense unit could be, for example, a sentence subject, an adjective-noun group, a verb group (perhaps with an adverb),
or a prepositional phrase of time or place.

1 | Look at how this sentence from the text has been divided up into sense units.

Firefighters / arrived quickly / after the alarm / and put out the flames / so fast / that no
more than / the seat coverings / were burned.

2 | Divide the following sentences from the text in the same way. There is more than
one way to do this.

1 The people in the Iroquois Theater and the Mecca tunnel behaved as people often do
when faced with unexpected and dangerous situations such as fires, earthquakes, and
floods: they panicked. (par. 4)

2 This fear is made worse if the people involved think they will be trapped or unable to
escape. (par. 5)

3 Typically, these are people whose desire to save themselves makes them ignore the fate
of others and of the dangerous consequences of their panic. (par. 5)

4 This is when numerous people engage in wild or frenzied activity without checking the
source of their fear. (par. 6)

3 | Read your sentences out loud to a partner. Compare your answers and discuss
why you divided the sentences the way you did.

Task 3 BUILDING VOCABULARY:
WORD MAPS FOR REMEMBERING NEW VOCABULARY

It is important to develop ways to remember the new words you meet in your reading. One good way is to make a "word map." This means that instead of simply writing words in a list, you write words organized by topic and subtopic on a visual "map."

1 The text contains many words related to the topic *panic* – the *situations* that might lead people to panic, the *feelings* people have when they panic, their *states of mind*, the *actions* they might take, and what might *result* from a panic situation.

Look back at the text and find words that you could place on the word map for *panic*, below. Add any other words you know.

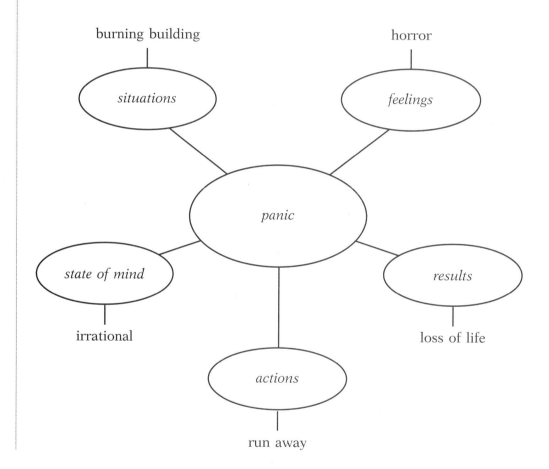

2 Work with a partner and compare word maps. Add some of your partner's words to your map.

Task 4 WRITING A LISTING PARAGRAPH

> Understanding how paragraphs are organized can help you read more effectively. The most basic type of paragraph organization is a *listing paragraph*. A listing paragraph usually starts with a general statement followed by a list. Typically, the general statement indicates how many reasons/factors/characteristics/kinds there are, with either a specific number (four, five, etc.) or a term such as *a variety of a* or *a range of*. The rest of the paragraph then gives some or all of these reasons/factors, etc.

1 Look back at the text and decide which paragraph is a listing paragraph. Take brief notes from that paragraph in the following way:

  • A heading that describes the list
  • A numbered list of items (1, 2, 3, 4, etc.) below the heading

2 Look at the following common patterns that can be used to write a listing paragraph.

  1 Patterns for writing the general statement.

There are	two (three, four etc.) many several a variety of a range of	reasons . . . characteristics factors . . . ways . . . types of . . . kinds of . . .

  2 Patterns for writing about the items in the list.

For two items in the list One is . . .	the other is . . .
For more than two items in the list One is . . . The first is . . . First, . . . These include . . .	Another is . . . The second (third, fourth, etc.) is . . . Second, (Third, Fourth, etc.) . . .

3 Think back to the situation that you chose as the most frightening in "Personalizing the Topic" on page 44. Write a listing paragraph giving the reasons that you chose this situation. Use some of the patterns from step 2 in your paragraph.

CHAPTER 2   WRITING ASSIGNMENT

Choose one of the following topics as your chapter writing assignment.

1   Write a set of guidelines for visitors to your country to help them understand how to behave and what to expect. You might want to focus on one area of behavior only (for example, eating and drinking).

2   "The peer group is both a positive and negative influence in our lives." Discuss this statement using information from the reading "Peer Group Pressure" in Section 2 of this chapter. Give examples from your own experience.

3   People in crowds sometimes act in a way they would not if they were alone. Give at least three examples of such behavior, based on your own experiences and observations, and then give your opinion of why people might act differently in crowds.

4   Many popular films are based on situations that would cause most of us to panic – for example, boats sinking at sea, fires breaking out in tall office buildings, and hurricanes destroying people's homes. Why do you think such films are popular? Mention any films like that you have seen, and describe your reaction to them.

Gender and Sexuality

In this unit we look at issues related to being male and being female. In Chapter 3, we look at some of the major influences on how we perceive our gender roles: the family, children's books, school, and the media. In Chapter 4, we look at gender issues that are current today – how being female or male affects people's lives in the home and at work.

Previewing the unit

Before reading a unit (or chapter) of a textbook, it is a good idea to preview the contents page and think about the topics that will be covered. This will give you an overview of how the unit is organized and what it is going to be about.

Chapter 3: Growing up Male or Female

In Chapter 3, you will read about how boys and girls are treated differently as they grow up. Discuss with a small group:

1 What jobs did you perform around the house when you were growing up?
2 Did you have certain jobs because you were a boy, or because you were a girl?
3 At school, were there any subjects or activities that only boys did, or only girls did?
4 Were your teachers mainly male or mainly female?

Chapter 4: Gender Issues Today

In Chapter 4, you will read about some of the difficulties that adult males and females have to overcome in their lives.

1 Study these survey results.

Do you think it is easier to be a man or a woman?		
	Females	**Males**
To be a woman	30%	21%
To be a man	59%	65%

(Survey results taken from Time Special Issue: Women: The Road Ahead, *Summer 1990, p. 12.)*

2 How would you answer the survey question above? Discuss your reasons with the class.

3 Ask five women and five men outside the classroom the survey question and bring your results back to class.

4 Add the class results together, and then compare them to the survey results reported in the box above.

Unit Contents 2

Preparing to read

SKIMMING

Remember that when you skim, you do not have to read every word. You just need to try to understand the main idea of a text and its organization. Pay special attention to pictures and captions. It is also a good idea to read the introduction and conclusion. Get into the habit of skimming all texts before you read them, especially when you are reading for study.

Skim the text, taking particular note of the pictures and their captions. Which of the following sentences do you think states the main idea of the text?

a Boys are usually brought up differently from girls.
b Parents are more likely now to bring up boys and girls in a similar way.
c There are good and bad consequences from bringing up girls and boys differently.

PERSONALIZING THE TOPIC

Look at these toys and discuss the following questions with a partner:

1 What is the toy?
2 Is the toy for boys or girls? Of what age?
3 Would you buy these toys for children you know? Why or why not?
4 What kinds of toys did you play with as a child? (for example, dolls, balls, toy cars)
5 Do you think the toys you played with influenced you as an adult in any way?

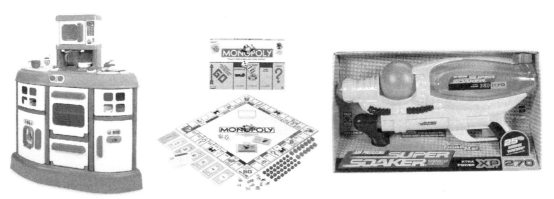

Now read

Now read the text "Bringing up Boys and Girls." When you finish, turn to the tasks on page 57

Growing up Male or Female

1 BRINGING UP BOYS AND GIRLS

Newborn babies do not know if they are boys or girls, but it does not take them long to find out. They very quickly learn the way that their society expects males and females to behave and think. That is, they learn their **gender roles.**

From the moment of birth, babies are usually treated according to their gender. In the United States and in many other countries, baby girls tend to be dressed in pink clothing and baby boys in blue. Baby girls are handled more gently than boys. Girls are cuddled and kissed while boys are bounced around and lifted high in the air. Girls are given dolls, whereas boys are given cars, trucks, and building blocks. Mothers think a lot about how pretty their little girls should look, but they are less concerned about their little boys' appearance.

When they start to talk, children are taught the difference between the words "he" and "she" and between "him" and "her." There are also differences in the way parents talk to their children. Parents use words about feelings and emotions more with girls than with boys, and, by age 2, girls use these words more than boys do. Furthermore, mothers and fathers talk differently, because of their socialization. Mothers tend to talk more politely ("Could you turn off the TV, please?") and fathers tend to use more direct language ("Turn off the TV.") By age 4, girls and boys have learned to imitate these conversational styles.

Girls are generally taught to be "ladylike" – polite and gentle. They are taught to rely on others – especially males – for help. They are allowed to express their emotions freely. Girls learn the importance of being pretty. They may even learn that they must rely more on their beauty than on their intelligence to attract men. Boys, on the other

1

gender roles
the way that society expects males or females to behave and think

2

3

4

Society teaches girls the importance of beauty and family.

Society teaches boys to learn about cars and to like sports.

hand, are taught to behave "like men." Boys are also encouraged to be independent and strong and to avoid being "mama's boys." They are told that boys don't cry. If they put on makeup and wear dresses during play their parents are horrified. Therefore, boys grow up with a fear of being feminine, and, as young men, try to keep up a "macho" image. They may also develop a negative attitude toward women in adult life (Elkin and Handel 1988; Power and Shanks 1989).

Parents also have different social expectations of daughters and sons. Daughters, more than sons, are socialized to think more about the family, for example, to remember birthdays, to spend time with the family on holidays, and, when they get older, to provide care for sick family members and relatives. Sons are not expected to do these things. They are expected to be more interested in the world outside the family and more independent of the family in social activities. Daughters are also thought to need more protection than sons. For example, parents may make their daughters come home earlier at night and forbid them to go to places that they might let their sons go to. Such protectiveness often encourages girls to be less active in exploring their environment.

In recent years, though, there has been a trend in many parts of the world to more **gender-neutral socialization**. Young parents, female professionals, and well-educated parents, in particular, are more likely to socialize their children into more equal gender roles. However, this is not always an easy task. One study of parents who wanted to bring up their children in a nonsexist way found that it was very difficult to do. The parents complained about toy stores being filled with **gender-specific toys** – war toys for boys and domestic toys for girls. They also commented that while they might be able to give their children gender-neutral toys themselves, it was difficult to get relatives and friends to do this. Almost all the children in the study owned and played with gender-specific toys given to them by other people. The parents also found it hard to fight against the gender lessons of books, the peer group, and school.

gender-neutral socialization

bringing up boys and girls the same way

gender-specific toys

toys made for boys only or for girls only

After you read

Task 1 NOTE TAKING: MAKING A CHART

It can be useful to make a chart (or table) when taking notes, especially when the text compares and contrasts two or more things.

1| Look back at the text and complete the chart below with information about the different ways boys and girls are brought up.

	Girls	Boys
Color of clothing	pink	
Way children are handled		
Types of toys children are given		
Amount of attention paid by parents to appearance		not so much
Language and conversation learned from parents	talk about feelings talk politely	
Behaviors taught		
Parents' social expectations		expected to be independent

2| Look at your chart and discuss with a partner how this chart might be different if it was about bringing up children in your country.

Task 2 LANGUAGE FOCUS: LINKING WORDS

1| Study the following common linking words that are often used to make comparisons and contrasts.

	Within a sentence	To begin a sentence
Comparison	and both . . . and . . .	similarly likewise in the same way
Contrast	while whereas but	on the other hand in contrast however

2| Look back at the text and find examples of these linking words.

3 Choose linking words from the chart to complete these sentences.

1 Adults tend to talk about girl babies as "sweet," "pretty," or "charming."

_____ , they speak of boy babies as "handsome," "tough," and "strong."

2 Boys are expected to prefer playing outdoors, _____ girls are expected to like playing indoors with dolls and housekeeping toys.

3 Some modern parents might encourage their daughter to play with cars,

_____ they might encourage their son to play with dolls.

4 Parents who think their unborn child is a boy tend to think of it as strong,

_____ if they think it is a girl, they think of it as graceful and gentle.

5 Children's books often present stereotyped gender roles. _____ , movies tend to show women as caregivers and men as adventurers.

6 In some families, _____ boys _____ girls are expected to do housework.

Task 3 WRITING A COMPARISON AND CONTRAST TEXT

You will often be asked to read and write comparison and contrast texts, so it is important to be familiar with their organization. There are two common ways to organize information when two (or more) items are being compared.

- *Linear method:* First, one item is described and then all the similarities and differences of the next item are described.
- *Zigzag method:* First, one aspect of an item is compared or contrasted with the same aspect of another item, then a second aspect is compared and contrasted, then a third, and so on.

Here is an example of how you could use each method to organize your ideas if you were comparing and contrasting bananas and apples.

Linear method   Zigzag method

bananas: **appearance:**
  appearance   bananas   apples
  texture
  flavor   **texture:**
               bananas   apples

apples:
  appearance   **flavor:**
  texture   bananas   apples
  flavor

1 In paragraph 2 of the text, the zigzag method is used to describe differences in how boys and girls are treated. The paragraph below includes the same information, but uses the linear method instead. Complete the paragraph with words or phrases from the text.

From the moment of birth, babies are usually treated according to their gender. In the United States and in many other countries, baby girls tend to be dressed in pink clothing. They are _____ gently, cuddled, and kissed a great deal and _____ as toys. Mothers think a lot about how pretty their little girls should look. Baby boys, in contrast, are _____ . They are not handled as gently as girls and are bounced around and _____ _____ . Boys are given cars, trucks, and building blocks as toys. Another difference is that mothers are less _____ .

2 Read the paragraph below. Discuss with a partner whether the zigzag or linear method is used.

Thorne (1993) found a number of differences in the way boys and girls interact with their same-sex friends. First, girls engage in more cooperative kinds of play, for example, jumping rope or practicing dance steps together. Girls also tend to say "Let's . . ." or "Why don't we . . ." to generate this play. In contrast, boys engage in competitive rough-and-tumble play and physical fighting. Boys also like to appear tough by making verbal threats (for example, "I'm gonna punch you"). These kinds of threats are sometimes made in anger but they are also made in the spirit of play. Second, girls like to spend time with only one or two best friends, whereas boys tend more to hang around with a larger group of casual friends. Third, when there is conflict among friends, girls talk about the undesirable behavior of playmates behind their backs rather than to their faces. As a result, a conflict between girls can take a long time to be resolved. Boys, on the other hand, are more direct and confrontational, so their conflicts are often over quite quickly.

3 Choose either the linear or the zigzag method of organization to write a paragraph comparing and contrasting the social lives of teenage boys and girls in your country. Here are some possible topic sentences for your paragraph:

- In X (name of country) teenage boys and girls have very different social lives.
- There are many differences in the way teenage boys and girls socialize in X.
- Apart from a few important differences, adolescent boys and girls have similar social lives in X.

4 Exchange your paragraph with a partner and see if you can tell which organizational pattern your partner used: zigzag or linear.

Preparing to read

THINKING ABOUT THE TOPIC

Look at this picture and the pictures on pages 61 and 64. They are from stories that have been told to children in English-speaking countries for hundreds of years. In English, these stories are called *fairy tales*.

1 Discuss with your class:
  1 What type of people do you think the characters in the pictures are? (for example, good, bad, strong, weak)

  2 When you were a child, did your storybooks have pictures like these? Did they have characters like these?

2 Tell a partner about one fairy tale you remember from childhood. Who were the characters and what were they like? What happened in the story?

BUILDING VOCABULARY: LEARNING WORDS RELATED TO THE TOPIC

> If you know the words related to a topic, you will find it much easier to read about that topic.

These words are frequently found in children's stories:

heroine	hero	handsome	prince	princess	dragon
magician	witch	beast	wicked	forest	monster
fairy	godmother	stepmother	evil	rescue	cruel
brave	slay	tower	cottage	castle	turn into

Place the words above under the correct headings below. Use your dictionary to help you.

People	Words to describe people	Nonhuman creatures	Places	Actions

Now read

Now read the text "Fairy-Tale Lessons for Girls." When you finish, turn to the tasks on page 63.

2 FAIRY-TALE LESSONS FOR GIRLS

Once upon a time, there was a beautiful young girl who lived with her father and wicked stepmother. Even though she was kind-hearted and worked very hard, her stepmother was very cruel to her and made her do all the hardest work. One day, she was out collecting wood in the forest, when she met a handsome young man . . .

Can you guess how this story ends? Most of us read many stories like the one above when we were children, and we know how they will end. In these stories, the female heroines are usually very beautiful. Because the heroines are beautiful, they marry the handsome prince at the end of the story. Their beauty is presented in a way that links goodness with beauty. Good girls and good women are beautiful. Bad girls and bad women are ugly. They are also powerful and strong.

The female characters share other features. The beautiful heroines are also usually very quiet and passive. They do not say very much. If they do, they are usually answering questions. They rarely ask questions themselves, and they rarely take action and make decisions. They spend a lot of their time indoors cooking and cleaning for the males in the story. While they are doing this, the males are having a very exciting time – having great adventures and facing danger at every turn. In one analysis of gender roles in children's books, males outnumbered females by a ratio of 11 to 1 (Weitzman et al. 1972 in Giddens 1989, p. 163). This study also found that women who were not wives and mothers were imaginary creatures such as witches or fairy godmothers. No women in the books analyzed had an occupation outside the home. By contrast the men were depicted in a large range of roles as fighters, policeman, judges, kings, and so on. More recent studies show some improvement in the balance of male and female characters, and in their roles and occupations. Even so, most studies show that males still appear more frequently in central roles, titles, and pictures.

feminists

supporters of equal rights and opportunities for women

stereotypes

fixed ideas about what members of a particular group of people (for example, women) are like

The portrayal of females as quiet and passive reflects the view of "good" women at the time when many of the stories were written, in the early nineteenth century (Bottigheimer 1986). However, these stories are still widely read. Many **feminists** have argued that these fairy-tale **stereotypes** of women are damaging for the little girls who read them today. The stories make girls want to be beautiful rather than strong, powerful, and clever. Others disagree. They argue that female roles in fairy tales may be viewed in more positive ways. Cinderella, for example, can be seen as clever. After all, she does manage to gain freedom from the kitchen and housework.

Many children's authors today are creating fairy stories in which the heroines are more aggressive than the stereotypical fairy-tale heroine. For example, in *Cinder Edna* (1994) by Ellen B. Jackson, Cinderella's practical neighbor wears comfortable shoes and takes the bus to the ball. In *Sleepless Beauty* (1996) by Frances Minters, Beauty fools the wicked witch by setting an alarm clock. In stories set in modern times too, more and more strong, clever female characters are appearing.

New fairy-tale heroines

These days, a new type of heroine can be found in children's films. These films are adaptations of old stories or new stories altogether. Walt Disney Productions, for example, has made many cartoon films in which the character of the original heroine has been changed to become strong, brave, and clever.

In Walt Disney's *Beauty and the Beast*, for example, Belle, the heroine, spends all her time reading books. She shows a complete lack of interest in the big, strong, handsome young man who wants to marry her. She thinks he is stupid and big-headed. Belle is also funny and brave. She rides off alone into the dark forest to search for her lost father, and fights to save the Beast's life. While the story ends traditionally with Belle marrying the Beast, who has now turned into a handsome prince, she has a much more active role in determining her future than in the original tale.

The Powerpuff Girls are cartoon examples of a new type of children's heroine: strong, brave, and clever.

After you read

Task 1 WRITING SHORT ANSWERS TO TEST QUESTIONS

> You will often be asked to write short answers to questions about texts you have read in college. It is important to stick to the question, including only relevant information in your answer. It is a good idea to use words from the question in your answer, to use only relevant information, and to give examples where possible. Remember to make use of your own experiences and observations where you can.

1 Read the question, text, and sample answer below. Study in particular the highlighted parts of the text, and how they are used in the answer.

Question: According to the text, what are some of the characteristics of "good" girls or women in traditional fairy tales? (Mention two or three.)

. . . In these stories, the female heroines are usually very beautiful. Because the heroines are beautiful, they marry the handsome prince at the end of the story. Their beauty is presented in a way that links goodness with beauty. Good girls and good women are beautiful. Bad girls and bad women are ugly. They are also powerful and strong.

The female characters share other features. The beautiful heroines are also usually very quiet and passive. They do not say very much. If they do, they are usually answering questions. They rarely ask questions themselves, and they rarely take action and make decisions. They spend a lot of their time indoors cooking and cleaning for the males in the story. ⟶ *words from the question*

"Good" girls or women in traditional fairy tales are usually very beautiful, and very quiet and passive. They rarely take action or make decisions, and they spend ⟶ *relevant information*
a lot of their time indoors cooking and cleaning for the males in the story. ⟶ *examples*

2 Answer each question below in one or two sentences.

1 According to the text, what types of roles (or occupations) have women often been given in children's books, and what types of roles have men been given?

2 According to the text, why do some people say these traditional stereotypes are bad for little girls?

3 According to the text, what sort of heroines are some authors and filmmakers creating in more recent years?

Task 2 APPLYING WHAT YOU READ

1 Read this fairy story.

Rapunzel

Long long ago, a good man and his wife lived happily in a little cottage at the edge of a wood. Next door to the cottage was a wonderful garden belonging to a witch. One day the wife fell very ill. She knew that the only thing that would cure her was an herb called "rapunzel" from the witch's garden. Every night the husband would climb into the garden and take some of the herb. But one night the witch caught him. The witch said that she would let him have the herb for his sick wife if he promised to give her their first-born child. The man was so worried about his wife that he agreed. The wife became well soon after and had a beautiful baby girl. Despite the couple's tears and cries, the witch immediately took the baby away.

The baby, who the witch named Rapunzel, grew into a beautiful young girl, but when she was 12 the witch locked her up at the top of a high, high tower deep in the forest so that no man would ever see her and want to marry her. Rapunzel was very lonely and often used to sit at the window and sing to the birds. Each day when the witch took food to the tower, she would call out, "Rapunzel, Rapunzel, let down your hair." Rapunzel would let down her long golden hair and the witch would climb up. One day, a prince heard the singing. He saw the witch and heard her calling out to Rapunzel to let her up. After the witch had gone, he repeated her words and was able to climb up the golden hair in the same way. When they met, Rapunzel and the handsome prince immediately fell in love. The prince came day after day to see Rapunzel.

One day the witch found out about the prince and flew into a rage. She cut off Rapunzel's hair and took her deep into the forest and left her there. When the prince returned to the tower, the witch let down Rapunzel's hair and caught the prince. She threw him out of the window and he fell and blinded himself on some prickly bushes. After many days, as he wandered lost and alone in the woods he heard Rapunzel's sweet voice. When Rapunzel saw him, she kissed and hugged him. Her tears fell on his eyes and suddenly he could see again. The prince took Rapunzel to his father's palace where they married and lived happily together for the rest of their lives. The wicked witch was never seen again.

2 Work with a partner. Find examples of any traditional stereotypes of females or males mentioned in the text.

3 Discuss with the class:

Do you believe that images like these stereotypes are harmful for young people? Why or why not?

Task 3 WRITING A PERSUASIVE TEXT

Writing a persuasive text is a common college writing task. In a persuasive text, you try to convince the reader of your view on a topic. Therefore, this type of text mainly consists of points that support your view. It is important, however, to show that you are also aware of the other side of the argument.

Think of a traditional children's story you know. Write two paragraphs arguing for or against the view that the story includes damaging stereotypes for girls or boys. Follow the steps below to organize your writing and use the "Frog Prince" essay as your model:

Steps	**The Frog Prince**

Paragraph 1

- Introduce the topic by giving the story's name and your point of view.
- Say what the story is about.

"The Frog Prince" by the Brothers Grimm is a traditional tale that presents a very harmful stereotype for girls. The story is about a beautiful young princess who loses a special golden ball in a deep pond, and promises to love an ugly frog if he will go in the pond to get it. She breaks her promise as soon as she gets the ball back, however, and is cruel to the frog. She changes her behavior only when her father finds out about the promise and forces her to keep it. In the end, the frog turns out to be a handsome prince who takes her away to be married and live happily ever after.

Paragraph 2

- Give two or three points to support your view; use linking words such as *first, second,* etc., to link your arguments.
- If possible, include an argument for the opposing point of view, and say why you do not agree with it.
- Write a sentence to sum up your view.

The princess is a very bad model for young girls. First, she is very cruel to the frog until she learns he is a prince. Second, she does not keep her promise to the frog until her father forces her. Third, even though she has been so cruel the prince falls in love with her. Some might argue that it would be natural for a young girl to dislike an ugly frog and that this excuses her bad behavior, but I do not agree. I believe that the story shows young girls that if they are beautiful, unkindness is acceptable, and can even lead to happiness.

Preparing to read

EXAMINING GRAPHIC MATERIAL

Remember that before reading a text, you should look at any graphs, tables (charts), or diagrams. By doing this, you can quickly get a good idea of the text's content.

1 Look at the graph in the text (Figure 3.1). Answer true (T) or false (F).

_____ 1 The "gender gap" refers to the difference in the academic performance of males and females.

_____ 2 The graph is about college students' performance on standardized tests.

_____ 3 On average, males in the study performed better than females.

2 Check your answers with a partner.

3 Discuss the following questions with your classmates.

1 Are you surprised by the results of the graph?

2 What do you think are the reasons for these results?

3 Were all the subjects listed in Figure 3.1 available to both girls and boys at your high school?

4 In general, who did better at your school – boys or girls? Why do you think that was?

5 What advice did your high school teachers give you about study and careers? Do you think their advice was related to your gender?

PREDICTING

1 Circle the word that you think will best complete each statement below.

1 Most teachers in the United States are men/women.

2 Most school principals in the United States are men/women.

3 In the United States, girls receive less/more attention in the classroom from their teachers than boys.

4 In Australia, young men are less/more likely to commit suicide than young women.

2 Check your answers to step 1 after you read the text "Learning Gender Lessons at School."

Now read

Now read the text "Learning Gender Lessons at School." When you finish, turn to the tasks on page 69.

3 LEARNING GENDER LESSONS AT SCHOOL

Thirty years ago, many schools in the United States still segregated courses on the basis of gender. Secretarial courses and cooking were for girls; business and mechanical courses for boys. High school teachers were not likely to encourage girls to go on to college, because they were expected to get married and stay home to raise children. If a girl was going to college, teachers advised her to choose a traditionally feminine career such as teaching, nursing, or social work.

These things do not happen now. American schools generally offer the same courses to all students and expect both boys and girls to have careers after they graduate. However, some gender-role differences are still common. Various studies have shown, for example, that from preschool through high school, girls are given less attention than boys. Teachers tend to ask boys to do things more often, and offer them more helpful criticism. They tend to allow boys to shout out answers, but scold girls for doing so, especially in math and science classes. Studies also show that because girls receive less attention from teachers, they suffer a further drop in self-esteem when they reach high school. At age 9 the majority of girls are confident, assertive, and positive about themselves. By age 14 less than one-third feel that way (Sadker and Sadker 1994). Perhaps partly as a result of this, high school girls score lower in most subjects on standardized tests than boys (see Figure 3.1).

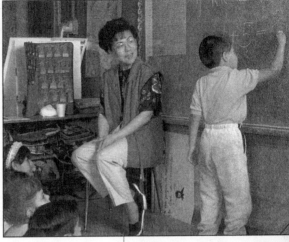

Boys often receive more attention from teachers than girls.

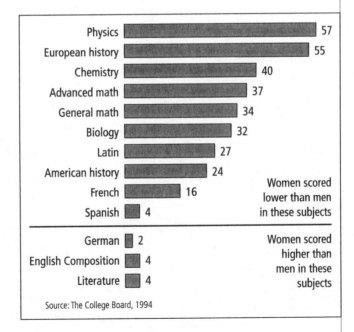

Difference in points between men's and women's average scores on standardized tests given to college-bound high school students in 1993

Subject	Difference
Physics	57
European history	55
Chemistry	40
Advanced math	37
General math	34
Biology	32
Latin	27
American history	24
French	16
Spanish	4

Women scored lower than men in these subjects

Subject	Difference
German	2
English Composition	4
Literature	4

Women scored higher than men in these subjects

Source: The College Board, 1994

Figure 3.1 The gender gap in academic achievement.

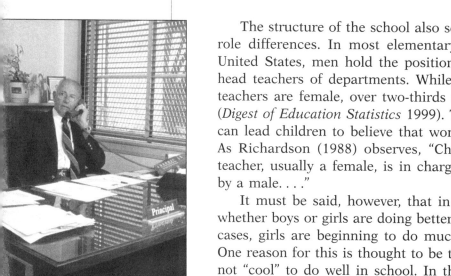

The majority of teachers are women but most school principals are men. This sends the false message to children that women are not capable of holding executive jobs.

The structure of the school also sends out a message about gender role differences. In most elementary and secondary schools in the United States, men hold the positions of authority as principals and head teachers of departments. While approximately three-quarters of teachers are female, over two-thirds of all school principals are male (*Digest of Education Statistics* 1999). This male-dominated atmosphere can lead children to believe that women need the leadership of men. As Richardson (1988) observes, "Children learn that although their teacher, usually a female, is in charge of the room, the school is run by a male. . . ." 3

It must be said, however, that in recent years the evidence about whether boys or girls are doing better in school is conflicting. In many cases, girls are beginning to do much better than boys academically. One reason for this is thought to be the attitude among boys that it is not "cool" to do well in school. In the United States and some other countries, concern about gender socialization in school years is shifting from girls to boys. Boys and young men have more social problems than girls and young women, both at school and after school. In Australia, for example, young men commit suicide at five times the rate of young women and have 300 percent higher death rates from automobile accidents. They are also more likely to drop out of high school, and more likely to end up in prison than young women (Legge 1995). 4

One conclusion from these findings is that schools should be encouraging boys to express their feelings. Some Australian schools are trying to address this issue with special programs. One type of program helps boys with their communication and social skills. Another type encourages boys in subjects that allow them to express their feelings, for example, art, public speaking, drama, and even dance. Other programs help teachers and parents understand boys' needs better, and give them more positive messages about education and achievement. 5

In the British movie *Billy Elliot,* Billy wants to become a professional ballet dancer despite the opposition of family members who do not think his career choice is appropriate for a boy.

After you read

Task 1 WRITING A ONE-SENTENCE SUMMARY

At college, you sometimes need to summarize a text in one sentence, for example, when writing a short answer to a test question, or when citing a research study in an essay. To write a one-sentence summary, you need to understand the main ideas covered by the text and then find a way to capture them in a few words.

1 Choose the best ending to complete a one-sentence summary of the text.

The text "Learning Gender Lessons at School" describes
a the many different ways that boys receive more attention than girls in schools.
b the ways schools give messages to boys and girls about gender roles and some recent concerns about boys.
c the many different ways that schools these days give messages to boys and girls about gender roles.
d how the structure of schools tells children about the different status of men and women in society.

2 Add two examples to the summary sentence you chose to make a short paragraph.

3 Write a one-sentence summary of the previous two readings in this chapter.

Task 2 BUILDING VOCABULARY: USING CONTEXT CLUES

Find the words in the left column (below) in the text, and use context clues to figure out their meanings. Match each one to a word or phrase with a similar meaning in the right column.

_____ **1** segregated (par. 1)   **a** confidence
_____ **2** scold (par. 2)   **b** forceful
_____ **3** self-esteem (par. 2)   **c** leave school before graduating
_____ **4** assertive (par. 2)   **d** not always in agreement
_____ **5** conflicting (par. 4)   **e** find fault with, criticize
_____ **6** shifting (par. 4)   **f** moving, changing
_____ **7** commit suicide (par. 4) **g** separated
_____ **8** drop out (par. 4)   **h** kill yourself

Task 3 PERSONAL WRITING

Journal writing is a good way to practice writing in a second language without worrying too much about accuracy. It also helps you remember what you read. When you read about a topic that interests you, take some time to write down your personal thoughts on the topic.

Write briefly about some of your school experiences with one or more of the gender issues discussed in the text.

Preparing to read

PREVIEWING ART IN THE TEXT

Look at the cartoon on page 71. Discuss the following questions with your classmates:

1 What is the woman doing? What is the man doing?
2 How would you describe the relationship between the man and the woman?
3 Do you think the images of the man and woman in this cartoon accurately reflect U.S. society? Why or why not?

SPEED-READING TECHNIQUES

College students often have very long reading assignments. They do not have time to read these slowly and carefully. Instead they have to develop a fast reading style known as "speed reading." Speed-reading techniques are also good general reading techniques:

- Do not say the words under your breath as you read.
- Try to focus on groups of words, not individual words.
- Try not to backtrack (go over the text again and again).
- Guess at the general meaning of words that you do not know.
- Skip over words that you do not know and that do not seem too important.
- Slow down slightly for key information, such as definitions and main ideas.
- Speed up for less important information, such as examples and details.

Quickly read the text that begins on the next page using the techniques above. Then see if you can answer these questions:

1 Which areas of the mass media are mentioned in the text?
2 What sort of advice did women's magazines give to women in the past?
3 In which two roles were women shown in TV commercials in the past?
4 What message do modern TV shows give about successful women?
5 Which aspect of the media did Spicher and Hudak research?
6 What was one thing that they found out from their research?

Now read

Now read the text "Gender Roles in the Media" again to check your answers to the questions in the task above. When you finish, turn to the tasks on page 73.

4 GENDER ROLES IN THE MEDIA

The mass media influences all aspects of our lives, including the learning of gender roles. Newspapers and magazines, television, and film all have an influence on the way we view the roles of women and men and on the way we think they should behave.

Four decades ago, traditional women's magazines such as *Good Housekeeping* and *Family Circle* talked to women as though they were children who needed to learn the basics of how to care for their families. Today, magazines do not do this. However, they still tend to define the female role in terms of homemaking and motherhood (see cartoon below), and to offer beauty advice to help women attract men and please husbands. There are now a few less traditional magazines such as *Ms.* that show women in a range of roles and that cover a much wider range of topics. However, the more traditional magazines still dominate.

Television commercials have also, until recently, presented women primarily as sex objects and as housewives. Young sexy women were shown admiring older men who smoked a particular cigarette brand. Housewives were shown smiling joyfully about their clean bathrooms, or looking guilty for not using the right laundry soap to wash their husband's clothes. These days advertisers are more careful about the way they present women, and they are presented in a variety of roles. However, it is still quite common to see advertisements where beautiful young women are dressed in sexy clothes to sell cars or other products. One study also found that the changes are mainly on nighttime television, with daytime commercials still tending to portray women doing household chores (Craig 1992).

"Gotta run, sweetheart. By the way, that was one fabulous job you did raising the children."

Prime-time television programs also often used to stereotype women. In past decades, women were usually shown as lovers, as mothers, or as weak, passive girlfriends of powerful, effective men. Today's TV programs are somewhat different. Women are more likely to be presented as successful and able to support themselves and their families, but the traditional stereotypes of women are still there. Even when women are shown to be successful professionals, the storylines suggest that they should be sexy as well.

Comic strips in the Sunday newspaper are another influence on gender-role socialization. In a content analysis of six Sunday comic strips, the researchers identified several themes. One of these was "if you are a woman and you want a happy home, do not have a career, and if you are a man, never marry a career woman" (Mooney and Brabant 1987, cited in Knox 1990).

TV cartoons

Research shows that there has been very little change since the 1970s in the gender stereotypes that America's young minds are watching in TV cartoons. In the 1970s, male cartoon characters on TV outnumbered female cartoon characters by almost four to one. In 1997, researchers Spicher and Hudak videotaped and categorized 118 cartoon characters from popular Saturday morning cartoons and found the ratio had not changed.

They found that male cartoon characters were more prominent in the cartoon stories than female characters and were more interesting personalities. Male characters were powerful, strong, smart, aggressive, and so on. Occasionally there were female cartoon characters, but they were colorless and boring. Although women's occupations have changed considerably over the past decades, in these TV cartoons there were still only a very small number of females shown in nontraditional occupations such as doctors or police officers (Spicher and Hudak 1997).

"Isn't that cute? He's reading his diplomas again."

TV and print media cartoons seldom show women in non-traditional occupations.

After you read

Task 1 READING FOR DETAIL

Complete the chart below with information from the text about how women were portrayed in the media in the past, and how they are portrayed today.

	In the past	Today
Women's magazines		
Television commercials		
Prime-time TV shows		
TV cartoons		

Task 2 LANGUAGE FOCUS: THE PASSIVE VOICE

> Sentences in the passive voice are found frequently in academic textbooks, so it is important to be able to recognize the passive voice and understand its use.
>
> The passive voice is used by writers when they want to do the following:
> - focus on the person or thing being acted upon
> - <u>not</u> focus on the person or persons doing the action
> - focus on the action itself

1 Find 5 examples of the passive voice in the text and discuss with a partner why the passive voice was used.

Housewives were shown smiling joyfully about their clean bathrooms . . .

(The focus is on the housewives, not on the television commercials that show the housewives.)

2 Rewrite the sentences below in the passive voice. Omit the active subjects, as in the example, if you think they are not necessary.

1 Filmmakers still typically cast men in stronger roles than women.
Men are still typically cast in stronger roles than women.

2 Advertisers these days often show men doing the washing and cooking dinner.

_____

3 TV producers use more men than women to anchor news programs.

_____

4 In the fifties, TV producers cast women only in roles as mothers and homemakers.

_____

5 Television directors increasingly show women in roles that have traditionally been men's.

_____

6 Advertisers still very often portray women in stereotypical gender roles.

_____

3 Look at some cartoons and advertisements in your local media. In what different ways are men presented? In what different ways are women presented?

1 Find one advertisement or cartoon that you think is typical of the way men and/or women are presented.

2 Write a paragraph about the role and image of the man and/or woman in the advertisement or cartoon you chose. Use the passive voice where it is appropriate. You can begin your paragraph like this:
In this advertisement/cartoon, the man/woman is...

Task 3 READING CRITICALLY

> Just because an argument is in print does not mean it is always true. When you read, you should read critically, that is, you should develop the habit of assessing if what you are reading is logical, or if it could be looked at in another way.

1 The text "Gender Roles in the Media" discusses gender stereotyping (presenting fixed, restricted images of women and men) in newspapers, magazines, and television. With a partner, find evidence in the text:

• to support the view that women are stereotyped in the media.
• to argue against or balance this view in some way.

2 Now think about your own experience of the media. Discuss the following questions:

1 What examples have you seen of the gender roles described in the text?
2 What examples have you seen of nontraditional gender roles?
3 Do you agree with the view that women are stereotyped in the media?

CHAPTER 3   WRITING ASSIGNMENT

Choose one of the following topics as your chapter writing assignment.

1   Imagine you are going to interview a group of people for a research project about gender roles and stereotyping in the home and at school. Write a list of questions you would ask them about their childhood experiences, based on the readings in this chapter.

2   Describe a character (male or female) that would, in your opinion, be an ideal model for a children's story – someone with the characteristics you think are important for men or women today. Talk about this character's appearance, personality, actions, and so on.

3   Describe a TV program that you know. Describe the characters and plot, and discuss any male or female stereotypes.

4   Read the following extract from a newspaper article:

Researcher Dr. Peter West, a long-standing critic of the way men are portrayed in the media, says, "Whenever there's someone doing something stupid on TV it's a man, and if a man is doing something good then he's young and sexy." However, he says that part of the problem is men themselves, because they dominate the writing and production of television programs. (Zuel 1999)

The extract suggests that men are stereotyped in the media just as much as women. Do you agree or disagree with this suggestion? How much do you think male stereotyping affects the way people think or behave?

Preparing to read

1 Look at these newspaper and magazine headlines. Discuss with a small group:

1 What do you think each article will be about?

2 What topic do all the articles have in common?

2 Look at the family situations listed below. For each situation, discuss with your class whether the husband or wife should do each of the following: cook, clean, take care of children, and pay the bills.

- The husband works and the wife stays home.
- The wife works and the husband stays home.
- Both husband and wife work, but the husband earns more.
- Both husband and wife work, but the wife earns more.

Now read

Now read the text "Balancing Home and Work." When you finish, turn to the tasks on page 80.

Gender Issues Today

Chapter 4

1 BALANCING HOME AND WORK

Here is one woman's story of balancing home and career. Rachel always   1
dreamed of having a large family and an interesting career. She now has
four children and works full-time.

I really have two full-time jobs. My job in the city is in investment banking and I really like it. It's interesting and important. My other job is at
home – raising four kids and keeping the household going. I like this job
too, and though it's not always interesting, I know it's important. But
when I'm not cleaning up the kitchen after a meal, or picking up the
kids' things from the floor for the millionth time, or feeding the dog, then
I'm falling asleep during my youngest daughter's piano practice. When I
do have some free time, I've usually got a headache. The reality is that,
most of the time, it's just too much.

Role overload

role overload

having too much to do and too many responsibilities as a result of combining two or more roles

Rachel has **role overload.** That is, she has difficulty combining the roles of worker and of wife and mother. Role overload is one of the disadvantages that today's women face. While both parents are more "stretched" when the woman of the household works, it is usually the woman who does most of the childcare and housework. Most studies investigating housework conclude that women (whether employed or not) do "the lion's share" of housework and childcare. An Australian study, for example, found that employed wives did 69.3 hours of unpaid work around the house during a two-week period while employed husbands did approximately 31.2 hours. A study by Bird (1999) shows a similar picture for U.S. households. In this study of 1,256 adults, Bird showed that while working women certainly want an equal share of housework, they "shoulder the main burden" by doing approximately twice as much as their spouses. Her study showed that after marriage, women gain 14 hours of household chores per week, while their husbands gain only 90 minutes.

2

Even if women work outside the home, they tend to do most of the housework.

Value of housework

There have been some attempts in the United States, Europe, and Australia over the past few decades to encourage governments to pay people for the housework they do. A U.S. organization called the Wages for Housework Campaign argued for many years that housework was boring and degrading because it was unpaid, and that payment would improve the status of women in society overall. More recently they have argued for housewives to be included in the labor force and for unpaid housework to be included in calculations of a nation's wealth, for example, the gross national product (GNP). They have argued that this would make housework more visible, and could possibly lead to greater investment in programs to help women.

3

So far, no government has seriously considered paying people for housework. This is not surprising when you consider how difficult it would be to implement such a scheme. The first problem would be to determine how much people would be paid. In 1995 the United Nations estimated the annual value of women's unpaid work at $11 trillion worldwide. An Australian government study in 1991 calculated that if someone was to be paid to do all the housework in one home it would be worth 400 Australian dollars a week (equivalent to about 250 U.S. dollars at that time). However, there would be more problems to "iron out." Would everyone get the same amount? Which tasks would and would not be paid for? How would the government know if the work was done?

4

Other consequences of being a woman

Role overload is not the only disadvantage women of today may experience. A negative self-concept and lack of self-confidence are other disadvantages. In a study in which women and men were told they were incapable of performing a mental task, the women were more likely than the men to believe that they were incapable (Wagner et al. 1986). Another study showed that women are more likely to think their success is due to luck than to their own ability (Heimovics and Herman 1988). A further problem for many mothers is the difficulty they have in finding new interests and activities when their children leave home.

But there are also advantages to being a modern woman. One is the likelihood of living longer. In 1998 in the United States, average life expectancy for men was 73.9, whereas for women it was 79.4. Other advantages are being able to express emotions more easily, having a closer bond with children, and not having one's identity tied to employment. One big advantage today is that women have so many options. It is socially acceptable to work full-time if you have children, but it is also acceptable to be a full-time mother and stay at home, or to work part-time.

Avoiding the housework

Jokes about men and housework are common in TV shows and newspaper comics. But research shows that there may be at least a little truth in these jokes.

Mackay (Kissane 1990) revealed four tactics that men sometimes use to avoid doing household chores:

- Helplessness – he agrees to cook but asks directions for every step.
- Getting the kids to do it – he insists that they are old enough to help and he is not needed.
- Going slowly – he hopes that his wife will find it more trouble than it is worth to ask him for help again.
- The "black-cloud" strategy – he does the chores, but so ungraciously that the wife feels angry and upset.

Men in this study justified their tactics by claiming that women "want it both ways." They also argued that they had never agreed to the concept of sharing housework.

After you read

Task 1 READING FOR DETAIL

1 | Answer the following questions.

  1 What is the point of Rachel's story?

  a that you should not work full-time if you are a woman with children
  b that it can be difficult to combine full-time work and raising a family
  c that women do most of the housework even if they work full-time

  2 What does research tell us about the way most men and women share housework?

  3 What information can you find in the text to suggest that governments will never pay people to do housework?

  4 Make a list of all the disadvantages and advantages of being a woman mentioned in the text.

  5 How do some men try to get out of doing housework?

2 | Compare your answers with a partner.

Task 2 LANGUAGE FOCUS: FIGURES OF SPEECH

When writers are using language in a way that goes beyond its normal, literal meaning, they often put these words or expressions in quotation marks (". . ."). This indicates that it is a figure of speech, not the normal usage.

Work with a partner. Find these figures of speech in the text and work out what they mean from the context and the words themselves. Then complete the sentences below using one of the words or expressions.

  a stretched (par. 2)
  b the lion's share (par. 2)
  c shoulder the main burden (par. 2)
  d iron out (par. 4)
  e want it both ways (boxed text)

  1 Kathy and Jim fought about the housework again. I hope they can

  _____ their differences.

  2 She's working at two jobs, raising a son, and going to night school. She must

  feel so _____ .

  3 Julia wants to be successful, and she wants to be a perfect mother. Women like

  Julia _____ .

4 In traditional families, the man is expected to _____ of supporting his wife and children.

5 Mark and Lola decided to switch roles in their marriage. Now she does most of the gardening and repair tasks, and he does _____ of the cooking and cleaning.

Task 3 PERSONALIZING THE TOPIC

1 Fill in this chart for your household (current or past). Check (✓) the appropriate column.

In your household who mainly does each job?	Male	Female	Shared equally
General straightening up of the house			
Vacuuming			
Cleaning bathrooms			
Washing floors			
Shopping for food			
Cooking meals			
Cleaning up after meals			
Childcare			
Taking children to school, sports, etc.			
Doing household repairs			
Paying bills			
Laundry			
Organizing social events			

2 Compare your answers with a small group and discuss:

1 Who does the most housework – males or females?

2 What jobs do males usually do?

3 What jobs do females usually do?

4 What jobs are usually shared?

5 What factors influence who does certain jobs?

3 Write two or three paragraphs to summarize your group discussion.

Preparing to read

PREVIEWING TEXT HEADINGS

> Before reading a text it is a good idea to look at any headings used and to think about what kind of information might be included underneath.

1 Read this list of headings from the text "It's Not So Easy Being Male." With a partner discuss what information might be in each section.

1 Required to make money
2 Inadequate development of other skills
3 Identity equals job
4 Emotional stereotypes
5 Adapting to the modern woman

2 Now read the following extracts with your partner and guess which part of the text each one comes from. Write the number of the heading from step 1.

_____ **a** Some men have never learned how to cook, wash clothes, or take care of a home.

_____ **b** Not only are men less likely to cry than women, but they are also less able to express feelings of depression, anger, and fear.

_____ **c** Of course not all men respond at the same speed to these changes in male-female relationships.

_____ **d** Because our culture expects a man to earn money, he may feel that his salary is connected to his self-esteem.

_____ **e** Ask a man who he is and he will tell you what he does.

3 Scan the text to check your answers.

Now read

Now read the text "It's Not So Easy Being Male." When you finish, check your answers to step 2 above. Then turn to the tasks on page 85.

2 IT'S NOT SO EASY BEING MALE

The male gender role is a complex one to fulfill. It is true that males
are likely to enjoy many advantages. For example, they generally have
a more positive self-concept, greater confidence in themselves, and a
greater status than women (Wagner et al. 1986). They are also less likely
than women to experience **discrimination** and **harassment** because of
their gender. In general, both males and females see more advantages
in being male than being female (Fabes and Laner 1986). However, men
do experience some disadvantages throughout their lifetimes.

1

discrimination

treating a person differently
from others because of
his/her gender, race,
religion, etc.

harassment

repeatedly causing a
person to feel
uncomfortable or
threatened

Required to make money

Just as the woman is more often pushed toward the role of wife and
mother, the man is pushed toward the world of employment to pay the
basic bills of the family. He has little choice – his wife, children, parents, in-laws, and peers expect it. Because our culture expects a man to
earn money, he may feel that his salary is connected to his self-esteem.
Additionally, the amount of money earned is equated with success. Our
society encourages us to think that the man who makes $50,000 a year
is more of a man than the one who makes $10,000. In other words, a
male in our society must earn money to feel good about himself.

2

Inadequate development of other skills

The pressure to make money may interfere with the development of
other roles and skills. Since most men were cared for by their mothers,
they may expect similar care from their wives. Some men have never
learned how to cook, wash clothes, or take care of a home. Because of
this, they feel dependent on a woman for their domestic needs.

3

Identity equals job

Ask a man who he is and he will tell you what he does. His identity **4**
lies in his work. In studies of unemployment during the Great Depression, job loss was regarded as a greater shock to men than to women, although the loss of income affected both. It is no different today – losing one's job can still be crushing to a man's self-esteem.

The identification of self through work also becomes a problem **5**
when it pushes other concerns – such as family life – out of the picture. Many men get too caught up in their jobs and do not allow enough time for their families. This can put a strain on their relationship with their wives and children.

Emotional stereotypes

Some men feel caught between society's expectations that they be com- **6**
petitive, aggressive, independent, and unemotional and their own desire to be more open, expressive, and caring. Not only are men less likely to cry than women, but they are also less able to express feelings of depression, anger, and fear (Snell et al. 1986). The film *Tootsie* illustrates how men do not feel free to express the gentle side of their personalities. Near the end of the film, Dustin Hoffman (who has been dressed up as a woman called Tootsie throughout the story) says to Jessica Lange (with whom he has fallen in love), "I was more of a man with you as a woman than I have ever been with a woman as a man . . . I just need to learn to do it without the dress."

Some men have no trouble reporting to a woman boss, but others find it difficult.

Adapting to the modern woman

There is a new equality in relationships between men and women. **7**
Women have changed and men must adapt to these changes. The new equality can be seen in attitudes to higher education, for example. A young married man no longer asks his wife "Where will you work to put me through school?" but "How will we finance our educations?" or "Do you want to finish your education before I finish mine?" Men also have to deal with the fact that modern women are more likely to challenge their opinions and attitudes.

Of course not all men respond at the same speed to these changes **8**
in male-female relationships. In one study of over 300 men, Astrachan (1986) concluded that no more than 5 to 10 percent of American men fit the media's description of the "new age" men – those who support women in the workplace and give equal time to new male roles such as child rearing.

After you read

Task 1 UNDERSTANDING PRONOUN REFERENCE

> When reading, it is important to keep track of how pronouns – for example, *he, she, it, they, this, that, these, those* – may be used to refer back to people, things, or ideas in a previous sentence.

Look back at the text to find the meaning of the word in *italics*.

1 He has little choice – his wife, children, parents, in-laws, and peers expect *it*. (par. 2)

2 Because of *this*, they feel dependent on a woman for their domestic needs. (par. 3)

3 *This* can put a strain on their relationship with their wives and children. (par. 5)

4 . . . *those* who support women in the workplace and give equal time to new male roles such as child rearing. (par. 8)

Task 2 APPLYING WHAT YOU READ

1 Read this newspaper article about a househusband – a man who stays at home and does housework and cares for the family's children.

Stan Richards is a Mr. Mom – he looks after four children while his wife goes to work. Stan believes he is very lucky to be able to get to know his children this way. "Most fathers don't get this opportunity. They're too busy working all day and too tired when they come home to really get involved with their kids."

Stan became a househusband by chance. He had a back injury and had to stay home for a few months to recuperate from his injury. In that time his wife, Marion, found a full-time job that paid more than Stan's had. Stan liked his new job and so did Marion, so they decided to continue with the role reversal for a little longer. That was two years ago.

Stan admits he was afraid and confused at first and took hours to do chores that took his wife ten minutes. Now he is extremely organized, and the house runs like clockwork. Stan says that changing roles has helped their marriage as well. They both know and appreciate what the other does all day. Stan also feels he is more able to express himself emotionally now. He thinks this is partly because he spends more time with his children. The main problem, Stan says, is the way other people treat him. Some women don't know how to talk to him anymore and some men – even his friends – make fun of him.

2 Discuss the following questions with your classmates, using ideas from the text.

1 What difficulties do you think Stan faced when he first became a househusband?

2 Why do you think some people might not know how to deal with Stan?

Task 3 PERSONAL WRITING

Write down your own ideas on one or two of the issues discussed in the text.

Preparing to read

THE SQR3 SYSTEM (PART I)

> **SQR3: Survey (S), Question (Q), Read, Recite, and Review (R3)**
> Many books about studying at college recommend the SQR3 approach to reading. The SQR3 approach helps you become an active reader. Active readers do not simply pick up a text and read it. They do tasks before reading, while reading, and after reading. These tasks help them understand and remember what they have read.

In this prereading activity, we will look at the first three steps only – survey, question, and read.

1 **Survey**   When you survey a text before reading it closely, you look at titles, headings, subheadings, highlighted words, pictures, graphs, and charts. You also look quickly through the text – perhaps reading some parts, such as the introduction and conclusion, more closely.

   • Survey the text "Inequality at Work." Report to the class about what you looked at and what you found out.

2 **Question**   Before you read a text, you should think about what the text will tell you. One way to do this is to make up questions you think will be answered by the text. As you read, you should keep checking to see if your questions are being answered.

   • On the basis of your survey, write down some questions that you think the text will answer. Look especially at any headings or highlighted words. One question, for example, might be "What is sexism?" Compare your questions with others in the class.

3 **Read**   You should read a text as if you are looking for the answers to your questions. Of course, you may not find the answers to all your questions because the answers may not be there. Also, you may find out much more than these answers as you read. But looking for answers is a good strategy to make you read actively.

Now read

Now read the text "Inequality at Work" with your questions in mind. When you finish, turn to the tasks on page 89.

Women won the right to vote in the United States in 1919, but they are still struggling for equality in the workplace.

3 INEQUALITY AT WORK

In the past, women have been denied the right to vote, to go to school, to borrow money, and to enter certain occupations. Women have, however, fought for their rights over the years and now **gender equality** is protected by a number of laws and rulings in many countries of the world. Nevertheless, inequalities still remain. Underlying these inequalities is prejudice against women that is based on **sexism**.

One of the areas where women fight for equality is the workplace. Since laws were passed to prohibit sex discrimination in employment more than thirty years ago, women have made some gains in the workplace. More women are employed than ever before and their pay is higher. Still, women are far from being equal to men economically. Women typically hold lower-status, lower-paying jobs. In many traditional female occupations – such as nursing, public school teaching, and secretarial work – women work in positions that are subordinate to those usually held by men. Thus, nurses are subordinate to doctors, teachers to principals, and secretaries to executives.

One of the reasons that women work in a narrower range of occupations than

gender equality
equal rights for men and women

sexism
prejudice and discrimination based on a person's gender

Positions	Percent held by women
Secretaries	99
Dental hygienists	99
Receptionists	97
Childcare workers	97
Cleaners and servants .	94
Registered nurses	94
Bank tellers	88
Librarians	88
Billing clerks	86
Elementary school teachers	86
Waiters	80

Source: Statistical Abstract of the United States

Table 4.1 Percent of lower-status, lower-paying positions held by women.

men is their commitment to the family. Schwartz (1989) has identified two types of women in the workforce – "career-primary" and "career and family" women:

> The majority of women . . . are what I call career-and-family women, women who want to pursue serious careers while participating actively in the rearing of children . . . most of them are willing to trade some career growth and compensation for freedom from the constant pressure to work long hours and weekends.

Many of these women, as a result, take jobs that are primarily clerical (for example, secretaries), operative (for example, machine operator), and service (for example, sales clerk). The pay is low and the opportunity for advancement is limited. The benefit, however, is that they can quit at any time, take care of their families as long as necessary, and then get another job when family demands decrease.

In recent years the participation of women in jobs traditionally held by males has increased. However, the number of women making their way up to higher management positions is still relatively small. A 1994 study, for example, found that women make up about 24 percent of officials and managers in industry. At the higher, vice-presidential level, women make up an even smaller proportion – less than 5 percent (Reskin and Padavic 1994; Kilborn 1995).

Even when women hold the same jobs as men, or have equal skills, training, and education, they tend to earn less. The state of Washington has tried to solve this problem by introducing a policy of *comparable worth*. This means that women are paid the same as men for doing different but equally demanding work. For example, office cleaning may be paid the same as truck driving. Some other states have followed Washington's lead with similar programs. Even so, among industrial nations, the United States has nearly the worst record in women's earnings, as Figure 4.1 shows.

Figure 4.1 The gender gap in earnings: a global view.

After you read

Task 1 THE SQR3 SYSTEM (PART II)

> The SQR3 approach to reading also includes two strategies to use after reading: Recite and Review.

1 **Recite**   When you recite, you say aloud from memory what you have read about. You can do this while reading, stopping after each paragraph and asking yourself: Now what did I just read? Do I understand the main ideas? Did the text answer my questions?

- Choose a paragraph from the text. Re-read it and then tell a partner what your paragraph was about. Listen to your partner tell you about a different paragraph.

2 **Review**   Reviewing means going back over the text and thinking about how much you understand. You can put a check (✓) next to the parts you understand and a question mark (?) next to the parts that are still unclear.

- Review the text now and put checks and question marks where appropriate. Discuss with a small group the parts you did not understand.

Task 2 BUILDING VOCABULARY: COLLOCATIONS

> When learning English it is a good idea to be aware of collocations. Collocations are combinations of words that often occur together. For example, some verbs are often followed by certain nouns. The more collocations you are aware of, the easier reading becomes.

Scan the text and find the nouns that occur with these verbs.

to deny _the right_	to pass _____	to take _____
to enter _____	to hold _____	to solve _____
to fight for _____	to pursue _____	to follow _____

Task 3 SUMMARIZING

> Reciting and reviewing, as in the SQR3 system, is one way to help you understand a text. Writing a summary is another good way. It also helps you to remember what you have read.

Write a one-paragraph summary of the text. Include only the main ideas and omit very specific details or supporting evidence. Include these words in your summary:

sexism   inequality   workplace
lower status   lower pay   "career and family"

Preparing to read

EXAMINING GRAPHIC MATERIAL

It is important to study any data presented in charts and tables. These often give additional information about the research reported in the text. Looking at them before you read can also give you an idea of what the text is about.

1 Read the questions in the first paragraph of the text and then look at Tables 4.2 and 4.3. Which question does each table answer?

2 Tell a partner one interesting or surprising thing you learned from each table.

THINKING ABOUT THE TOPIC

1 Read the following remarks made by a married male boss to a single female office worker. Check (✓) if you think the remarks are *OK, Somewhat inappropriate (SI), Sexual discrimination (SD)* or *Sexual harassment (SH)*.

	OK	SI	SD	SH
1 Hey, you're really looking great, today. I love that dress.				
2 I'm starving. How about getting some lunch? We could go to the coffee shop on the corner.				
3 Would you like to have dinner with me tonight? I'd really like to get to know you better.				
4 Here, I've bought you a little present. I hope you don't mind. It's just a pair of earrings. Why don't you try them on?				
5 This is completely wrong. I knew I should have asked a man to do the job if I wanted it done right.				
6 Come on. Give me just one kiss. No one will ever know.				
7 Be a honey, would you and look this up for me? I'm really busy and you know I'm hopeless with computers.				
8 I'm sorry I didn't give you the promotion, but I didn't think you could cope with the job because of your home commitments – especially now with your new baby.				
9 Let me open the door for you.				
10 In our company, we expect female staff members to look like females. So the rule is that you wear a dress or a skirt every day.				

2 Compare your answers in a small group.

Now read

Now read the text "Sexual Harassment." When you finish, turn to the tasks on page 94.

4 SEXUAL HARASSMENT

What is sexual harassment? How often does it occur? And what are the consequences for the individuals and organizations involved? Sexual harassment is difficult to define. Its meanings range from telling a sexual joke to a co-worker to one individual putting pressure on another for sex (Mazer and Percival 1989). Here, we define sexual harassment as unwanted sexual advances.

Sexual harassment affects both men and women, but in general, women report that they have experienced sexual harassment more often than men. In a survey of 1,232 women and men in Los Angeles County, researcher Barbara Gutek (1985) provided the data shown in Table 4.2.

Is the woman in this picture being harassed by her boss? Sexual harassment is not always easy to define.

Have you ever experienced sexual harassment?	
Women:	53.1%
Men:	37.3%
Have you ever talked to a co-worker about sexual harassment?	
Women:	22.5%
Men:	5.5%
Have you ever transferred to another department because you were sexually harassed?	
Women:	5.1%
Men:	0.2%
Have you ever quit a job because you were sexually harassed?	
Women:	9.6%
Men:	1.2%
Have you ever lost a job because you refused sex?	
Women:	6.9%
Men:	2.2%

Table 4.2

Sexual harassment is:	
Expected sexual activity Women: 98.0% Men: 94.5%	Insulting looks, gestures Women: 80.3% Men: 61.1%
Expected socializing Women: 95.8% Men: 91.1%	Complimentary comments Women: 33.5% Men: 21.9%
Insulting comments Women: 85.5% Men: 70.3%	Complimentary looks, gestures Women: 28.9% Men: 18.9%
Sexual touching Women: 84.3% Men: 58.6%	Nonsexual touching Women: 7.3% Men: 6.6%

Table 4.3

Table 4.3 indicates the percentage of women and men in Gutek's survey who defined a particular behavior as sexual harassment. Notice that women are more likely than men to label each of the categories of behavior as sexual harassment.

One of the causes of sexual harassment in the workplace is "sex role spillover" – that is, what happens when expectations about behavior are carried over from other domains (for example, the home) into the workplace. One example is a female employee being expected to serve as a helper or assistant without ever advancing to a top managerial position. Another is a male employee being automatically expected to act as a leader in a mixed-gender group. Gutek observed that a main reason for sex role spillover is that we tend to define a person more by their gender than by their work. Try to think of a person you know without being aware of their gender. It is impossible to do. Yet it is easy to think about some people without thinking about their work role. Another explanation for sex role spillover is that some females may feel more comfortable with a stereotypically female role. Some men may also be more used to interacting with females in stereotypical roles – as wives, daughters, sisters, or mothers – and may only feel comfortable relating to women this way.

Sexual harassment has negative consequences for the individuals involved and for the companies they work for. It affects job satisfaction and career advancement of workers, especially female workers. It also affects companies. They may not be able to find employees willing to work for them. Customers may stop buying their products. Employees may feel less committed to the company and even leave. On top of all this, sexual harassment lawsuits are usually very costly. Sexual harassment has been estimated to cost the country's 500 largest companies an average of $6.7 million annually.

While sexual harassment law and policies have generally been welcomed by society, there are still some concerns about them. In workplaces, many workers (especially men) are worried that their normal, friendly behavior could be considered sexual harassment. Can they compliment a co-worker about his or her appearance? Can they ask a co-worker out on a date? Should they avoid being alone with another worker? Some critics fear that the policies will affect normal professional relationships between men and women because of these sorts of concerns. Others see that the laws deny individual rights – telling individuals how they should behave and even how they should speak. Some women fear that making sexual harassment a crime will make women less powerful, because they will be seen as weak creatures who need special handling. They believe that women should learn to handle such situations themselves. Others say that putting nonsexist people in management positions is more effective than making laws against sexual harassment (for example, Gutek 1985). Whatever their view, most people would agree that the issue is an extremely complex one.

Some people are concerned that sexual harassment issues may limit sociability in the workplace.

After you read

Task 1 SCANNING

Look back at the text to find

1 the definition of sexual harassment adopted in this reading.
2 the researcher who surveyed men and women in Los Angeles County in 1985.
3 the percentage of men and women who had quit a job because of sexual harassment.
4 the definition of "sex role spillover."
5 the percentage of men and women who consider "insulting comments" a type of sexual harassment.
6 a typical question that workers (especially men) may ask themselves because they are worried that they might be accused of sexual harassment.

Task 2 LANGUAGE FOCUS: EXPRESSING NUMERICAL DATA

In assignments at college you will often need to draw upon research data expressed numerically – in numbers, fractions, or percentages. When you write about this research, however, it will often be more useful to the reader if you *approximate* the numerical data.

In this text, for example, we are told that 53.1 percent of the women surveyed had experienced sexual harassment. We could approximate this finding as "Just over half the women surveyed had experienced sexual harassment."

1 Look at this chart of words and expressions that we can use to express numerical data.

(just) over more than less than roughly approximately	half a quarter three-quarters 60%	of the women/men/etc.
most a (large) majority a (very) small number a (very) large number	of the women/men/etc.	

2 Use the words and expressions in the chart to write five sentences about the research discussed in the text.

Task 3 READING CRITICALLY

Textbooks are filled with the *results* of research, but quite often, little or no information is given about how the research was done (the *methodology*). Research methodology includes:

- where the research was done
- how many subjects were involved
- how the subjects were chosen
- who the subjects were
- how their responses were obtained (for example, individual interview, group interview, written survey)
- what they were asked
- how their answers were recorded.

When you read research results, it is important to think about how the methodology might have affected the results. This will, in turn, affect how you use the results yourself in assignments and essays.

Imagine, for example, that you are reading about a research study on women's attitudes toward work. If you read that the research was done in only one small workplace, you should bear in mind that the particular work situation (for example, the type of work the women did, and whether or not they liked their boss) may have affected the way these women answered questions about work in general. Therefore, you should probably use the study only as an example of research on the subject. You would not want to use it to draw conclusions about the attitudes of all working women.

1 | Look back at the text and find as many references as you can to Barbara Gutek's research. Then answer these two questions:

   1 What do you know about the methodology of Gutek's research?

   2 What more would you like to know to help you evaluate her results?

2 | Look back at one other text in this chapter. Scan the text to find a report of research results. Discuss with a partner who chose the same research results what you would like to know about the methodology of the research, and what confidence you have in the reported results.

Task 4 THINKING ABOUT THE TOPIC

Discuss your views on these questions about sexual harassment with other students:

1 Are sexual harassment policies necessary in workplaces?
2 Do sexual harassment laws and policies give women power or take power away from them?
3 Do sexual harassment laws and policies deny individual rights? How?
4 Do you agree or disagree with the way men and women defined sexual harassment in Gutek's survey?
5 What reasons in addition to "sex role spillover" could explain why sexual harassment is such a problem in today's workplace?

CHAPTER 4 WRITING ASSIGNMENT

Choose one of the following topics as your chapter writing assignment.

1 Think about what you have read in this chapter and write an answer to the survey question in "Previewing the unit" on page 52, "Do you think it is easier to be a man or a woman?"
2 "People should be paid by the government to do housework." Do you agree or disagree with this statement? Explain your answer.
3 Write about your own personal experiences and views on balancing work or study with home life. You could write about yourself or about someone you know.
4 What do you think are the most important gender issues in today's workplace (for men, or women, or both)? Write about at least two.

Unit **3**

Media and Society

I n this unit we look at the media, including radio, television, newspapers, magazines, and the Internet. In Chapter 5, we consider
how and why we use the media. We look at the kind of information
the media contains, who and what gets reported, and how accurate
that reporting is. We also look at the role of advertising in the media,
and the strategies used by advertisers to sell their products. In Chapter 6, we consider notions such as privacy, freedom of expression,
and censorship. We also look at the influence of TV on children,
especially the impact of showing violence on TV.

Previewing the unit

> Before reading a unit (or chapter) of a textbook, it is a good idea to preview the contents page and to think about the topics that will be covered.

Read the contents page for Unit 3. Then work with a partner and do the activities below.

Chapter 5 Mass Media Today

1 | Write a one-sentence definition of the term *mass media*. Use these excerpts from dictionary definitions of the words *mass* and *media* to help you.

mass (adj) . . . affecting a large number of individuals . . .
media (noun, pl) . . . methods of communication . . .

Begin your definition like this:

The term mass media refers to . . .

2 | Compare your definition with a partner. Then, with your partner, make a list of as many different kinds of mass media as you can think of.

_____   _____

_____   _____

_____   _____

_____   _____

3 | Read the first paragraph of the first text in Chapter 5, "The Role of Mass Media," on page 101. Compare your definition and your list of mass media with the definition and list in the paragraph. Find the similarities and differences.

Chapter 6 The Influence of the Media

1 | Find out the meanings of the following words used in this chapter.
- censorship
- privacy
- truth
- propaganda

2 | Discuss with other students what issues and problems are connected with censorship, privacy, truth, and propaganda in the mass media.

Unit Contents 3

Preparing to read

PERSONALIZING THE TOPIC

> Thinking about your own personal connections to a topic before you read will help you absorb new information on that topic.

Think about your own use of the mass media. Complete the following chart. Then compare your answers in a small group.

MEDIA	On average, how many hours per week do you spend using these media?	What are your main purposes for using the media? • Information • Education • Entertainment • Other	Which media do you use most often to get the news? Put the media in order from 1 to 5. 1 = most often used 5 = least often used
TV			
Radio			
Newspapers			
Magazines			
Internet			

BUILDING VOCABULARY: LEARNING WORDS RELATED TO THE TOPIC

1 Work with a partner, and describe each type of television program. Give some examples.

talk shows	soap operas
news	cartoons
prime-time movies	comedies
late-night talk shows	documentaries

2 At what time of the day is each type of program likely to be shown on television?

early morning	early afternoon	evening
mid-morning	late afternoon	late evening

3 Compare your answers with those of another pair of students.

Now read

Now read the text "The Role of Mass Media." When you finish, turn to the tasks on page 104.

Mass Media Today

1 THE ROLE OF MASS MEDIA

The term *mass media* refers to the channels of communication *(media)* that exist to reach a large public audience (the *mass* of the population). Mass media includes newspapers, magazines, television, radio, and more recently, the Internet. It informs people about events that they would otherwise know little about. Mass media communication is usually rapid, because the media will report an important event as quickly as possible after it happens. In fact, some television reporting is live; that is, the viewers can see the events as they happen. It is also transient; that is, the focus on one event doesn't last long. This is captured in the expression "there is nothing as old as yesterday's news." 1

The mass media is an important part of life in the United States and most Americans are exposed to the media daily in the form of print, sound waves, and pictures. Over 55 million newspapers are circulated each day. There are over five radios per household, and it is estimated that radio reaches 77 percent of people over the age of 12 every day. The radio listening time for those over 12 is more than three hours each day. Most households also have two or more television sets, with a total viewing time of about seven hours per day. The amount of time that people spend in front of their television sets varies with age, gender, and education, but on average it amounts to three to four hours a day. 2

While most of us make use of some form of the media on a daily basis, we may not think about the functions or purposes the media serves in our society. One important function is entertainment. On television, in particular, the variety of entertainment programs is extensive, ranging from soap operas, to comedy, to talk shows, to sports. Even advertising, where the main purpose is to sell things to the public, may sometimes be seen as entertainment.

Another function is education. A quick look through a television or radio guide will reveal many programs with an educational focus. These include documentaries on a wide range of topics such as animal behavior, geography, history, or art. They also include a wide variety of instructional programs such as cooking, home decorating, or investing. Some children's programs are also educational, teaching children to count or recognize words, or introducing them to different societies and cultures.

The media can provide important community information in the form of warnings. For example, the media can warn of the danger of an approaching hurricane or tornado. These warnings provide up-to-the-minute information on the location of the bad weather and alert people to take the necessary precautions. Without such warnings there would be a greater danger of loss of life and property. Warnings may also be given for other hazards such as air or water pollution. Periodically, the media raises questions about water quality, suggesting that the water we drink is not safe. How much these water scares are motivated by commercial interests is unknown. However, bottled water is a 2-billion-dollar business and growing.

In addition to these functions, the media has an important role in shaping our beliefs. Sometimes information contained in the media is

Politicians use the media to shape the public's opinion about them. Here former Vice President Al Gore chats with popular talk show host Oprah Winfrey.

deliberately presented in such a way that it encourages us to believe certain things or to form certain opinions. This practice is referred to as *propaganda*. When we think of propaganda, we usually think of political forces, but commercial interests may also use the media to propagandize. Advertisements, for example, encourage us to believe that certain products will change our lives in amazing ways. The media can also influence what we believe is possible. For example, 43 percent of American adults believe that UFOs (Unidentified Flying Objects) may be space vehicles from another planet, and most Americans think that alien visitors would be like E.T. from the movie by Steven Spielberg. TV and movies are likely to be responsible for these views (Miller 1987).

A further function of the mass media is that of socialization. This is the process by which a society transmits cultural values about what is appropriate behavior to its members. People may be socialized into behaving in certain ways in response to a personal problem, because they have frequently seen others on the news or in soap operas behaving that way in similar circumstances. Finally, for some people the media offers companionship. Television personalities and talk show hosts may be seen as "friends" by their viewers, particularly if those viewers are socially isolated, aged or invalid, and in need of companionship.

The range of functions or purposes of the media in society are many and varied, and the influence on our lives is considerable. The media influences how we spend our time and our money, what we get to see and hear about, and the way we understand those events. It helps to shape our beliefs, our opinions and our behaviors.

What's on commercial television?

The content of commercial television tends to follow a pattern. Early morning programs consist of news, interviews, and occasional movie reviews. Mid-morning programs usually include more talk shows, with some exercise and re-run shows. The early afternoon is devoted to "soaps," while late afternoon programming is mainly re-runs of old programs. There is evening news, and then from 8 p.m. to 11 p.m. is prime-time television with movies, situation comedies, and specials. There is usually late news followed by late-night talk shows, entertainment shows and movie re-runs. Scattered throughout the week are televised sporting events. The expansion of television stations through public broadcast, satellite and cable means that there are now many stations that specialize in particular kinds of programs.

After you read

Task 1 LINKING IDEAS IN A TEXT

Sometimes large sections of a text (several paragraphs) will provide a series of examples of something. This kind of organization of a text is often signaled in ways such as these:

There are a number of kinds of/examples of/functions of . . . One is . . .

The functions of/causes of . . . are many. They include . . .

Linking expressions may be used to show that another idea is being added to the list. Some common words used to link ideas in a text include: *another, further, also, and, secondly, finally, in addition to.*

If it is clear that a text is presenting a series of ideas, simply adding a new sentence or paragraph without using a linking expression is sometimes sufficient to signal that this is the next idea in the list. Understanding these organizational features will help you to follow the meaning of the text.

1 Underline the part of the text in paragraph 1 that signals to the reader that a list of different types of media will follow.

2 Paragraphs 3 to 7 list and explain the main functions or purposes of the media. Complete the chart with the functions and the linking expressions used to introduce them. If there is no linking expression write "none."

Par.	Functions of the media	Linking expressions
3		
4		
5		
6		
7		

3 Review the notes on writing a listing paragraph in Chapter 2 on page 49.

Use the list of media functions from the chart and some of the linking expressions to write a listing paragraph. Begin like this:

The media fulfills many functions in our daily lives. . . .

Task 2 APPLYING WHAT YOU READ

1 | Read the boxed text again. Compare the information in the boxed text with your answers in step 2 of the task "Building Vocabulary" on page 100.

2 | Find a TV viewing guide in a local newspaper. Do the programs follow the pattern identified in the boxed text?

3 | Discuss with a small group. Why do so many commercial TV channels follow this pattern in programming? Think about who the main viewing audience is at different times of the day.

Task 3 HIGHLIGHTING

Highlighting is a useful strategy for quickly recording important information in a text when you are studying for a test or doing research. However, simply highlighting information will not necessarily help you to recall it. You will need to review that information and perhaps make notes from it.

1 | The paragraph below is taken from the text. It presents facts and figures on media use in the United States. Highlight the media mentioned and the relevant facts and figures.

The mass media is an important part of life in the United States and most Americans are exposed to the media daily in the form of print, sound waves, and pictures. Over 55 million newspapers are circulated each day. There are over five radios per household, and it is estimated that radio reaches 77 percent of people over the age of 12 every day. The radio listening time for those over 12 is more than three hours each day. Most households also have two or more television sets, with a total viewing time of about seven hours per day. The amount of time that people spend in front of their television sets varies with age, gender, and education, but on average it amounts to three to four hours a day.

2 | Record the highlighted information in note form in the space below.

Form of media	Facts and Figures
1) *Newspapers*	
2)	
3)	

Preparing to read

THINKING ABOUT THE TOPIC

If something is *newsworthy*, it means that it has value or *worth* as news, and the public will probably be interested in hearing or reading about it in the media.

1 Put a check next to the events below that you think would be newsworthy to an American living in San Francisco.

☐ A fire destroys a church in a town in Brazil.
☐ The U.S. president trips on the sidewalk and falls over.
☐ A man drives his car into a parked van in a suburban street in Chicago.
☐ An elderly couple celebrates their 50th wedding anniversary with family and friends.
☐ A traffic accident stops traffic for three hours in Berkeley, a city across the bay from San Francisco.
☐ An earthquake occurs in Mongolia.
☐ An earthquake occurs in Los Angeles.
☐ It snows in Florida in May.

2 Discuss your choices with a small group. Why are some stories newsworthy and others not? Make a list of factors that make a story newsworthy.

SKIMMING

> Remember that skimming involves reading parts of a text such as sub-headings, opening sentences of paragraphs, or words in italics or bold.

1 Skim the text looking at the words in italics. Write down the words you recall.

_____   _____
_____   _____
_____   _____

2 Repeat the exercise. This time look quickly for information to explain the terms.

Now read

Now read the text "What Is Newsworthy?" When you finish, turn to the tasks on page 109.

2 WHAT IS NEWSWORTHY?

From all that is happening in the world, very few events or people are selected for the news. Why? What makes an event or person *newsworthy*? Research has identified a number of factors that influence the selection and shaping of news stories.

Negative events are more likely to be reported than positive ones. News of current events is often bad news. Such news includes disasters or accidents that involve damage, injury, or death. Consider how much news is about conflict between people, political parties, or nations. Once an event is selected for the news, the negative aspects of the event can then be highlighted through the use of strong negative language in the headline or story.

Time is also important. The best news is something that has just happened. The language of the story and of the headline tends to stress the immediacy of events. Headlines in the news most frequently make use of the present tense, rather than the past tense, for example "Bomb explodes in mall." This makes the event seem closer in time. The print media and the main TV and radio news programs operate on a daily cycle. Shorter events that fit into this time span are more likely to be reported than those that last longer. Therefore, the murder is more newsworthy than the police investigation; the verdict is more likely to be reported than the whole trial (adapted from Bell 1991).

An exception is when the person involved in a trial or other event is very *famous*. Famous people are more newsworthy than others. Sometimes an event can become news just because a politician or a movie star is involved. If it were about ordinary people, it would simply be ignored. Take, for example, the trial of O. J. Simpson, the famous American football player and media personality accused of murdering his wife. The trial became one of the most widely broadcast of all times, and millions of people around the world tuned in day after day to watch and listen, because he was a celebrity.

Geographic proximity or closeness is also a key factor. The closer the place, the more news value the event has. A minor accident may be reported in the place where it happens, but not 100 miles away. A major catastrophe can be reported from the other side of the world. The issue of proximity can also apply to cultural associations (Galtang and Ruge in Bell 1991). In the English language media a story from an English speaking nation is likely to be considered more newsworthy than a similar story from a non-English speaking nation. When a bomb exploded in a market in the Irish town of Omagh in 1998, killing 30 people and injuring 200, it was reported at length in one English language newspaper, with long stories and photographs. A few months later when a bomb exploded in a market in an Algerian town, the complete news report in the same newspaper consisted of the following:

Negative events – such as this hurricane in Belize that left 13,000 people homeless – are more likely to be reported than positive events.

Photojournalists, reporters, and TV crews turned football star O.J. Simpson's trial for murder into a sensational event.

MARKET BOMB KILLS 29

Algiers: A bomb exploded in a market in Tiaret, south of the Algerian capital, killing 29 people and injuring 110. (*South China Morning Post* 1998)

The media also prefers stories that are *clear and unambiguous*, and contain many *facts and figures*. These may be facts about place and time, people's names and occupations, and figures to do with numbers of people involved, amounts of money, or measurements of various kinds. In general, too, *the unexpected or unusual* are more newsworthy than the ordinary and routine (Bell 1991).

Rescue workers spent long hours looking for victims of the World Trade Center Disaster.

September 11, 2001

The destruction of New York's World Trade Center on September 11, 2001, received a huge amount of coverage in the media throughout the western world and in many other parts of the world as well. This was an event that combined all the factors necessary to become *newsworthy*. It was a disaster that occurred unexpectedly on a beautiful day in early autumn, taking thousands of lives. Geographically, the World Trade Center buildings were in the heart of the financial district of one of the largest cities in the world. Furthermore, although the World Trade Center was located in New York City, many international companies had offices in its buildings, which meant that a large number of people from countries around the world were personally affected. Leading figures in the business community were killed alongside people less well known. Prominent politicians and community leaders commented publicly on the event, and famous artists performed at memorial services or made special appearances to raise money for families of the victims.

News coverage of the World Trade Center disaster also had another side that doesn't often get reported in tragedies. Shortly after the news of the actual collapse of the buildings, the media began to report on the heroism of rescue workers – the fire fighters, medical personnel, and police who rushed to the site and, in many cases, lost their own lives in trying to help others.

After you read

Task 1 APPLYING WHAT YOU READ

1 | Work with a partner. Re-read the text quickly. Find and list all of the factors for newsworthiness mentioned in the text.

2 | Read the following news headlines. Which factors from your list make each story newsworthy?

1 Blast Injures 2
2 $40 Million-Drug Bust In Los Angeles
3 Hurricane Rips Into Miami
4 Elsie Is 110 Today!
5 10,000 Homeless After Turkish Quake
6 Movie Star's Daughter Arrested For Drunk Driving
7 Hottest Winter's Day On Record

3 | Read the front page of a local English-language newspaper. Decide why each news item was included.

Task 2 READING NEWS STORIES

The main facts and figures in a news story are usually presented in the opening sentence or "lead." This first sentence answers "Wh" questions like Who? What? Where? When? and questions such as How? How much/many? Keep these question words in mind as you read the first sentence of a news story. Then read the rest of the story to find out the details.

1 | Read the following openings to news stories. Work with a partner and write as many "Wh" and "How" questions as you can from the information given for each story.

Story 1: A late winter storm hit New York yesterday, dumping fourteen inches of snow on the city and forcing airlines to cancel up to 50 percent of their flights.

Story 2: First prize in Sunday's state swimming competition at Texas State College went to a senior from the College of Abilene who took first place in the 100- and 200-meter races.

2 | Imagine you are reporting a bank robbery that has happened in your town.
- Write an opening sentence for a news story about the event that includes answers to "Wh" and "How" questions.
- Compare your sentence with that of another pair of students.

Preparing to read

REVIEWING PREVIOUS READINGS

Sometimes your reading of a longer text is interrupted for a period of time. When you begin to read again, it is a good idea to go back and review the previous section to remind yourself of the main points.

Quickly review the content of the previous text, "What is Newsworthy?" Give a brief summary of the main points to a partner.

BUILDING VOCABULARY: PREFIXES

A prefix is a part added to the beginning of a word to change its meaning in some way. For example, the prefix *sub* means *under* or *below*, so *submarine* is a vessel that goes *under the sea*, and a *subheading* is a heading that appears *below the main heading*.

It is a good idea to build up your knowledge of prefixes and suffixes to help you guess at the meanings of words you don't know.

1 In the examples below, the words in italics contain the prefix "mis":

- The article *misreports* the facts. The thief stole $1,000, not $10,000.
- I *misheard* you. I thought you said you came from Austria, not Australia.
- The governor was *misquoted*. She didn't say, "I will resign." She said, "I may resign."

From the context guess what each word means. How does adding the prefix "mis" to the beginning of a word change the meaning?

2 In the chart below, there are three more words that appear in this reading. Each has a prefix. Discuss the meaning of each word and its prefix. Check a dictionary to confirm the meaning. Finally, add two more words based on the same prefix under each word in the chart.

centimeters (par. 3)	**rearranging** (par. 6)	**unverified** (par. 7)

Now read

Now read the text "Reporting the Facts." When you finish, turn to the tasks on page 113.

3 REPORTING THE FACTS

Should you believe what you read or hear in the media? What is presented as fact is not always so. Sometimes errors occur because the reporters and editors did not check the facts properly. Sometimes news reporters misreport or misrepresent information in an effort to make a story more newsworthy. Changing the facts a little can make the story either more serious or more sensational.

1

Failing to check the facts

There have been some embarrassing examples where major newspapers and TV networks have published false information because reporters have not checked it for accuracy. One such example was the publication of a report of the death of the elderly comedian, Bob Hope. A U.S. Congressman apparently misheard someone talking about Bob Hope. He stood up in Congress and announced the death of the comedian. This was then picked up and published widely in the media. When reporters called Mr. Hope's home to follow up the story, his daughter was very surprised and assured them that he was at that moment happily eating his breakfast.

2

Misreporting

Research into the accuracy of media reporting has revealed some interesting findings. One media researcher (Bell 1991) collected and studied newspaper articles about climate change. His study revealed a number of examples of errors in the way that units of measurement were reported in the media. In one article about the rise in sea level, it was reported that the sea level was rising at 1 to 2 *centimeters* per year, when

3

the interviewee had (correctly) said *millimeters*. Another story predicted that the annual rainfall would increase 8 *centimeters* rather than *millimeters*. The researcher argued that these mistakes did not occur at random. If they were random we would expect to find units of measurement that were both smaller and larger than the correct ones. But all these incorrect measurements made the figures larger, not smaller. The exaggerations helped to build up the news value of the stories.

Misquoting

sources

people or organizations that provide reporters with information for a story

Misquotation of **sources** is a common complaint about news stories. In the study mentioned above (Bell 1991), 34 percent of sources believed they had been misquoted, that is, the sources did not really say what was reported in the news story. When you read a direct quotation in a news story, you probably think you are reading someone's exact words. But often the part of the text in quotation marks is actually a summary of what was said, put together by the reporter (van Dijk in Bell 1991). In some cases, sources that are quoted in media stories have never even spoken to the reporters.   4

A well-known case of misquotation occurred in the U.S. media in 1999. Al Gore, the U.S. vice president at the time, was speaking to a group of secondary school students about efforts to clean up toxic waste. He was referring to a community where the issue had been taken up by local residents and said, ". . .that was the one that started it all." One prominent newspaper reported his words as "I was the one that started it all." As this misquotation was re-reported by other newspapers around the country, Al Gore faced enormous criticism for trying to claim credit for things he had not done.   5

Misquotation is also possible in broadcasting (radio and television). Technology makes it possible to edit what someone says so that it sounds like continuous speech, when in fact some phrases or sentences have been removed. Broadcasters argue that this is sometimes necessary. They say that if they are quoting someone who is not a very skilled speaker, they have to edit the talk. Another issue is the rearranging of questions and answers, so that a question receives an answer that was originally given to another, though similar, question.   6

Rumors on the Internet

The Internet is the source of many rumors, or unverified stories. Rumors are generally spread from one person to another by word of mouth, and the story evolves or changes in the process. But the Internet has allowed rumors to spread much further and faster than ever before. In fact the Internet has begun to be used as a deliberate strategy to circulate rumors, often for political purposes and often with a serious impact. In 1998, false reports of riots in Malaysia sparked panic that prompted people to stock up on food and lock themselves indoors (*South China Morning Post* 1998).   7

After you read

Task 1 SCANNING

1 Scan the text and find the subsection in which each news story appears.

_____ **1** Annual rainfall will increase by 8 centimeters.

_____ **2** Al Gore said about toxic waste, "I was the one who started it all."

_____ **3** There were riots in Malaysia.

_____ **4** Bob Hope is dead.

a Failing to check the facts
b Misreporting
c Misquoting
d Rumors on the Internet

2 Each story in step 1 is false. Scan the text and find what is inaccurate in each one.

3 Explain how each inaccurate story is a good example of the main idea of the subsection in which it appears.

Task 2 ASKING FOR CLARIFICATION

It is important to be able to ask questions when you are not sure about the meaning of something in a text that you are reading. Furthermore, in some college classes, you will take part in discussion groups where you will be encouraged to talk and ask questions about difficult concepts and texts.

1 Look at some ways you could ask for clarification about parts of this text.

1 _I am not sure what the author means when she says that_ "these mistakes did not occur at random." (par. 3)

2 _Could you give me examples of what the author means when she says that_ "the exaggerations helped to build up the news value of the story"? (par. 3)

3 _Could you explain what the author means when he says,_ "edit what someone says so that it sounds like continuous speech"? (par. 6)

4 _I don't think I understand what the author means by_ "unverified stories." (par. 7)

2 Work with a partner. Discuss how you would answer the above requests for clarification.

3 Find other parts of the text where you would like to clarify the meaning. Take turns with your partner asking for and giving clarification.

Task 3 BUILDING VOCABULARY: COLLOCATIONS

Remember that, when learning vocabulary in English, it is useful to understand collocations or combinations of words that often occur together. There are, for example, some adjectives and nouns that frequently occur together, or collocate. Learning groups of words as collocations can help you expand your vocabulary more quickly.

1 The nouns below and the adjectives in the chart are from "Reporting the Facts."

criticism
information
complaint
impact
words
strategy

Collocations					
common	**false**	**enormous**	**deliberate**	**serious**	**exact**
criticism		*criticism*		*criticism*	

Work with a partner and decide which nouns can make collocations with the adjectives in the chart. In some cases, it is possible to use more than one noun with the same adjective.

2 Scan the text to find the actual collocations used.

3 Which of the following verbs can combine with the adjective-noun collocations you made above? You may need to add an article (a/an/the).

to publish
to have
to make
to plan
to record
to give

Task 4 **SUMMARIZING**

> Remember that summarizing is an essential study skill. Writing a good summary is a way of showing that you have understood what the text is about and what the most important points are.

Use eight of the words listed below to complete the summary of the text.

reporters	misquoted
accurate	questions
facts	sources
error	rumors
newsworthy	edited
exaggeration	strategy

News reports in the media sometimes contain information that is not _____. This may result from simple slips or insufficient checking of _____, or it may be the result of deliberate _____ to make the story more _____. People are sometimes _____, that is, they are reported as using words they did not use, or they are reported as giving answers to _____ that they were not actually asked. Sometimes people are reported as saying something when they have never even spoken to _____. The Internet is not always reliable. It is a source of _____, where unchecked facts are picked up and circulated widely around the world.

Preparing to read

THINKING ABOUT THE TOPIC

1 Think about an advertisement from television or a magazine.

   1 What was the product or service being advertised?

   2 Why do you think you remember this advertisement?

   3 Did it influence you to buy the product or service?

2 Discuss these questions with a small group:

   1 Are advertisements shown on television in your country?

   2 Are tobacco products advertised on television or in newspapers and magazines?

   3 Is alcohol advertised in the media?

   4 What kinds of products are advertised using images of families?

   5 What kinds of products are advertised using images of young people?

READING AROUND THE TOPIC

> Reading newspapers and magazines regularly will make your college reading easier. Articles, advertisements, and letters to the editor or to advice columns, for example, can provide examples of behaviors, attitudes, and events that you are studying.

Read the following news story on TV advertisements. Then discuss the questions below.

TV advertisers try the one-second sell

For many people the sight of a TV commercial is a prompt to visit the kitchen or hit the remote control. The length of a traditional 60-second TV advertisement has been halved a couple of times to keep up with our shortening attention spans and because they cost less. Now some advertisers are experimenting with the snack-proof and zap-proof advertisement – a one-second ad.

    This kind of commercial has been called a "blink ad." It is cheaper to buy and cheaper to make, but can you sell anything in one second? Advertisers say blink ads cannot introduce a product but they can certainly reinforce well-known logos and symbols such as McDonald's Golden Arches.

(*Source: Time*, Aug. 3, 1998, p. 43)

---

   1 Why is a one-second advertisement called a "blink ad"?

   2 What does it mean to be "snack-proof" and "zap-proof"?

   3 What company symbols or logos could be used in a blink ad?

Now read

Now read the text "Advertising in the Media." When you finish, turn to the tasks on page 120.

Your hammock is waiting . . .

4 ADVERTISING IN THE MEDIA

Most television networks, radio stations, and newspapers depend for their income on selling advertising time or space. As a result, advertising is a very common feature of all our daily media. In fact, in most daily newspapers, advertising makes up the majority of the content. Very large amounts of money are spent on the production of advertising – far more than is spent on media programs such as soap operas or the news. A television commercial can easily cost many thousands of dollars per second.

Like other texts in the media, advertisements have to attract the audience's attention, and there are many different strategies used in advertising to do this. Some advertisements provide information about a product or service in order to influence the audience to buy that product or service. They tell us what the product is made of, or what it is useful for, or how much it costs. But there is a growing number of advertisements that provide very little information about the product. Instead they are designed to create an image, an image that appeals to our desires and tastes. In the pages of glossy fashion magazines there are, for example, advertisements for perfumes, for jewelry, for watches, or for brand name clothes in which there is nothing more than a brand name or a logo and picture. The picture is often one that presents an image of beauty, wealth, an idyllic location or lifestyle (see the picture above), romance or popularity, things that we as the audience are assumed to desire or to want to be associated with.

What are some features in the design of advertisements that encourage us as the viewer to feel attracted and involved? One is eye contact. Models used in advertisements may look directly into the camera. This will give the impression that the model is looking at the viewer, which encourages the viewer to feel more involved than if the

model is looking away. Close-up photographs that clearly show the viewer the face and eyes are considered to be more involving than photographs taken from a distance.

4 Color is also an important issue in the design of advertisements. Bright, bold colors create a different impression from pale, pastel colors, and certain colors carry certain cultural associations and meanings. Red, for example, may mean danger or passion. It is generally described as a *warm* color, along with orange and yellow. Green and blue, on the other hand, are *cool* colors and are associated with a clean, fresh image. White is the color of purity and innocence, but also elegance, and gold is wealth.

5 Another strategy in advertisements is to feature famous or glamorous people wearing or using a product. The suggestion is that if we, too, wore or used this product we could share in some of the qualities that make them popular or famous or glamorous.

6 Where there is language as well as pictures, the words are often chosen to make some pattern or play on words. For example, in the advertisement below for Toyota there are examples of alliteration, where sequential words begin with the same letter or sound: Today . . . Tomorrow . . . Toyota.

Advertisements also make cultural references, which, if you are a part of that culture, bring to mind other ideas or associations. To make full sense of the following advertisement, for example, you would need to recognize that the two women are sisters and famous American tennis stars. You would need to know that "doubles" is the form of tennis where one pair of players competes against another pair. You would also need to know that in perhaps hundreds of American movies and TV shows a character walks to a bar and says "Make mine a double," meaning a large-size drink.

After you read

Task 1 APPLYING WHAT YOU READ

1 Look again at the advertisements in the text and discuss these questions with a partner.

   1 What strategies mentioned in the text are used in the design of these advertisements?

   2 Who do you think is the target audience for these advertisements? Why?

2 What meanings, if any, do you associate with the following colors?

Blue _____

Pink _____

Yellow _____

Black _____

3 Find other advertisements in local newspapers or magazines. Discuss the following questions in a small group:

   1 What strategies are used in the advertisements you found?

   2 Who do you think is the target (intended) audience for these advertisements? Why?

   3 What colors are used and what impression do they give?

Task 2 BUILDING VOCABULARY: DEALING WITH UNKNOWN WORDS

1 Work with a partner and make a list of at least four different strategies you can use when you come across a word you do not know. If you want to review the strategies presented in previous tasks, look back at Chapter 1, Task 2 on page 7 and Chapter 2, Task 3 on page 43.

_____

_____

_____

_____

2 Now find the following words in the text. Figure out the meaning of each word. Tell another pair of students which strategy you used for each word.

glossy (par. 2)
brand name (par. 2)
logo (par. 2)
idyllic (par. 2)
glamorous (par. 5)
sequential (par. 6)

Task 3 DRAMATIZING THE TEXT

Imagine that you are asked to develop a television commercial that advertises a new product. Work in a small group.

1| Decide on the following:

- the product
- the target audience
- the length of your commercial
- strategies you will use to sell your product

2| Develop a commercial for your product.

3| Rehearse the commercial.

4| Perform the commercial for your class.

CHAPTER 5 WRITING ASSIGNMENT

Choose one of the following topics as your writing assignment.

1 Write about your favorite TV program. Say what kind of program it is, describe what it is about, and explain why you like it.

2 Consider each form of mass media. Write about the advantages and disadvantages of each for communicating news to the public.

3 Choose a recent news event that has received a lot of attention in the media. Describe the news event and explain why it has received so much attention.

4 "Advertising is a necessary evil." Do you agree with this statement? Why or why not?

Preparing to read

PREDICTING

Work with a partner. Look at the photographs below.

1 | Who are these people? What do you already know about them?

2 | These people are mentioned in the text you will read. Why do you think they might be mentioned in a text about privacy and the media?

THINKING ABOUT THE TOPIC

Work in a group. Imagine that you are members of the editorial board of a newspaper. You have photographs of the following events:

- a politician passionately kissing someone other than his or her spouse
- a person threatening to commit suicide by jumping off a building
- a movie star punching a news reporter in the street
- a wild dog attacking someone
- the arrest of a teenager for shoplifting
- a movie star sunbathing in a bikini in the backyard of her private residence

Discuss and decide which of these photographs, if any, you will publish in your newspaper. What factors did you consider in making your decisions?

Now read

Now read the text "Privacy and the Media." When you finish, turn to the tasks on page 126.

The Influence of the Media

Chapter 6

1 PRIVACY AND THE MEDIA

Journalists are often faced with difficult decisions about whether or not to print a story or a photograph. There are a number of **ethical issues** they need to consider. Is the material too violent? Will it upset people because it tells about acts or events that are against their moral values? Does it represent an invasion of someone's privacy, that is, does it present to the public something that should remain private? Journalists must decide what responsibility, if any, they have to society and if that responsibility is best fulfilled by publishing or not publishing.

An interesting question related to invasion of privacy is whether or not the public has the right to know about the private lives of people who are public figures. In 1987, one U.S. presidential candidate, Gary Hart, was forced to drop out before the election because of press stories about his affair with a woman. Now, all candidates for the office

1

ethical issues
questions of what is morally right and wrong

2

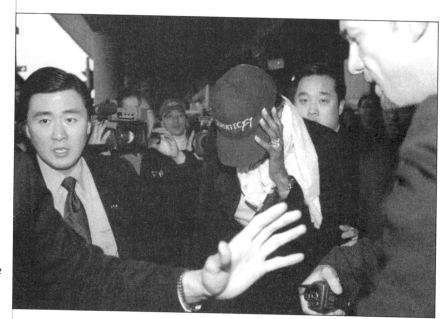

Does everyone have a right to know about the private lives of public figures?

of president can expect to have their personal lives watched closely and with interest by the media. In 1998, the story of the relationship between President Clinton and Monica Lewinsky dominated the media for many months. The public was presented with very personal details of the relationship, and the scandal almost forced the president to resign. A basic question for the media is whether a politician's personal life is relevant to his or her performance in the job. One point of view suggests that if a person is not honest and faithful to his or her spouse, that person will not be honest and faithful to his or her country. Another view says that if you get rid of everyone who has broken a moral law, there will be no one left to serve in public office.

Politicians are not the only ones whose private lives are of interest to the media. Famous people of various kinds, including movie stars and royalty, are often closely followed by the press. There have been stories of journalists digging through garbage bins to find little bits of information on the private lives of the rich and famous. Some press photographers try to take photographs of famous people in their most private moments to sell to the world's media. They often use very powerful long lenses so that they can take photos from a distance and spy into people's homes, for example. These photographers are called *paparazzi*.

Paparazzi have been around for decades, but the business has grown in recent years as there are now more magazines that focus on the lives of famous people. New technology such as digital videos and cameras also allows for the photos to be sent much more quickly to one publisher or to many publishers around the world. There is a lot of money to be made and this means that some of the paparazzi are becoming even more aggressive in their efforts to get a "good" photo. Some paparazzi have been accused of deliberately starting fights with movie stars in order to catch them on film in embarrassing situations.

In 1997, when Princess Diana died in a car accident in Paris, her car was being chased by paparazzi. This started a big public debate about the behavior of paparazzi and the issues of privacy and the media. There was much public criticism of the paparazzi and of the newspapers and magazines that published paparazzi photos. One member of the paparazzi argued, "I feel no responsibility, legal or moral. Of course I'm sad, because someone we all adored is dead. But when you become Princess Di, you are a public person." Many magazine editors say that when they are deciding whether or not to use paparazzi photos, they consider each case separately. They decide whether the news value of a picture is more important than the person's right to peace and privacy. **5**

Some critics have called for laws to limit the actions of paparazzi. However, the campaign against the paparazzi has its dangers. Journalism necessarily involves some degree of unwelcome observation, that is, the journalist's job is to investigate matters that some people would rather not be publicized. Moreover, famous people often use the paparazzi for their own purposes. They look for as much media coverage as possible to keep them in the news, in order to maintain their fame and popularity. **6**

Australian model Elle MacPherson seems to be enjoying and encouraging media attention at this event. Famous people may complain about press attention but they often rely on it to maintain their fame.

After you read

Task 1 READING FOR MAIN IDEAS

1 Each of the following statements summarizes one of the six paragraphs in this text. Number the statements 1–6 according to the number of the paragraph each statement summarizes.

_____ **a** There are several reasons why there are more paparazzi today.

_____ **b** There is a question as to whether the press should write about the private lives of public figures.

_____ **c** Journalists face many ethical questions before they decide whether or not to publish a story in the media.

_____ **d** Criticizing the actions of the paparazzi may have its dangers.

_____ **e** Journalists and photographers have many different tricks to get pictures and find out private things about celebrities.

_____ **f** The death of Princess Diana led to a debate on what journalists should and should not be allowed to do.

2 Read statement **b** above. Can you think of any recent examples in the news in which the press has damaged the careers of one or more of the following: a politician, a sports figure, a movie star, a TV personality? Discuss your example with a partner.

Task 2 BUILDING VOCABULARY: GUESSING THE MEANING FROM CONTEXT

Read the passages below that are from the text and use the context to work out what the word in bold probably means. Choose the answers from the following definitions.

a causing shame and discomfort   **d** not wanted   **g** quit
b using strong, forceful methods   **e** a shocking event   **h** attention
c was most important   **f** on purpose   **i** examine

In 1987, one U.S. presidential candidate, Gary Hart, was forced to **drop out** before the election because of press stories about his affair with a woman. Now, all candidates for the office of president can expect to have their personal lives watched closely and with interest by the media. In 1998, the story of the relationship between President Clinton and Monica Lewinsky **dominated** the media for many months. The public was presented with very personal details of the relationship, and the **scandal** almost forced the president to resign.

_g_ **1** drop out

_____ **2** dominated

_____ **3** scandal

There is a lot of money to be made and this means that some of the paparazzi are becoming even more **aggressive** in their efforts to get a "good" photo. Some paparazzi have been accused of **deliberately** starting fights with movie stars in order to catch them on film in **embarrassing** situations.

_____ **4** aggressive

_____ **5** deliberately

_____ **6** embarrassing

Some critics have called for laws to limit the actions of paparazzi. However, the campaign against the paparazzi has its dangers. Journalism necessarily involves some degree of **unwelcome** observation, that is, the journalist's job is to **investigate** matters that some people would rather not be publicized. Moreover, famous people often use the paparazzi for their own purposes. They look for as much media **coverage** as possible to keep them in the news, to maintain their fame and popularity.

_____ **7** unwelcome

_____ **8** investigate

_____ **9** coverage

Task 3 WRITING A DISCUSSION PARAGRAPH

A discussion paragraph is often organized in the following way:

1 statement of the issue

2 argument for one side

3 argument for the other side

Understanding this structure will help your reading and your writing.

1 Work with a partner.

- Re-read the extract from the text below.
- Underline the part that describes the topic being discussed.
- Highlight in one color the argument for one side.
- Highlight in a different color the argument for the other side.

A basic question for the media is whether a politician's personal life is relevant to his or her performance in the job. One point of view suggests that if a person is not honest and faithful to his or her spouse, that person will not be honest and faithful to his or her country. Another view says that if you get rid of everyone who has broken a moral law, there will be no one left to serve in public office.

2 Discuss this question with a partner. Think of one main argument in favor and one main argument against.

Should the media be able to broadcast the coverage of a trial live from a courtroom?

3 Use the same structure as in the extract in step 1 to write a discussion paragraph on the topic of live broadcast of trials from a courtroom. Begin like this:

One question concerning privacy is whether the media should be able to broadcast the coverage of a trial live from a courtroom.

Preparing to read

READING AROUND THE TOPIC

Read the passage below to find answers to the following questions:

1 What is the Internet?
2 How did it begin?
3 Why do people use the Internet today?

The Internet is a global network of hundreds of thousands of linked computers that pass information back and forth. It was originally developed by the U.S. military. The network later began to be used by academics and researchers around the world so that they could share information. In recent years there has been an explosion in the use of the technology by the general public, and the Internet now reaches offices, schools, and homes around the world. People use the Internet for many different communication needs including commercial, political, educational, entertainment, and personal.

PERSONALIZING THE TOPIC

Discuss the following questions with a partner:

1 Do you use the Internet? If so, how often and for what purpose? If not, why not?
2 Is your use of, and attitude about, computers different from that of your parents?

SPEED READING

When you are studying, it is important to be able to read quickly. You do not have time to read everything slowly and carefully. Review the speed-reading techniques in Chapter 3, page 70.

Practice the speed-reading techniques as you read "Internet Issues." Time yourself (or your teacher will time you). Try to read the text in four minutes. Then tell a partner two or three main ideas you understood from the text.

Now read

Now read the text "Internet Issues." When you finish, turn to the tasks on page 132.

2 INTERNET ISSUES

The Internet is an amazing information resource. Students, teachers, and researchers use it as an investigative tool. Journalists use it to find information for stories. Doctors use it to learn more about unfamiliar diseases and the latest medical developments. Ordinary people use it for shopping, banking, bill-paying, and communicating with family and friends. People all over the world use it to connect with individuals from other countries and cultures. However, while there are many positive developments associated with the Internet, there are also certain fears and concerns.

One concern relates to a lack of censorship or control over what appears on the Internet. Anyone can put information on the Internet that can then be read by anyone else, at any time. This makes it very different from television or radio. With television and radio there are editors to check the accuracy or appropriateness of the content of programs, and with television there are restrictions on what kinds of programs can be broadcast and at what times of the day. With the Internet, parents cannot check a published guide to determine what is suitable for their children to see. While **software** can be used to block access to certain **websites,** such as those displaying pornography, this can never be completely effective.

software

programs used to operate a computer

website

a location where information is published on the World Wide Web

If you shop on the Internet, it is possible for others to trace every site you visit. This information could be used to your disadvantage.

on-line
| connected to the Internet

browse
| to look through something
(in this case, various sites
on the Internet) without
searching for anything in
particular

There are also concerns about privacy and control of communication on the Internet. For example, when you use e-mail communication or participate in chat groups, it is possible that your private messages may be read by others without your knowing. If you buy things **on-line** or simply **browse** the Internet, it is possible to trace all the websites that you visit. Someone may be looking over your shoulder "electronically." Such information can be used to build up a profile of your interests and habits. One purpose for such a profile is to provide information to companies who sell on-line advertising space. If they know your habits and interests, they can select particular advertisements to send to you when you are on-line. The advertisements are chosen to match your profile. One potential danger is that the information could be used by others to your disadvantage. For example, an employer could use such information to decide that you are not a suitable applicant for a job.

A further issue relates to the misuse of the Internet in the workplace. Many companies are now finding that they need to establish policies to control when employees use the Internet and for what purposes. Recent surveys undertaken in the United States have revealed, for example, that:

- 47 percent of employees send up to five personal e-mails per day, 32 percent send up to ten personal e-mails daily, and 28 percent receive up to twenty personal e-mails per day.
- On-line industry analysts predict that Internet misuse will cost companies an estimated 1 billion dollars in lost productivity.
- In companies that use software to monitor employee use of the Internet, 60 percent of the managers said they had disciplined employees for on-line misuse, and 30 percent had fired people for such behavior, which included shopping or gambling on-line and **downloading** pornography.

downloading
| moving data from the
Internet or a computer
network onto a personal
computer

A fourth and growing area of concern is that of Internet addiction. 5
An Internet addict is someone who is unable to control his or her own
use of the Internet and whose behavior threatens to overwhelm his or
her normal life. Internet addiction can result in many problems including a lack of sleep, lateness for appointments, neglect of work responsibilities, and the disintegration of marriages and families. Internet
addiction is not just a matter of how much time a person spends on-
line. It is more a matter of how much damage Internet use causes in
a person's life.

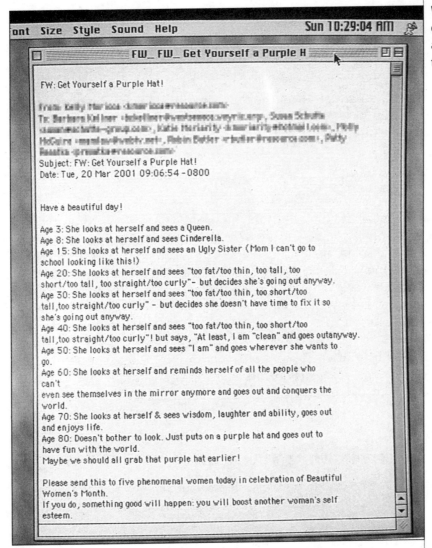

Workers often send each other humorous e-mails, a practice employers try to discourage.

After you read

Task 1 READING FOR MAIN IDEAS

1 Quickly re-read paragraphs 1 to 5. Write a few words or phrases to record the main idea of each paragraph.

Paragraph 1: _____

Paragraph 2: _____

Paragraph 3: _____

Paragraph 4: _____

Paragraph 5: _____

2 Work with a partner. Read the following list, which relates to the last paragraph of the text you have just read. Write a topic sentence that might be used to introduce the information the list contains.

_____

_____

- Set an absolute time limit for how long you will spend on the Internet.
- Force yourself to stay away from the Internet for several days at a time.
- Set an absolute policy for yourself of never signing on to the Internet at work (unless this is required for your job).
- Establish meaningful (but not harmful) consequences for yourself for failing to keep your word.
- Force yourself to do other things instead of spending time on the Internet.
- Ask for help whenever you feel you are not being successful.
- Avoid people or environments that might encourage you to return to your addictive behavior.

Task 2 APPLYING WHAT YOU READ

1 Take the Internet addiction test, and calculate your score. Then read the "Analysis of results" section and discuss your results with other students.

An Internet Addiction Test

To assess your level of addiction, answer the questions below. Consider only the time you spend on-line for nonstudy or non-job-related purposes. For each question, give yourself a score using the following scale:

0 = Never   1 = Rarely   2 = Occasionally   3 = Often   4 = Always

How often do

1 _____ you find that you stay on-line longer than you intended?

2 _____ you neglect household chores to spend more time on-line?

3 _____ you form new relationships with fellow on-line users?

4 _____ others in your life complain to you about the amount of time you spend on-line?

5 _____ you spend so much time on-line that your study or work suffers?

6 _____ you check your e-mail before something else that you need to do?

7 _____ you feel that life on the Internet is more interesting than life off-line?

8 _____ you lose sleep due to late-night use of the Internet?

9 _____ you try to cut down the amount of time you spend on-line and fail?

10 _____ you choose to spend more time on-line rather than going out with others?

Add the numbers you selected for each response to obtain a total score.

Your total score: _____

Analysis of results The higher your score, the greater your level of addiction. Here's a general scale to help measure your score:

10–19 points: You are an average on-line user. At times you may spend a bit too much time on the Internet, but you have control over your usage.

20–29 points: You are experiencing occasional or frequent problems because of the Internet. You should consider the Internet's full impact on your life.

30–40 points: Your Internet usage is causing significant problems in your life. You should evaluate the impact of the Internet on your life and address the problems caused by your Internet usage.

2| Discuss with a partner: Are the behaviors mentioned in the test good indicators of an addiction? Are there other questions you could add to the test?

3| Work with your partner. Discuss other points you could add to the list of ways to control Internet addiction in step 2 of Task 1.

Task 3 THINKING ABOUT THE TOPIC

At present, it is possible for anyone to access websites that broadcast the following:

- "hate" literature that is directed against certain groups in society
- material that encourages violent behavior
- untrue information or rumors about people
- pornographic material

Discuss with a small group: Should there be controls on what can appear on the Internet? If not, why not? If so, by whom and for what kinds of material?

Preparing to read

THINKING ABOUT THE TOPIC

1 Different newspapers may report the same event in very different ways.
For each headline on the left find a matching headline on the right that reports the same story.

_____ **1** Peaceful Protest Ends In Arrests

_____ **2** Army Chiefs Say Only Military Targets Hit

_____ **3** President Replies To Critics Of Foreign Policy

_____ **4** Unemployment Rising Says Job Report

a Government Outlines New Plans To Support Jobless

b No Clear Direction In Foreign Policy

c Demonstrators Disrupt City Traffic – Police Restore Order.

d Women And Children Flee U.S. Bombs

2 Work with a partner. Compare each pair of headlines in step 1. Discuss how they are different and why.

3 Discuss with your partner what you think the word *propaganda* means. Check your ideas by looking in a dictionary. What new information did you find?

SKIMMING

1 Skim the text quickly for one minute. Look especially at the subheadings and at any words or phrases in italics or bold.

2 Match each question on the top to an answer on the bottom.

"Why doesn't propaganda always work?"

"How does propaganda work?"

"What is propaganda?"

"Communication that is intended to shape our views or change our opinions"

"We do not rely on just one source of ideas. There are many different influences on our thinking."

"By using language or visual images that encourage us to think positively or negatively about an idea"

Now read

Now read the text "Propaganda and the Media" more carefully. When you finish the text, turn to the tasks that begin on page 137.

3 PROPAGANDA AND THE MEDIA

What is propaganda?

Politicians want to win our hearts and minds, and businesses want to win our dollars. Both these groups use the media to manipulate public opinion and to try to gain mass support. This deliberate manipulation of public opinion is called "propaganda." It may be true or false, but what sets propaganda apart from other communication is that it is intended to shape our views or change our opinions.

How does propaganda work?

A number of methods of propaganda are used in the media. One is giving positive or negative *labels*. If something is given a negative label, then the audience might reject the idea or person without questioning the label. Likewise, a positive label might encourage people to support an idea. For example, a public rally may be described in the media as "peaceful" or as "disruptive." The different labels will give different impressions. People who favor limits on gun possession may be described as "voices for gun control" or "anti-gun activists." Some labels encourage a favorable response and others a negative one.

We can also be influenced by *visual images* in the media. A newspaper editor may have several photographs of a famous person to choose from. An attractive picture may be chosen to create a good impression, or an unattractive one to have the opposite effect. For example, the photograph below of a smiling politician meeting the public and holding a baby presents a positive and sympathetic image.

President George W. Bush presents a positive image for the cameras.

Another method of propaganda is to have a beautiful or famous person promote some idea or product, or link the product to other concepts that are admired or desired. At election time, politicians often look for support from movie stars or famous sports people to campaign for them. Similarly, in advertising, products are promoted by beautiful, expensively dressed people. The audience is encouraged to make an association from the attractiveness of one image to the other.

Another method used by promoters is to create the impression that everyone supports the product or idea. Soft-drink companies use commercials to show a crowd of young, happy people all drinking their product. This is propaganda because it puts pressure on the audience to conform to this behavior because it is seen as popular.

Why doesn't propaganda always work?

There are limits on the role of propaganda. The **propagandist** cannot simply make us believe in something, or easily get rid of beliefs or opinions we already hold. There are at least three factors that limit the influence of the media on public opinion. One is the fact that independent organizations can present us with different points of view, so the influence of one can cancel out or balance the influence of another. A second is that media owners are interested in making a profit, so the media often presents what the audience already wants to see or hear. The third is that there is often a two-step process of influence: we may hear an analysis of an issue on television, but we often accept or reject it after being influenced by other opinion leaders – people in the community whom we respect.

propagandist
person who produces propaganda

Actor Chuck Norris campaigns for George W. Bush.

After you read

Task 1 READING FOR THE MAIN IDEA

1 | Which of the following best states the main idea of this text?

   a We are often persuaded to buy a product because of the attractive image we see in advertising, or because we are told that everyone likes this product.

   b Politicians and businesspeople use propaganda to manipulate public opinion.

   c Propaganda uses a variety of strategies to try to shape our opinions of products or ideas.

   d The effects of propaganda are limited by other influences in our lives.

2 | Find which parts of the text are summarized by the remaining three statements.

3 | Compare your answers with a partner.

Task 2 BUILDING VOCABULARY: COLLOCATIONS

> There are many common collocations of verbs and nouns in English.
> Make a note of new collocations as you learn them. The more you are
> aware of collocations, the easier reading becomes.

1 | The following verbs and nouns occur in the text. Write the verb that you think collocates with each noun. For some nouns and verbs more than one collocation may be possible.

Verbs		Nouns
to manipulate	**1** _____	our hearts and minds
to shape	**2** _____	a good impression
to win	**3** _____	a profit
to gain	**4** _____	mass support
to create	**5** _____	public opinion
to make	**6** _____	our views

2 | Scan the text to find the actual collocations used.

Task 3 APPLYING WHAT YOU READ

Find photographs from news stories in your local media. Discuss each image with a partner: Is the photo propaganda? Why or why not? Then choose one of the photographs. Write a paragraph describing the photo and explaining the impression it creates for you.

Preparing to read

READING AROUND THE TOPIC

1 There are frequent articles in the press about our television viewing habits and the effects of television on behavior. Read the selections below.

- If you watch more than 30 hours of television a week, some psychologists would consider you to be a television addict. Television addicts may show some of the following symptoms. They may not be selective in what they watch; in other words they will watch anything. They may feel a loss of control when viewing. They may feel angry with themselves for watching so much, but are not able to stop watching, and they may feel miserable when they are stopped from watching.

- A study has found a link between high levels of teenage TV watching and their consumption of junk food. And the less children watched television, the more likely they and their parents are to eat apples.

- A spokesperson for the National Coalition on Television Violence suggested the government should require the television industry to run a 30-second public service announcement daily to educate viewers on TV violence. Such announcements should show us how to recognize when violence is being made glamorous or when violence is used to entertain, and suggest that when we see such violence, we should change channels or turn off the TV.

2 Work with a partner and discuss the following questions.

1 The selections in step 1 suggest certain social problems associated with TV viewing. What are they?

2 What do you consider to be the positive and/or negative impact of television on your own life?

PREDICTING

1 Make a list of words and expressions you might expect to find in a text entitled "Television and Children." For example, you might think about program types, attitudes and behaviors that are modeled, and positive and negative effects. Try to make a list of at least ten words.

2 Work with a partner. Compare your lists and discuss what topics and ideas might be included in the text.

Now read

Now read the text "Television and Children." When you finish, turn to the tasks on page 141.

4 TELEVISION AND CHILDREN

Over the past thirty years or so, the influence of television has been increasing. In the United States, 99 percent of all homes have a television set turned on for about seven hours a day, and on average children in the United States watch television for more than twenty hours a week *(www.tvb.org; www.bizjournal.com)*. A recent study found that two-thirds of children 8 years or older have a TV set in their bedroom. Among this age group, two-thirds also said the TV was usually on during meal times and that their parents had no rules for watching TV, *(The Henry J. Kaiser Family Foundation* 1999). It is estimated that by age 18, the average U.S. child born today will have watched some 10,000 to 15,000 hours of television. They will have spent more time watching television than on any other activity except sleep. They will have seen some 300,000 commercials, 200,000 acts of violence, and 16,000 murders *(www.cme.org)*.

Given the large amount of time that children spend watching TV, it is not surprising that there have been many research studies on the effects of television programs on behavior, especially the relationship of TV violence to aggressive behavior in children. Violence is defined as the threat or use of physical force, directed against the self or others, in which physical harm or death is involved. Television drama is highly violent. Matthews and Ellis (1985), for example, analyzed 1,600 television programs and found that 80 percent contained violence. On average there are 7.5 violent acts per hour in television drama. Children's programs show even higher levels of violence, although killing is less commonly shown. Cartoons contain the highest number of violent acts of any type of television program.

Does this violence on TV influence the audience? Tan (1985) claimed that by watching violence we become less sensitive to it. That is, we become more tolerant of violence. Other studies have suggested that children who observe adults being aggressive toward each other usually increase the frequency with which they are aggressive. However, not all the research studies undertaken in this area have produced the same results. A recent review of sixty-seven studies that investigated the influence of TV violence on aggression in children found that three-quarters of the studies claimed to find some association. In 20 percent of cases there were no clear-cut results, and in 3 percent of the studies the researchers concluded that watching television violence decreases aggression.

Some researchers suggest that it is not just a question of whether or not violence is shown on TV. It is also important to consider how violence is portrayed. For example, in many crime dramas and children's cartoons that contain violence, there are underlying themes of justice and punishment, that is, the "bad guys" do not usually win. A far higher proportion of those who act violently are brought to justice in crime dramas than happens in real life, and in cartoons harmful or threatening characters usually tend to lose in the end.

Some researchers have also pointed out that children's responses to TV are not simply passive. Children do not just copy the behaviors they see. They interpret or "read" what they see. If this is the case, then it may not be the violence as such in television programs that has effects on behavior. Instead, it may be the way that violence is presented and dealt with, and also the attitudes and values that the child has already developed (Giddens, 1991).

Whatever the research shows, parents and young adults seem to think there is a connection. Marklein (1989) found that 60 percent of parents surveyed believed that television promotes violent behavior. And one recent survey of 18- to 25-year-olds found that 70 percent believed that the level of violence portrayed in the mass media affects the level of violence in the community, although only 18 percent supported an increase in media censorship.

Fiction and reality

Studies have found that children do not easily understand the difference between fiction and reality in their TV viewing. This is of concern to many parents. Mothers interviewed in a study reported that they had to explain to young children that getting hurt on television was not real. They pointed out, for example, that although a cartoon character could fall off a high cliff and soon be walking and talking again, real people or animals can't recover from accidents in this way. They also had to explain that monsters and witches don't really exist, and that real people can't fly. One mother observed her youngsters jumping up and down on the sofa in an effort to achieve flight – they had just been watching *Superman*.

In *Superman* dramas the wires that help Superman "fly" are not visible. Children who watch these shows may think humans really can fly.

While movies shown on TV often have lots of violence, "the good guy" usually wins.

After you read

Task 1 TEST TAKING: ANSWERING TRUE/FALSE QUESTIONS

True/false questions are sometimes given in tests to check your under-standing of a reading passage. Read this list of strategies for answering them.

- Answer every question. You always have a 50/50 chance of being right.
- Pay special attention to statements with negatives in them. These are often tricky to answer. Remember that a negative statement that is correct is true.
- Pay attention to words like *always*, *never*, and *all*. Statements that represent extreme positions are usually false. On the other hand, more tentative statements are more likely to be true.
- Read all parts of a statement carefully. Some parts may be true, but if any part of it is false, then the whole statement is false.
- In any series of true/false questions, there are usually about the same number of true statements as false ones.

Decide if the following statements are true or false according to the information in this text. Write *T* or *F* next to each statement.

_____ 1 The author suggests that the average child spends more time watching television than sleeping.

_____ 2 One analysis of 1,600 television programs found that 80 percent contained violence.

_____ 3 The type of television program containing the most violent acts is television drama.

_____ 4 All studies of the relationship between TV violence and aggression in children conclude that there is some connection.

_____ 5 A far higher proportion of those who act violently are punished in TV crime dramas than are punished in real life.

_____ 6 The effect of TV violence on a child's behavior will depend in part on the attitudes and values he or she already has.

_____ 7 Most young adults don't believe that TV violence increases violence in the community.

Task 2 READING CRITICALLY

Much research about TV's effect on children investigates the relationship between different factors, such as hours of TV watching and diet, or amount of violence on TV and child aggression. It is important to read such research findings carefully and critically. Do the findings suggest that factor A *causes* factor B? Or do they simply report some *correlation:* that where you find A, you tend to find B?

1 Read the excerpts from research reports below. Notice the underlined words that signal a relationship between factors. Decide whether each extract presents a cause/effect (CE) relationship or a correlation (CO) between factors.

   1 "... A study has found <u>a link between</u> high levels of teenage TV watching and their consumption of junk food." __*CO*__

   2 "... There have been many research studies undertaken to investigate <u>the effects of</u> television programs on behavior." __*CE*__

   3 "... research undertaken to investigate <u>the relationship of</u> TV violence to aggressive behavior in children" _____

   4 "... Tan (1985) claimed that <u>by</u> watching violence we <u>become</u> less sensitive to it." _____

   5 "... children who observe adults being aggressive toward each other usually <u>increase the frequency</u> with which they are aggressive." _____

   6 "... three-quarters of the studies claimed to find <u>some association</u>." _____

   7 "... in 3 percent of the studies the researchers concluded that watching television violence <u>decreases</u> aggression." _____

   8 "... 60 percent of parents surveyed believed that television <u>promotes</u> violent behavior." _____

   9 "... a survey of 18- to 25-year-olds found that 70 percent believed that the level of violence portrayed in the mass media <u>affects</u> the level of violence in the community." _____

2 Compare your answers with a partner.

Task 3 LANGUAGE FOCUS: REPORTING VERBS

When writers report on research, they make use of a variety of *reporting verbs* to introduce the findings or results. The reporting verbs they choose signal how certain they are about the results. For example, if a text says, "Study X **showed** that ..." this implies certainty about the results. If a text says, "The results **suggest** that ..." or "The researcher **claimed** that ...", there is some doubt or uncertainty about the research results.

1 Work with a partner. Look at the reporting verbs in bold below. Say whether they signal high certainty (+) or less certainty (−).

1 "... A study has **found** a link between high levels of teenage TV watching and their consumption of junk food." ____+____

2 "... Tan (1985) **claimed** that by watching violence we become less sensiive to it." _____

3 "... Other studies have **suggested** that children who observe adults being aggressive toward each other usually increase the frequency with which they are aggressive." _____

4 "... in 3 percent of the studies the researchers **concluded** that watching television violence decreases aggression." _____

5 "... Some researchers have also **pointed out** that children's responses to TV are not simply passive." _____

2 Choose a different reporting verb for each statement above to change the degree of certainty. For example, number 1 could be changed to "A study has **suggested** a link between ..."

Task 4 CITING STUDIES IN YOUR WRITING

In an essay or research report you may want to cite a study you have read about. Review the information on citing studies in Chapter 1 on page 27.

The examples below show two different ways to include information on author and year of publication.

a Matthew and Ellis (1985) found that 80 percent of TV programs contain violence.

b It has been found that 80 percent of TV programs contain violence (Matthew and Ellis 1985).

In example **a**, the authors of the research are the subject of the sentence and the year of publication of the study appears in parentheses after their last names. In example **b**, the sentence reports the research findings. In this case, the authors' last names and the year of publication of the research appear in parentheses at the end of the sentence.

1 Find other places in the text in which research findings are cited.

2 Change the method used to cite the research findings from **a** to **b** or vice versa.

CHAPTER 6 WRITING ASSIGNMENT

Choose one of the following topics as your chapter writing assignment:

1 Does the public have the right to know about the private lives of politicians? Write your opinion and give your reasons.

2 The growth of the Internet in recent years has sometimes been described as a "revolution" in communication. Why is it described in this way?

3 Define *propaganda* and say how it works. Give an example of how the media reported a recent political event to illustrate your answer.

4 Look at the following cartoon. Describe the cartoon and the message it conveys. Explain why you agree or disagree with this message.

Breaking the Rules

In this unit we look at crime in society. In Chapter 7, we focus on different kinds of crime and criminals. We also look at some new ways of solving crime with the use of developments in science and technology. In Chapter 8, we consider ways of preventing or controlling crime in society. We look at different means of punishing criminals, including the ultimate punishment, the death penalty. We also look at the role of the law and how it can be used to help prevent crime.

Previewing the unit

Read the contents page for Unit 4 and do the following activities with a partner.

Chapter 7: Crime and Criminals

1 The first two sections of this chapter look at the kinds of crimes that commonly occur in most Western industrialized societies, and who the criminals tend to be. Read each statement and circle the word that you think makes it correct.

1 (More/Fewer) males are arrested for crimes than females.

2 People of higher socioeconomic status are (more/less) likely to be arrested than those of lower socioeconomic status.

3 Younger people are (more/less) likely to be involved in crime than older people.

4 One of the (most/least) common crimes is burglary.

5 Homicide, or murder, is mostly committed by (strangers/people known to the victim).

6 Homicide is most often committed on (weekdays/weekends).

Review your answers after you have completed Sections 1 and 2 of Chapter 7.

2 The last two sections look at some developments in solving crimes. Look at this picture of the famous fictional detective, Sherlock Holmes, and discuss: What changes in crime-solving techniques have happened since his times (late 1800s–early 1900s)? Review your answer after you have completed Sections 3 and 4 of Chapter 7.

Chapter 8: Controlling Crime

In this chapter, we look at what stops us from committing crimes, such as punishment of people who break the law.

1 Work in a small group. Think of five different kinds of punishment for criminals. For each kind of punishment think of a type of crime that should be punished in this way.

2 Discuss the following question with your group: Are there forms of punishment that should never be used?

Unit Contents 4

Preparing to read

THINKING ABOUT THE TOPIC

1 Check the meanings of *deviance* and *crime* in a dictionary.

2 Work with a partner. Think about the relationship between deviance and crime. Discuss the following questions:

1 How would you define *deviant behavior*? Write a definition, beginning with:
Deviant behavior is behavior that . . .

2 How would you define *criminal behavior*? Write a definition, beginning with:
Criminal behavior is behavior that . . .

3 List some examples of deviant and criminal behavior.

4 Complete the table with behaviors that relate to the issues listed on the left.

Table 7.1 Some behaviors that are generally considered normal, deviant, or criminal in most Western industrialized societies			
Issue	Normal	Deviant but not criminal	Deviant and criminal
Use of the streets	Crossing the street at the traffic light		Failing to stop after a traffic accident
Use of alcohol	Moderate social drinking	Alcohol abuse	
Making money	Earning a living as an adult	Begging on the streets	

Source: Knox, 159. (adapted)

5 Think of another culture you know well. Would the behaviors in the table above be considered normal, deviant, or criminal in that culture?

Now read

Now read the text "Deviance and Crime." When you finish, turn to the tasks on page 151.

Crime and Criminals

Chapter 7

1 DEVIANCE AND CRIME

Have you ever . . .

> crossed the street against the traffic light?
> driven through a stop sign without stopping?
> drunk or bought alcohol as a **minor**?
> cheated on a test?

If so, you have broken a socially accepted norm or practice, and you could therefore be considered deviant. *Deviant behavior* is behavior that is considered to be unacceptable, or outside the norms for that society.

There are, of course, degrees of deviance and not every member of a society will agree on what is deviant behavior and what is normal behavior. For example, while many people believe that prostitution is deviant, others see it as a legitimate way for people to earn a living. Also, what is seen as deviant behavior will change over time and vary from place to place. Drinking alcohol, for example, has been regarded as deviant or as acceptable in the United States at different times in the past. In fact, in the 1920s, alcohol was considered to be so unacceptable in the U.S. that it was illegal to sell, buy, or consume it. Now drinking in moderation is accepted by the majority of the population as normal social behavior for adults.

minor

someone too young to be legally considered an adult; punishments for minors are usually different than those for adults

What is considered to be deviant may also vary from culture to culture. In most cultures, but certainly not in all, it is regarded as deviant for a man to have more than one wife at the same time. However, there are some religious groups and cultures where polygamy is an accepted practice.

Some acts of deviance may simply result in a person being regarded as odd or unusual, while other deviant behaviors actually break the law. These behaviors are seen as *crimes*. Crimes can be grouped into different categories. One category is violent crime. This includes murder, rape, robbery, and assault. Another is property crime, such as theft, arson, or burglary. There is also a category of victimless crime, so-called because such crimes do not involve harm to people other than the criminals themselves. Examples of victimless crimes include gambling, prostitution, and drug abuse. Another category is white-collar crime, which includes tax evasion and embezzlement.

In 2000, there were 11.6 million reported crimes (excluding traffic offenses) in the United States. According to a report by the FBI (Federal Bureau of Investigation), in 2000 the following crimes occurred at the rates shown (*www.disastercentre.com/crime/uscrime.htm*):

This man has been arrested and charged with a crime. He is being searched for weapons before going to jail.

Robbery: 46.5 per hour
Burglary: 234 per hour
Violent crime: 163 per hour
Rape: 10.3 per hour
Murder: 1.8 per hour
Vehicle theft: 133 per hour

It should be noted, however, that these figures are based only on crimes that are reported. Actual crime rates may be two or three times higher than the official figures.

Murder, or homicide, is the most serious crime, and reports on crime show that it is also mostly a personal crime. That is, homicide is far more likely to be committed against acquaintances, friends, or relatives than against strangers. It also occurs most frequently during weekend evenings, particularly Saturday night. As a crime of passion, homicide is usually carried out under overwhelming pressure and uncontrollable rage.

While the public perception may be that the crime rate, especially for violent crime, is continuing to rise, there has in fact been a decline over the past decade. In 1991, there were 1.9 million violent crimes reported in the United States. By 1998, this figure had dropped to 1.5, million. Murder rates in the same period dropped from 24,700 to 16,914.

After you read

Task 1 BUILDING VOCABULARY: TECHNICAL TERMS AND DEFINITIONS

1 Match the crimes on the left with the definitions on the right.

_____ **1** homicide	**a** spying
_____ **2** burglary	**b** sexual attack on a person
_____ **3** robbery	**c** murder or killing
_____ **4** hijacking	**d** a violent attack
_____ **5** espionage	**e** the deliberate burning of property
_____ **6** assault	**f** breaking into a building to steal
_____ **7** arson	**g** dealing in or selling drugs
_____ **8** prostitution	**h** using force to steal
_____ **9** drug trafficking	**i** forcing someone to give you control of a vehicle
_____ **10** rape	**j** having sexual relations in exchange for money

2 Write definitions for the following crimes, using a dictionary if necessary.

fraud   tax evasion   embezzlement

Task 2 UNDERSTANDING IMPLIED MEANINGS

The information you need to answer a question about a text is not always directly or explicitly stated in the text. Sometimes you need to figure out for yourself the meaning that is suggested, or implied. Use what you know from your experience and from information you are given in the text to answer questions about implied meanings.

The following questions are not answered directly in the text. Work with a partner to figure out the answers.

1 Why is burglary a more frequently occurring crime than robbery?
2 Where does the term "white-collar crime" come from?
3 What are some of the reasons that victims of crime may not report the crime?
4 Why is Saturday night the most likely time for homicides to occur?

Task 3 PERSONALIZING THE TOPIC

Discuss these questions with your classmates:

1 What are the most frequent types of crime in your country/city?
2 How safe do you feel in your country/city?
3 What is the most dangerous city in your country?
4 Have you ever been the victim of a crime?

Preparing to read

USING THE SQR3 SYSTEM

> You were introduced to the SQR3 approach to reading in Chapter 4. Remember that SQR3 stands for Survey (S), Question (Q), Read, Recite, Review (R3). It is a useful system for academic reading that helps you to become an active reader and to understand and remember what you have read.

In this pre-reading activity, we will look at the first three steps in the SQR3 system: survey, question, and read.

1 Survey

- Survey this text before reading it closely.
- Look at the title, subheadings, boxed text, and pictures.
- Skim through the text, reading the beginnings and ends of paragraphs.
- Report back to the class on what you looked at and discovered.

2 Question

- Before you read this text, think of questions that you expect the text will answer. One trick is to look at the subheadings and key terms that you noticed in your survey and turn them into questions. For example, the subheading "Age group" might prompt the question, "Which age group is most likely to commit crimes?"
- Write your questions in the margins.
- Compare your questions with a small group.

3 Read

- As you read, think about the questions you wrote in the margins.
- See if you can answer your questions.

Now read

Now read the text "Who Commits Crime?" When you finish, turn to the tasks on page 156.

2 WHO COMMITS CRIME?

Reports on crime can't give us a complete picture of who commits crimes because not all crimes are reported. Furthermore, law enforcement agencies don't always share their information. However, available information on reported crimes can give us information about the people who commit crimes. If we consider all categories of crime together, the most likely people to commit crimes are young men from lower socioeconomic backgrounds.

Young males from lower socioeconomic backgrounds are the most likely people to commit crimes.

Age group

Young people have the highest rates of arrest for reported crime. Almost half of all people arrested are under the age of 25. Older people may gradually move away from crime or they may become skilled in not getting caught. Younger people are more likely to be involved in crime because they have fewer relationships that encourage them to follow conventional behavior. A married person with two children and a steady job is less likely to commit a crime than an unemployed, single, child-free person.

Recent figures show a worrying increase in violent crime and homicide among youngsters under age 18. In 1995, some 5,280 children and youths died from gun-related injuries, and a recent study revealed that U.S. children are fifteen times more likely to die from guns than their counterparts in the twenty-five other major industrialized countries combined. Clearly, guns are only a part of the problem. Poverty, deprivation, and gangs are directly related to much of the crime. In addition, the way this generation of American parents is raising their children should be examined. One psychologist argues that "the fundamental problem is that kids these days are not getting the social and emotional learning they need. Parents aren't around as much, so there's not as much modeling of how to behave, or as much emotional support."

Gender

According to FBI (Federal Bureau of Investigation) reports, 78 percent of all those arrested for crimes are males. Males are also responsible for about 83 percent of violent crime and 70 percent of all property crimes. Females are arrested for criminal behavior in only 21 percent of all arrests. (Percentages for males and females don't add up to 100 percent because of rounding of numbers.) Although women commit all types of crime they are most likely to be involved in prostitution, petty theft, shoplifting, passing bad checks, domestic theft, and welfare fraud. They are less likely to be involved in the more profitable crimes of burglary, robbery, embezzlement, and business fraud. In

FBI statistics show that males are responsible for the majority of violent crimes and property crimes.

other words, women are more likely to commit crimes that reflect their less powerful position in society. Most women criminals are unemployed, uneducated, single mothers with small children.

Why is it that the figures for males and females are so different? 5 Sociologists suggest that it is more socially acceptable for males to be deviant and involved in crime than it is for females. Women are under a greater social pressure to conform than men are. If they do not conform to the expected social roles of wife and mother, they are more likely to be assigned extremely negative labels. It has also been suggested that women have fewer opportunities to get involved in criminal behavior. Compared to males, potential female criminals are less likely to be selected and recruited into criminal groups, have a more limited range of criminal career paths open to them, and have fewer opportunities for learning criminal skills (Steffensmeier 1983). In other words, like employment opportunities, criminal opportunities are still much less available to women than to men. A further argument is that in a male-dominated society, women are socialized differently from men. Consequently, women are less interested in achieving material success and more interested in achieving emotional fulfillment through close personal relations with others. A drive for material success, it is argued, can lead people into crime if they lack other opportunities to gain such success.

Socioeconomic status

socioeconomic groups

people grouped by sociologists according to social status, jobs, and amount of money earned

The majority of those arrested are also from lower **socioeconomic** 6 **groups** in the community. Without money, it is harder to keep out of trouble. You are more likely to do your gambling, for example, in a public place rather than in the safety of a suburban living room, and you cannot afford a private attorney to represent you if you do get caught. The poor are far more likely than the well-off to be arrested.

Females tend to commit crimes such as shoplifting, petty theft, or welfare fraud.

If they are arrested, they are more likely to be **charged**. If they are charged, they are more likely to be **convicted**, and if they are convicted, they are more likely to be sentenced to prison (Reiman 1979).

However, there is a whole category of crime – corporate crime – that is committed by people of high social status who work as company officials. Examples of corporate crime include disregard for safety in the workplace, the production of unsafe products, and violation of environmental regulations. Such crimes are committed without the obvious use of force, and the effect of the crime on the victims cannot be easily traced to the offender. The people who are involved in corporate crime often have a great deal of power that they use to avoid conviction. Much corporate crime escapes punishment. If a miner dies of lung disease, for example, it is difficult to prove beyond a reasonable doubt that he died because the employer broke the law by not providing adequate safety in the mine.

charged

officially accused of committing a crime

convicted

found guilty of committing a crime

After you read

Task 1 USING THE SQR3 SYSTEM

> The SQR3 system continues after reading a text. The fourth step is to recite, or say aloud from memory, and the last step is to review.

1 Recite
- Look again at the subheadings in the text. Choose one.
- Re-read that section, and then give an oral summary of the main ideas to a partner.

2 Review
- Go back and skim the text, placing a check (✓) next to the parts of the text that you are sure that you understand and a question mark (?) next to those parts that are still unclear to you and that you need to study further.
- Return to the sections of the text where you placed a question mark. Underline any difficult words in those sections. Try to figure out the meaning of the words from the surrounding context. Then check the dictionary.
- Discuss with a small group any parts that you still do not understand.

Task 2 LANGUAGE FOCUS: COMPARING DATA

> In academic writing it is common to compare one thing with another. When comparing data, you can often state the same information in different ways.

1 State the comparisons below in a different way. Change the underlined words to their opposite meaning and change other information as necessary.

1 ~~Younger~~ *Older* people are ~~more~~ *less* likely to be involved in crime than ~~older~~ *younger* people.

2 Young people have <u>fewer</u> relationships that encourage them to follow conventional behavior than older people do.

3 Women are <u>less</u> likely to be involved in the more profitable crimes of burglary and robbery than men are.

4 It is <u>more</u> socially acceptable for males to be involved in crime.

5 Women are under <u>greater</u> social pressure to conform than men.

2 Complete these sentences with the correct word from the parentheses.

1 The _____ are far less likely than the _____ to be arrested. (poor/rich)

2 Criminal opportunities are still much less available to _____ than to _____.
(women/men)

3 People from _____ socioeconomic groups in the community are more likely to
be arrested than those from _____ socioeconomic groups. (higher/lower)

4 _____ are more likely to be selected and recruited into criminal groups.
(Women/Men)

Task 3 READING ACTIVELY

Remember that when you read actively, you do not simply read to
understand the words on the page. You think about how the ideas
relate to what you already know, and you think about the implications
of those ideas.

1 Re-read paragraph 2, which is about youth crime. Write down any thoughts you
have while you are reading the text. Discuss your thoughts with a small group.

2 Discuss the following questions with the group.

1 Why do you think there is so much violence among today's youth, especially in
the United States?

2 What do you think should be done about the problem?

Preparing to read

THINKING ABOUT THE TOPIC

What kinds of crime are associated with computers?

1 Work with a partner. Make a list of kinds of crime that involve computers.

_____

_____

_____

_____

2 Compare your list with another pair of students.

BUILDING VOCABULARY: LEARNING WORDS RELATED TO THE TOPIC

1 The words in the left column below relate to computers; those in the right column relate to computer crime.

Discuss the meanings of the words with other students. Check an up-to-date dictionary if you are unsure.

Computers	Computer Crime
Internet	hacking
software	identity theft
homepage	virus
database	illegal copying
_____	_____
_____	_____

2 Add to the lists several other words that you expect to find in the text.

Now read

Now read the text "Computers and Crime." When you finish, turn to the tasks on page 161.

Advances in computer technology have created opportunities for new kinds of crime.

3 COMPUTERS AND CRIME

In 1993, the head of the foreign transfer department of a bank in the Netherlands used the bank's computer to move nearly $100 million in funds into outside accounts over a two-year period. In 1995, a U.S. government employee was charged with stealing money from pay checks. Using the computer system, she had diverted ten cents from each of hundreds of thousands of pay checks into her own account every month for nearly twelve years and had managed to steal more than 5 million dollars.

Advances in technology, especially the extensive use of computers in business and for private use, have brought with them new kinds of crime, such as the crimes of stealing reported above. And it is not only money that is stolen by computer. It is estimated that approximately 2 billion dollars worth of computer software is stolen from the Internet each year. Then there is the theft of information. The U.S. government estimates that 250,000 attempts were made in 1996 to hack (gain illegal entry) into the computers of its defense installations. While many of these attempts to gain illegal entry may be carried out just for the thrill or the challenge, others no doubt are attempts to steal information.

There are also crimes associated with selling over the Internet. For example, a fake company can set up a website and offer goods for sale, goods that don't actually exist. The unsuspecting consumer may be tricked into sending money or credit card details to the company. Or the goods for sale may be counterfeit. One U.S. company that investigates businesses on the Internet estimates that up to 20 percent of all brand-name goods sold over the Net are fakes.

Computer criminals can also cause harm in other ways. Computer "viruses" can be deliberately written into programs and documents. The viruses attack and cause damage to any computers onto which they are copied. In 1999, a virus called Chernobyl crippled hundreds of thousands of computers around the world. A 24-year-old man was eventually tracked down as the author of the virus.

> Scan Result: Virus *W32.Sircam.Worm@mm* found. File **NOT** cleaned.
>
> This file contains a computer worm, a program that spreads very quickly over the Internet to many computers and can delete files, steal sensitive information, or render your machine unusable
>
> ---
>
> This attachment has a virus that may infect your computer. It cannot be cleaned. We recommend that you **DO NOT** download this attachment.

Anti-virus software can scan computer files and alert users to the presence of a virus.

Computer-related crime of such kinds is growing at a rapid rate around the world, and police are faced with a difficult job in preventing it. One reason is that many computer crimes, especially thefts from companies, are not reported to the police. A 1996 survey conducted in the United States suggested that only 17 percent of **high-tech crimes** are reported to authorities. Although companies that are the victims of this kind of crime are likely to suffer huge financial losses, they tend to keep quiet about it. One explanation is that they want to protect their reputations. They do not want the public to think that they are vulnerable to such crimes, as the public may then lose confidence in the company. It is also difficult for police to keep up with the necessary technological skills. They need special training and equipment to fight computer crime effectively.

But while computer crime presents police with new problems in solving crimes, computers also help police in some ways. For example, law enforcement agencies in the United States are developing a national computer database on recorded thefts. They can also display photographs of suspects and wanted criminals on the Internet. These photographs have already led to the arrest of people on the FBI's most wanted list.

5

6

high-tech crimes

crimes involving advanced technology, such as computers

Law enforcement agencies use computer databases to help them find criminals.

Has computer technology changed our ideas of what is right and wrong?

A recent study found that one in every six people in the United States believes that traditional ideas of right and wrong have been changed by new technologies.

- Virtually everyone (96 percent) agrees that certain extreme behaviors are wrong, for example, deliberately damaging your employer's computer systems or data.

But on other activities, opinions are divided. For example,

- 35 percent do not think it is wrong to copy company software for home use, even though that is usually against the law.
- 34 percent do not think it is wrong to use an employer's computer to search for a new job.
- 46 percent think it is all right to use office computers for personal shopping on the Internet.

After you read

Task 1 SUMMARIZING FROM THE MAIN IDEAS

1 Look back at the text, including the boxed text, to find which part expresses each main idea below. Write the paragraph number (or "BT" for boxed text) next to the main idea.

_____ **a** using computers to solve crimes

_____ **b** problems in fighting computer crime

_____ **c** kinds of computer crime

_____ **d** attitudes to computer crimes

2 Make some brief notes of key information given in the text for each main idea.

3 Write a one-paragraph summary of the text, based on your notes. Begin like this:

Advances in technology have led to new kinds of crime....

Task 2 CONDUCTING A SURVEY

> Surveys are frequently used in academic research to gather information about people's attitudes and behaviors. When conducting a survey, there are some things you should keep in mind:
>
> - Keep your questions short and clear.
> - Try out the questions on a small number of people first to see if they can be easily answered, and to see if they give you the information you want.
> - Revise the questions if necessary.

Conduct a survey based on the ideas in the boxed text on page 160. Work in a small group.

1 Look again at the information in the boxed text. Write four yes/no questions that the interviewer probably asked.

2 Write the language you will use to do the following:

- introduce yourself; explain where you are from and what your survey is about
- ask if the person agrees to be surveyed
- thank the person for answering your questions

3 Use the language from step 2 and your questions from step 1 to survey twenty other students or friends. Record the answers to each question.

4 Organize your data, analyze the results, and write up your findings.

Preparing to read

BRAINSTORMING

One way to activate your background knowledge before you start reading is to brainstorm. When you brainstorm, you try to think of as many ideas as you can. You do not try to evaluate or organize your ideas; you just quickly make a list.

Think of television programs and movies you have seen about detectives solving crimes. Use those memories and the pictures below to do the following task.

1 Work in a small group. For five minutes, brainstorm different ways to solve crimes. Make a list.

2 Compare your list with another group of students.

BUILDING BACKGROUND KNOWLEDGE OF THE TOPIC

Acquiring information about important concepts that appear in a text helps you to build your background knowledge. Such background information will enable you to read more effectively.

In the text that follows, one of the methods of crime detection discussed involves the use of DNA.

1 Read the following description of DNA.

DNA stands for deoxyribonucleic acid. These are the molecules that make up the chromosomes that are a part of every cell in our bodies. Everyone has a different DNA code.

2 Discuss with a partner how you think DNA might be useful in solving crime.

Now read

Now read the text "Techniques for Solving Crimes." When you finish, turn to the tasks on page 165.

4 TECHNIQUES FOR SOLVING CRIMES

There are many methods of crime detection. Detection methods include the study of handwriting to find out who was the author of an incriminating document and the use of a lie detector test that indicates whether suspects are telling the truth by measuring their breathing and pulse and skin movements. Detectives can even use insects to help solve a murder case! By knowing how long it would take certain insects to break down body tissue, scientists can estimate the time of death. Insects can also be used to solve drug crimes. Insects are often found in illegal shipments of drugs. Detectives can use knowledge about where the insects come from to trace the drugs back to a particular location in the world.

One of the most important and reliable kinds of evidence that can be used in solving crimes is still the fingerprint. A person's fingerprints are the swirled patterns of ridges and valleys in the skin on the tips of the fingers. These patterns are unique, that is, no two people have identical patterns, and the patterns do not change over time. Criminal investigation agencies all over the world have large collections of fingerprints to use in crime detection and these are now computerized to make it easier to search for matching prints. If fingerprints are found at a crime scene, they may be entered into a computer bank to search for a match with the prints of a suspected criminal.

Fingerprints are made when someone touches a surface. Sweat and amino acids from the body transfer to the surface and leave an impression. Sometimes it is only a partial impression, but that can be sufficient. Many prints are invisible under normal circumstances, but they can be made visible using a variety of techniques, such as dusting powders and chemicals. The prints are then photographed and lifted with a tape. Today, prints are often examined in darkness using high-powered lasers, and they can be retrieved from almost any surface – even plastic bags or human skin.

Of course, some crime scenes may contain no fingerprints. When the New York City police arrested a murder **suspect** in June 1998, they had no physical evidence tying him to the killing. Only days later they were able to link him to that homicide, plus two other homicides – and it all came down to a cup of coffee. The man, who had been arrested on a petty theft charge, was given coffee by detectives while they were questioning him. After the suspect left the room, detectives used the saliva he left on the cup to obtain his DNA. Testing then showed that his DNA matched not only the DNA found at the crime scene, but DNA associated with other crimes as well. Another case involved a DNA sample from a popsicle. Detectives who had been following the suspect picked up the popsicle from a trash bin. In this case, however, the suspect was found not to be connected to the crime.

DNA analysis is based on the fact that every person (except an identical twin) has certain elements in his or her DNA that are unique. A sample of DNA can be taken from a person and matched to a sample of DNA taken from a crime scene – from a drop of blood or a strand

Fingerprints are one of the most important and reliable kinds of evidence used in solving crimes.

suspect
a person who police think may have committed a crime

5

10

15

20

25

30

35

40

45

of hair, for example. New methods of DNA testing mean that it is now a much faster and cheaper process, and large banks of DNA test results can be stored in computers, just as fingerprints are. When DNA is collected from a crime scene, the computers can search for a test result that matches the sample. Now, in New York City, detectives are being instructed to pick up such discarded items as gum, tissues, Band-Aids, and, in some cases, the spit of suspects, in order to get samples of their DNA. If detectives can match the DNA to DNA recovered from the crime scene, chances for a guilty plea or conviction are higher. If there is no match, suspects can be eliminated.

The analysis of DNA is another example of how science and technology are transforming crime fighting. However, there are some difficulties with this method. While some see it as a positive technological advancement – a tool that helps police to find and charge the guilty and to free the innocent – others see it as a serious invasion of privacy, suggesting it is like a police search of a person or place without permission. United States law regards DNA like other "property" that someone has abandoned. If a suspect leaves saliva on a glass in a restaurant, or a cigarette butt on a sidewalk, or in some other public place, this is abandoned property. If someone drinks from a glass in a restaurant and then leaves the restaurant, he or she is, in legal terms, "abandoning" the DNA left on the glass.

There is also the issue that DNA can be used to reveal much information about a person's genetic code. It can show, for example, whether the person has genes that relate to particular illnesses or to particular kinds of behavior. For reasons of privacy, therefore, it is important that DNA testing be strictly limited to simply identifying the person, and not used for other purposes without the person's permission. Special legislation may be needed to protect this genetic information.

Table 7.2 Determining DNA
The specimen amounts needed and the estimated likelihood of finding usable cells in them in order to determine a person's DNA profile

Specimen	Source or amount needed	Likelihood of usable cells
Blood stain	Size of a dime	More than 95%
Hair	Single hair with root and follicle Single hair without root	More than 90% Less than 20%
Saliva	On used gum or cigarette butt On used soda can or ground	50–70% Less than 50%
Mucus	On used tissue paper	Less than 50%
Skin cells	From socks, gloves, or other clothing used repeatedly From doorknob From handle of knife or pistol found at crime scene	30–60% Less than 20% Less than 10%

Source: NY City Medical Examiner's Office.

After you read

Task 1 UNDERSTANDING THE FUNCTION OF DIFFERENT PARTS OF A TEXT

A text will often contain different parts that have different functions. One part might recount past events, for example, while another part argues a point of view. Recognizing the function or purpose of different parts of a text helps you to understand more quickly what you are reading.

1 Look at the following list of functions that different parts of a text might have:

- to **discuss** different sides of an issue
- to **argue** a point of view
- to **tell a story** or **recount** past events
- to **report** data
- to **give facts and explain** them

2 Match the parts of the text "Techniques for Solving Crimes" indicated below with the appropriate function from the choices given.

1 Lines 1 to 10: data / (facts and explanations) / a point of view
2 Lines 11 to 29: past events / facts and explanations / a point of view
3 Lines 30 to 42: discussion of an issue / a point of view / past events
4 Lines 43 to 56: past events / facts and explanations / a point of view
5 Lines 57 to 62: discussion of an issue / a point of view / data
6 Lines 63 to 68: past events / facts and explanations / a point of view
7 Lines 69 to 75: discussion of an issue / a point of view / past events
8 Table 7.2: past events / data / a point of view

Task 2 EXAMINING GRAPHIC MATERIAL

1 Complete the following sentences, using information from Table 7.2, on page 164.

1 The most useful source of DNA is *a blood stain the size of a dime or larger*.
2 Saliva on _____ or _____ is more useful than that found on _____ or _____ .
3 The least useful source of DNA is _____ .
4 Mucus on used tissue paper is not as useful as, for example, _____ .

2 Write another three sentences of your own using information in the table.

Task 3 WRITING A CHRONOLOGICAL PARAGRAPH

Academic texts often include passages that tell about a series of events. This could be a story given to illustrate a point, or it could be an account of how someone conducted an experiment or a piece of research. These events are told in the order they happened, that is, in *chronological* order. Words like *then, later, after,* and *while* are used to help you keep track of the order of the events.

1 Re-read this extract from the text. It tells the story of how some New York City police officers solved a crime. Notice the underlined words that indicate time.

When the New York City police arrested a murder suspect in June 1998, they had no physical evidence tying him to the killing. Only days later they were able to link him to that homicide, plus two other homicides – and it all came down to a cup of coffee. The man, who had been arrested on a petty theft charge, was given coffee by detectives while they were questioning him. After the suspect left the room, detectives used the saliva he left on the cup to obtain his DNA. Testing then showed that his DNA matched not only the DNA found at the crime scene, but DNA associated with other crimes as well.

2 Answer the following questions:

1 Which words indicate that events occurred at the same time?

_____

_____

_____

2 Which words indicate that the events did not occur at the same time?

_____

_____

3 Imagine that you are a detective. You have been involved in solving a crime using DNA. Now you must write up your report. Tell the story of how you collected the DNA and how it helped you to find the criminal. Use the guide questions below to help you get started. The information in this section and in previous readings in this chapter will provide ideas.

1 What was the crime?
2 Who was the suspect?
3 How did you collect the DNA?
4 Then what happened?

CHAPTER 7 WRITING ASSIGNMENT

Choose one of the following topics as your chapter writing assignment.

1 Why is there an increase in youth crime in many industrialized countries? Suggest some possible solutions to the problem.
2 Look at the information from the U.S. Department of Justice in Table 7.3. Describe some of the information it contains, and give some possible explanations for the data.

Table 7.3 Who is in U.S. prisons?	
Gender:	92.8% men
	7.2% women
Age:	8.9% 18–24 years
	36.6% 25–34 years
	30.6% 35–44 years
	16.3% 45–54 years
	7.6% 55 or older
Education:	61.6% less than high school degree
	38.4% twelve years or more
Marital status:	30.4% married
	1.7% widowed
	5.8% separated
	20.5% divorced
	41.6% never married
Types of offenses:	47.2% violent crime
	22.0% property
	20.7% drug
	10.0% public order

Source: U.S. Dept. of Justice, Bureau of Justice Statistics, 1997. Sourcebook of Criminal Justice Statistics.

3 Compare the nature and extent of crime in your country with that in the United States.
4 How have advances in science and technology resulted in new kinds of crime as well as new kinds of detection?

Preparing to read

PERSONALIZING THE TOPIC

1 | Some of the reasons people do not break the law include the following:

a They have a strong moral belief that it is wrong.
b They fear the disapproval of their family and friends.
c They fear the embarrassment of being caught.
d They would have to pay a fine if they were caught.
e They are afraid of having a criminal record.

Which, if any, of the reasons above would deter or stop you from doing the following things?

_____ **1** parking illegally
_____ **2** copying computer software illegally
_____ **3** speeding
_____ **4** smoking in public places where it is prohibited
_____ **5** buying illegal copies of CDs or computer games
_____ **6** lying about your age to get into a bar or club

2 | Compare your answers with a partner.

SPEED READING

Remember that when you practice speed-reading techniques you should use these reading strategies:

- Do not say the words under your breath as you read.
- Try to focus on groups of words, not individual words.
- Try not to backtrack (go over the text again and again).
- Guess at the general meaning of words that you do not know.
- Skip over words that you do not know and that do not seem too important.
- Slow down slightly for key information, such as definitions and main ideas.
- Speed up for less important information, such as examples and details.

Practice speed-reading techniques as you read "What Stops Us from Committing Crimes?" Time yourself (or your teacher will time you). Then tell a partner two or three main ideas you understood from the text.

Now read

Now read the text "What Stops Us from Committing Crimes?" When you finish, turn to the tasks on page 171.

Controlling Crime

1 WHAT STOPS US FROM COMMITTING CRIMES?

If a society is to continue to function smoothly, then the members of
that society need to behave in orderly ways: they need to follow certain norms and obey certain rules. How does it happen that most people in a society agree to obey the rules? According to sociologists, there
are two kinds of controls that influence the way an individual behaves.
These are referred to as *internal controls* and *external controls*.

1

Internal controls

Imagine you are in a music store and you see a CD that you want. The
price is $20. You have only $5 with you, but the thought of stealing the
CD does not occur to you. Why not? The answer is internal controls.
Internal controls are those you impose on yourself based on your values, beliefs, and fears.

2

One of the values you hold is that stealing is wrong and that hon-
esty is right and good. To continue to feel good about yourself, you
don't steal. So the first aspect of internal control is how you feel about

3

yourself. The second aspect of internal control is the possible disapproval of friends and family who might become aware of your stealing. You do not want to have to talk with your parents or husband or wife or children or friends about why you stole a CD. The third factor operating to discourage you from stealing is the fear of being arrested. Many shops display signs such as "This store prosecutes shoplifters to the full extent of the law" and employ store detectives to identify shoplifters. Finally, social forces such as whether you are employed full-time may influence whether you steal or not. You may be afraid of social consequences, such as losing your job or losing the trust of your work colleagues. In a study of national property crime arrests, researchers compared the percentage of arrests within two populations: people with full-time jobs and people who were not employed. The researchers found that the percentage arrested among those who were not employed was much higher.

External controls

For some individuals internal controls will not be enough to deter them 4 from breaking the law. Most societies also impose external controls or punishments of some kind to discourage people from committing crimes. There are three main kinds of external controls: public embarrassment; the payment of money, or fines; and imprisonment. If a police officer stopped you for speeding, you would probably be embarrassed as other passing motorists stared at you. If you were going fast enough, you would also be asked to pay a fine as well as court costs. If you were driving while drunk, you would be taken to jail, fined, and have your driver's license taken away from you.

There are a number of factors that influence the effectiveness of 5 these external controls in stopping people from committing crimes. Their effectiveness depends, for example, on how certain it is that the crime will be punished. If there is little likelihood of being caught, the external controls may be weak or ineffective. It also depends on how severe the punishment is. The threat of being sent to prison is more likely to prevent people from breaking the law than the threat of paying a small fine. For some crimes, external controls do not seem to be very effective. For example, a person who commits a "crime of passion" is in a state of uncontrollable rage or feels overwhelming pressure and may not give any consideration at all to the consequences of his or her actions.

Fines for speeding aren't very large, but if you get speeding tickets frequently you can lose your driver's license.

After you read

Task 1 HIGHLIGHTING

Remember that highlighting sections of a text is a useful way to begin making notes from a text.

Find and highlight the following in the text:

- a definition of internal controls
- four kinds of internal controls
- a definition of external controls
- three kinds of external controls

Task 2 LANGUAGE FOCUS: DESCRIBING INTERNAL AND EXTERNAL CONTROLS

Here are some verbs that are used in the text to describe internal and external controls on behavior:

discourage (par. 3 & par. 4)   prevent (par. 5)
deter (par. 4)   stop (par. 5)

They are commonly used in a pattern like this:

		breaking the law
A fear of _____	discourages someone from	stealing
	deters someone from	speeding
The threat of _____	prevents someone from	cheating on a test
The thought of _____	stops someone from	committing a crime

Use the pattern to write some sentences of your own.

A fear of getting caught stops me from speeding.

Task 3 APPLYING WHAT YOU READ

As a college student, one of the things you must not do is to copy someone else's work and present it as your own. This is called *plagiarism*.

Discuss with other students:

1 What internal controls discourage you from plagiarizing?
2 What external controls exist to prevent plagiarism? (Find out if your school or college has rules about plagiarism and, if so, what they are.)

Preparing to read

READING AROUND THE TOPIC

The following statistics on people in prison were published by the U.S. Federal Bureau of Prisons in 2000.

Table 8.1 Sentence imposed	
Less than 1 year:	1.7%
1–3 years:	13.4%
3–5 years:	14.3%
5–10 years:	29.6%
10–15 years:	19.3%
15–20 years:	9.0%
More than 20 years:	9.7%
Life:	3.0%

Table 8.2 Type of offense	
Drug offenses:	58.1%
Robbery:	7.9%
Firearms, explosives, arson:	9.3%
Extortion, fraud, bribery:	5.1%
Property offenses:	5.8%
Homicide, aggravated assault, and kidnapping:	2.3%
Immigration:	6.6%
Other:	4.9%

Table 8.3 Inmates by security level*	
Minimum:	24.3%
Low:	34.5%
Medium:	23.6%
High:	10.5%

Additional inmates have not been assigned a security level.

Source: http://www.bop.gov/inmate.html.

1 Work with a partner and analyze the information in each table. Take turns making statements about the key information.

According to Table 8.1, the most common prison sentence imposed in the United States is 5 to 10 years.

2 Now discuss with your partner which data in these tables surprise you and why.

THINKING ABOUT THE TOPIC

Discuss with a small group:

1 Have you ever visited a prison? If so, where? What was it like? If not, what do you imagine a prison to be like?

2 Are there different types of prisons in your country? What are they?

3 Do prisons in your country try to rehabilitate prisoners, that is, prepare them for a normal, useful life after prison?

4 In your country can people be let out of prison early for good behavior?

Now read

Now read the text "Prisons." When you finish, turn to the tasks on page 175.

2 PRISONS

One long-serving prisoner described his first impression of prison in the following way: "Entering prison for the first time can be a frightening experience. The noise level is what strikes you and it is unlike any noise you have ever heard before. It's human noise and clamor. That, coupled with the sight of those dreary bars, made me think, 'Man, what have I gotten myself into here?!' When you enter prison, you have entered a world of its own. . . . Prison is a confined place, packed with living bodies of every shape, color and size. You will find yourself closer to other human beings than you ever have been before, many of whom you won't like."

The writer went on to describe his view of the different kinds of prisoners that are found in prisons. The first group are prisoners who may actually feel "at home" in prison. "They are conditioned for prison life from childhood. Starting out in juvenile correctional facilities, they later made the transition to youth reformatories and adult prisons. . . . They are **institutionalized** and would rather be in prison than out. . . . Prison's safe, controlled environment is best suited to them, a place where they are clothed, fed and told what to do. Outside life is too difficult to grapple with for these individuals."

A second group are people whose circumstances lead them unintentionally into prison, which becomes a kind of "homeless shelter" to them. They may be "unskilled, homeless and destitute, [and] they enter jails and prisons for an array of minor crimes to be fed and rested up. Prison gives them a needed break from homelessness and crack [drug] addiction." They are men and women whose economic and social conditions have led them into drugs and crime.

institutionalized
conditioned by many years of living in an institution so that the individual can no longer operate outside of one

A third group are those who are dedicated to a life of crime. "Crime is their vocation and they take coming to prison all in stride. For them prison is an occupational hazard. . . . They make no excuses for what they did and openly discuss what they will do once back out on the streets. . . . Their time in prison is just an extension of their criminal lives on the outside. Many continue to profit from [crimes] while in prison." (Ibraheem 1995)

Given the different circumstances that lead people to crime, and the different kinds of crime for which people are sentenced to prison, what should be the function of a modern prison? Should it be mainly to punish wrongdoers, to protect the society or its citizens, or to rehabilitate prisoners, that is, to move them away from criminal tendencies and prepare them for life back in the society?

There are different kinds of prisons, based on the level of security and the control over prisoners. This range of security includes minimum, low, medium, and high security. Each has different rules, and different kinds of prisoners will be sent to each. In most prisons there is some effort to rehabilitate prisoners. This may take the form of educational programs or vocational training, and some prisons employ prisoners in their own factories or on behalf of other companies. There are also systems of short-term work release into the community, and there is *parole*. If prisoners are put on parole, they are released back into the community under supervision before they have finished their sentence. They may be required to report periodically to a parole officer or to the police.

However, by their very nature prisons work against rehabilitation. They force people to be cut off from outside society. The habits and attitudes that prisoners learn may be the exact opposite of those they are supposed to learn. In prison they may learn to accept violence as normal. They will also mix with other criminals and learn new criminal skills. Over 60 percent of all men set free after serving prison sentences are re-arrested within four years. The problem is that if prisons are made more pleasant places to be, this may assist in achieving the rehabilitation of some prisoners, but it may also mean that a prison sentence becomes less of a deterrent to those who may commit crimes.

Probation officers routinely check on their clients.

There are some alternatives to prison as a means of punishment. For example, instead of being sent to jail, some offenders are put on *probation*. This means that they are allowed to remain in the community under some kind of supervision. They may have to follow certain rules of behavior or do some community service such as cleaning the parks or helping elderly people. New technologies, including security bracelets, can now assist in this supervision. The security bracelets enable the authorities to identify the location of offenders at all times. So, for example, offenders may be given a probationary sentence on the condition that they go nowhere near a certain part of the city, or that they do not leave their house except between certain hours. The security bracelets allow the authorities to monitor the wearers' movements.

After you read

Task 1 READING FOR DETAIL

Answer the following questions:

1 What are three kinds of prisoners found in U.S. prisons?
2 What are three possible functions of modern prisons?
3 What are three ways in which prisons may help to rehabilitate prisoners?
4 Why does rehabilitation often fail?
5 What does *probation* mean?

Task 2 BUILDING VOCABULARY: RECOGNIZING WORD "FAMILIES"

1 Find a word in the text that is related to each of the following words.

prison	*prisoner*	punishment	_____
deter	_____	homeless	_____
crime	_____	rehabilitate	_____

2 Complete the sentences below choosing an appropriate form of one of the words from step 1.

1 For some people, prison may offer an escape from _____.
2 While people are in prison, they may learn new _____ skills.
3 The _____ of prisoners is often unsuccessful and many return to crime when they are released.
4 Many people believe the main function of a prison should be to _____.
5 If prisons are uncomfortable, this may have a _____ effect.

Task 3 APPLYING WHAT YOU READ

1 Discuss in a group: If the people below are found guilty, what, if any, punishment do you think each should receive? Should they be sent to prison? Why or why not? If so, for how long? If not, what should be their punishment?

- A 16-year-old boy is arrested for stealing a car. It is the fourth time he has been arrested for this type of crime.
- An elderly woman was driving under the influence of alcohol. She caused an accident and someone was killed. It was the first time she had been arrested.
- A man finds that $1,000 has been transferred into his bank account by mistake. When the bank discovers the problem, they demand the return of the money. The man refuses. He is charged with stealing $1,000.
- A 22-year-old woman is arrested in a supermarket for shoplifting. The store detective finds the following items hidden in her handbag: a lipstick, a child's toy, several cans of food, and 3 CDs.

2 Write a paragraph explaining your opinion on one or more of the cases above.

Preparing to read

PERSONALIZING THE TOPIC

This text begins with the following words:

> Many Americans believe that the death penalty is effective in deterring people from committing murder. However, . . .

Discuss the following questions with a partner:

1 How do you think the second sentence will continue?
2 Does/Did your country have the death penalty? If yes, for what crimes?
3 Are you for or against the death penalty? Give reasons for your position.

SKIMMING

> Readers often skim a text to get the main idea before reading it more carefully. Skimming a text also gives you an idea of how a text is organized and the functions of the different parts of the text. This helps you to read more effectively.

1 The text you are about to read, "The Death Penalty," contains a discussion of a controversial issue. Such texts can be organized in different ways. Skim through the text and decide in which way this text is organized.

   a It only presents arguments for the death penalty.
   b It only presents arguments against the death penalty.
   c It presents a balanced discussion, arguing both sides of the issue.

2 When a writer presents an argument there are different types of evidence that can be included to support his or her position. Skim through the text to find which of the following are included as evidence:

   • personal stories
   • statistical data
   • the opinions of people who have specialized knowledge

3 Compare your findings with a partner.

Now read

Now read the text "The Death Penalty." When you finish, turn to the tasks on page 180.

3 THE DEATH PENALTY

Many Americans believe that the death penalty is effective in deterring people from committing murder. However, others disagree, and many sociologists argue that the evidence does not support this view. The evidence they provide includes the following:

a The United States is the only industrialized nation that still executes murderers and yet it has the highest murder rate in the industrialized world.

b In states of the United States that have retained the **capital punishment**, the homicide rates are generally much higher than in states that have abolished it. For example, Georgia, Louisiana, Mississippi, and Texas, which still use the death penalty, have considerably higher murder rates than Iowa, Maine, Minnesota, and Wisconsin, which have abolished capital punishment. This suggests that the death penalty does not deter murder.

c In states that have abolished the death penalty, homicide rates generally did not go up after the death penalty was abolished. Moreover, where capital punishment was restored in states that had earlier abolished it, it did not lead to any significant decrease in homicides.

d If the death penalty has a deterrent effect, then the execution of convicted murderers should scare potential killers and discourage them from killing. The number of homicides in the area should therefore decline. This may sound logical but the reality contradicts it. In Philadelphia during the 1930s, for example, the number of homicides remained about the same in the period from sixty days before to sixty days after a widely publicized execution

capital punishment
another term for the death penalty

of five murderers. This finding, among others, suggests that the death penalty apparently does not frighten potential killers and prevent them from killing.

e A study of the impact of the death penalty across fourteen nations concludes, "If capital punishment is a more effective deterrent than the alternative punishment of long imprisonment, its abolition ought to be followed by homicide rate increases. The evidence examined here fails to support and in fact repeatedly contradicts this proposition. In this cross-national sample, abolition was followed more often than not by absolute decreases in homicide rates, not by the increases predicted by [the] theory [of deterrence]" (Archer and Gartner 1984). In other words, when the death penalty was abolished, the majority of countries experienced a decline in homicide rates.

Some of this evidence is questionable. For example, regarding point **b**, the existence or not of capital punishment may not be the only difference between the states mentioned. Other differences, such as poverty levels or other population features, may account for the variation in murder rates. There is also the question of what is meant by the death penalty. Does it mean simply that in a certain state it is possible for a convicted murderer to be sentenced to death? Or does it mean that murderers have actually been sentenced to death? This difference could well affect the degree of deterrence.

Nevertheless, there is still considerable evidence to suggest that the death penalty does not deter murder, or, more accurately, that it is no more effective than life imprisonment in deterring murder. But why not? One reason is that murder is a crime of passion, most often carried out under the overwhelming pressure of an explosive emotion and uncontrollable rage. People in that condition usually cannot stop and think calmly about the death penalty. Another reason is that other factors, which may lead people to commit murder, such as having been brutally abused in childhood, are simply too powerful to be overcome by the threat of capital punishment.

While capital punishment may not deter people from committing murder, it can be effective for other purposes. It is obviously effective in preventing the murderer who is executed from doing harm to others again. It also succeeds in satisfying the emotion of outrage against the crime. Many Americans seem to advocate the death penalty for these reasons. As public opinion polls have shown, more than half of the U.S. adult population would still favor capital punishment even if they knew that it did not deter murder (Gallup 1999). This public support is reflected in the increasing number of executions up to 1999, as represented in the figures provided in Figure 8.1. However, the reduction in numbers since 1999 may reflect a shift in public opinion.

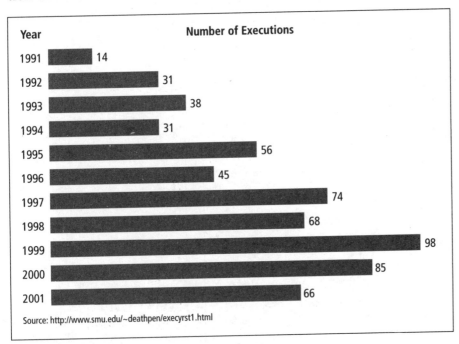

Figure 8.1 Executions in the United States 1991–2001

After you read

Task 1 READING FOR DETAIL

1 | This text presents detailed evidence to support the position that the existence of the death penalty does not deter people from committing murder. Complete the following statements of evidence.

1 In states that have abolished capital punishment, the murder rates _____

_____

2 When some states returned to using the death penalty, _____

_____

3 After widely publicized executions of criminals in Philadelphia in the 1930s, _____

_____

_____

4 The evidence from other countries _____

_____

2 | Figure 8.1 indicates that the number of prisoners executed in the United States increased five times from 1991 to 1999. The number then declined for two years in a row. What explanation for the recent decrease is suggested in the text?

_____

_____

Task 2 BUILDING VOCABULARY: SYNONYMS

Synonyms are words that have a similar meaning. Grouping words as synonyms can help you to remember new vocabulary. Using synonyms in your writing avoids repetition.

Find and underline the words from the text given below. Then find a synonym for each word. Begin by checking the text to see if the writer has used a synonym in a different place. If you don't find a synonym in the text, try to think of one. Use a dictionary if you need help. Write your synonym next to each word.

death penalty _____   accurately _____

homicide _____   powerful _____

deter _____   preventing _____

go up _____   outrage _____

decline _____   advocate _____

Task 3 READING CRITICALLY

Before reading the text you were asked to think about your opinion on the death penalty. Now, after reading the text, discuss the following questions with a partner:

1 What do you know that you did not know before?
2 Have you changed your views in any way? Why or why not?

Task 4 CONDUCTING A SURVEY

Conducting your own survey is a good way to deepen your understanding of a topic that you are studying. It can also give you fresh, original data to include in a paper that you may have to write.

1 Review the guidelines on page 161 for preparing questions to ask when conducting a survey.

2 Survey as many classmates and friends as you can to find out how many are in favor of the death penalty and how many are opposed. Use the charts below to record their answers. Place a check (✓) in the appropriate box for each person you ask.

Males	under 20 years old	20–40 years old	over 40 years old
For			
Against			

Females	under 20 years old	20–40 years old	over 40 years old
For			
Against			

3 Calculate the following:
- the percentage of people for and against
- the percentage of males and females for and against
- the percentage of people in each age category for and against

4 Write several statements reporting your results.

Preparing to read

1 The expressions below are used in the text. Discuss with a partner what they mean. Underline the ones you do not understand and ask other students or use a dictionary for help.

the war on drugs
the drug problem
drug dealing
drug addicts
drug related homicides
drug overdose
drug education programs
drug treatment
drug abuse
legalization of drugs

2 Compare your answers with the class.

PREDICTING

Trying to predict what information will be in a text before you read it is a good habit. It motivates you to read the text, and encourages you to pay attention to what you read to find out if your predictions were correct.

In this text you will read about the debate on whether or not to make some drugs legal. Work in a group. Use your own knowledge of the topic to predict what will be said in the text. Use the following questions as a guide.

1 What drugs do you think will be discussed?
2 What arguments for legalizing drugs do you think will be presented?
3 What arguments against legalization do you think will be presented?

Now read

Now read the text "The War on Drugs." When you finish, turn to the tasks on page 185.

Say **NO** to drugs

A MESSAGE FROM TEENS WHO CARE ABOUT TEENS.

4 THE WAR ON DRUGS

Over the last few decades, the drug problem in the United States (and   1
in many other industrialized countries) has become considerably
worse. In 1981, there were about 3 million drug addicts in the United
States; today there are around 6 million. The number of drug overdose
deaths and drug-related homicides has also increased. This is in spite
of the fact that the government has spent more and more money in trying to solve the drug problem. The fight against drugs is often referred
to as a "war" or "battle," and most experts now believe the battle
against drugs has been a failure. They say it has failed because the government has focused on controlling the problem through laws and punishments, rather than through drug education and treatment.

The failure of the law-enforcement approach has led to calls for   2
other approaches to solving the problem, including the decriminalization and the legalization of drugs. Advocates of decriminalization think
that drug users should no longer be labeled as serious criminals and
that the punishments for drug use should be significantly reduced.
Advocates of legalization believe there should be no restriction on drug
use at all, and that individuals should be able to buy drugs the same
way they buy cigarettes and alcohol today.

Those who are in favor of legalization argue that the current drug   3
laws do more harm than good. They argue that the current laws waste
police time because while police officers are busy arresting people for
smoking marijuana, they are not doing the work of arresting robbers
and murderers. Further, they argue that the high cost of illegal drugs
and the enormous amounts of money to be made from drug dealing
encourage more serious crimes. For example, many drug users turn to
stealing to support their habit and police can sometimes be bribed to

"look the other way." Finally, those who support legalization believe that if drugs were legalized, the huge amounts of money currently spent on law enforcement could be used for drug treatment and education, which would drastically reduce drug use.

Those who oppose legalization respond that, if drugs are legalized, drug use and addiction will skyrocket. They point to the experience with alcohol, which was prohibited in the United States in the 1920s. At the end of this period, called **Prohibition**, the consumption of alcohol apparently soared by 350 percent (Bennet 1989). Others feel that the use of drugs is a stepping stone to other crimes – that, for example, the use of marijuana leads to the use of heroin or cocaine, and on to more serious crime. If drug use is stopped, this trend will be prevented.

Another aspect of the debate on whether or not drugs should be legalized involves the question of individual rights. Some people call for legalization because they feel they have the right to take drugs – that it is none of the government's business. They think that laws governing this behavior are an invasion of individual rights. On the other hand, others argue that the government should try to protect us from harming ourselves.

Finally, there are those who believe that the problem of widespread drug abuse and crime can only be solved when the government attacks the root causes of the problem: poverty, racism and inequality (Currie 1993). They propose that the government should deal with the factors that cause the problem by providing employment for all, increasing the minimum wage, improving health care for the poor, offering paid family leave, and providing affordable housing.

Prohibition

the period (1920–1933) when the sale and consumption of alcohol was illegal in the United States.

The Shadow of Danger

If you believe that the traffic in Alcohol does more harm than good - *help stop it!*

After alcohol was decriminalized in the U.S., its consumption increased. Would decriminalizing drugs lead to an increase in drug use?

After you read

Task 1 NOTE TAKING: MAKING A CHART

1 Re-read the text to find and highlight the arguments *for* and *against* the legalization of drugs.

2 Make a chart with two columns. Write *For* at the head of one column and *Against* at the head of the other. In note format, put the arguments you found in step 1 in the appropriate column.

3 Compare the arguments with the predictions you made before you read.

Task 2 VARYING YOUR LANGUAGE

> Good writers vary the language they use so that their writing does not sound too repetitive.

1 Look back at the text and find the verbs listed below. Notice how the writer has used different words to provide variety.

- Verbs used to express an opinion
  think   believe   say   feel   argue

- Verbs used to take a position on an issue
  be in favor of   call for   propose   oppose

- Verbs used to discuss causes and consequences
  cause   encourage   lead to

2 Fill in the blanks in the text below with one of the verbs given above, in the appropriate form. Vary the verbs you use. Then compare your answers with a partner.

Many drug experts now (1)_____ the legalization of drugs. They (2)_____ that making drug use illegal only (3)_____ other social problems. They (4)_____ that it can, for example, (5)_____ police corruption, and (6)_____ more crime. Some people also (7)_____ that the money spent on fighting drug use would be better spent on fighting other crimes. Others (8)_____ that drug use is a question of individual rights. However, some people (9)_____ tough drug laws because they (10)_____ that drug use is morally wrong or because they (11)_____ drug use will (12)_____ people to commit other crimes. Others (13)_____ fighting the underlying factors of poverty and unemployment, which (14)_____ the problem of drug use.

3 Write a paragraph about what you think should be done about the illegal drug problem in the United States or your own country. Use some of the expressions given above.

Task 3 BUILDING VOCABULARY: FIGURATIVE LANGUAGE

Sometimes a writer uses figurative language – language that causes a picture to come to your mind. If you imagine this picture, it will help you understand the meaning of the expression that the writer is using.

1 Find a figurative expression in the text (paragraph indicated) to match the illustrations below. Write the expression next to the illustration.

1

(par. 1)

the battle against

drugs

2

(par. 3)

3

(par. 4)

_____

_____

_____

_____

4

(par. 4)

_____

_____

_____

_____

5

(par. 6)

_____

_____

_____

_____

2 Work with a partner. Explain what each expression means.

CHAPTER 8 WRITING ASSIGNMENT

Choose one of the following topics as your chapter writing assignment.

1 Write an essay that is an argument on what should be done to help control the level of crime in your community or a community you're familiar with. Use some of the ideas you have read about and discussed in this chapter.

2 Compare and contrast the kinds of crimes you hear about and read about in the United States with the kinds of crime that are most common in your country. Explain some of the differences.

3 Write an essay discussing the arguments for and against capital punishment.

4 Look at the information in Figure 8.2. Write a paragraph explaining what the graph shows and reporting some of the information it contains. Offer some possible explanations for the data.

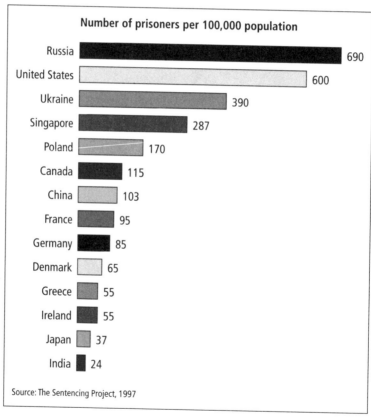

Figure 8.2 Imprisonment around the world

Changing Societies

I n this unit we look at change in society. In Chapter 9, we look at examples of how societies vary from place to place and over time. We also look at recent changes in technology and in the workplace, and how they are affecting many people's lives. In Chapter 10, we look at our whole planet. We begin with population issues: the growing number of people on our planet and how more and more people are moving to cities. We then explore an important issue for our survival – the environment. The chapter ends with speculation about what the future might bring.

Previewing the unit

Read the contents page for Unit 5 and do the following activities.

Chapter 9: Cultural change

Look at these pictures. What tells you that they are pictures of different cultures?

Chapter 10: Global issues

Circle what you think is the correct answer to complete each sentence. You will be able to check your answers as you read this chapter.

1 For 10,000 years, the population of the world grew by about 750,000 per century. Today, the population grows by nearly 750,000 _____.

  a every 3 days   **b** every 3 months   **c** every 3 years   **d** every 30 years

2 The population of the world today is _____.

  a 1 billion   **b** 6 billion   **c** 20 billion   **d** 100 billion

3 In 1900, only one-tenth of the world's population lived in cities. Today, for the first time in history, _____ of the world's population lives in cities. (Rogers 1998).

  a a quarter   **b** a third   **c** half   **d** three-quarters

4 Although they make up less than 6 percent of the world's population, each year people in the United States consume about _____ of the world's energy and raw materials.

  a 10 percent   **b** 30 percent   **c** 50 percent   **d** 75 percent

5 Surveys in the United States over the last decade reveal that roughly _____ of the population believes in the existence of life on other planets.

  a a tenth   **b** a quarter   **c** a third   **d** half

Unit Contents 5

Preparing to read

PREVIEWING ART IN THE TEXT

1 Look at the photographs in "Cultural Change and Variation" and read any captions that accompany them.

2 Work with a partner and discuss which photographs connect to which of the three subheadings in the reading. Give reasons for your choices.

- What is culture?
- Cultural variation
- How cultures change

3 Compare your ideas with those of other students in the class.

THINKING ABOUT THE TOPIC

1 Read these opening sentences of "Cultural Variation and Change."

What is culture?
The word *culture* appears frequently in the media and in academic texts. We read about cultural events, traditional cultures, youth culture, cultural values, and cultural differences.

- Discuss with a partner the meaning of the word *culture.*
- Share with your partner one behavior or value that is part of your culture.

2 Skim the second subsection of the text, "Cultural variation."

- Discuss with a partner the meaning of the term *cultural variation.*
- Share with your partner different ways that people get married in cultures that you are familiar with.

3 Skim the last subsection of the text, "How cultures change."

- Discuss with a partner the meaning of the term *cultural change.*
- Share with your partner some aspect of your culture that has changed in the past twenty years.

Now read

Now read the text "Cultural Variation and Change." When you have finished, turn to the tasks on page 196.

Cultural Change

Chapter 9

1 CULTURAL VARIATION AND CHANGE

What is culture?

The word **culture** appears frequently in the media and in academic texts. We read about cultural events, traditional cultures, youth culture, cultural values, and cultural differences. What is culture? To a sociologist, culture refers to the systems of signs, meanings, and worldviews of particular groups of human beings. It is everything that the members of a group learn to do, think, use, and make as part of growing up in the group. Culture in this sense has two levels: material and non-material. *Material culture* refers to all the objects, or artifacts, that have meaning to the members of a society or that are used by them. Artifacts include tools, clothes, buildings, weapons, and art objects. *Non-material culture* refers to the norms, customs, behaviors, beliefs, values, attitudes, knowledge, and language of the society.

culture

culture refers to the systems of signs, meanings, and worldviews of particular groups of human beings

Material and nonmaterial cultures are related in that the artifacts of the material culture reflect aspects of the nonmaterial culture. Some examples are given in the chart below.

Material Artifacts and their Meaning	
football stadium	value of sporting competition
textbook	value of knowledge and learning
wedding ring	custom of the marriage ceremony
microscope	the study of science
church	belief in a god or gods
clothes	ways of dressing
exercise machine	concern for fitness
cell phone	desire for fast communication

Cultural variation

In all cultures, even those that appear from the outside to be very uniform or homogeneous, there is a great deal of variation in attitudes and values. There are many factors that contribute to this diversity. They include differences in age, in education, in social status or class, and in gender, as well as factors such as whether people live in the country or in a town or city.

Some cultures are more tolerant than others of differences in values and behaviors among their individual members and subgroups. For example, in the United States there is generally a great deal of variation in what are considered acceptable ways to get married. Most people still get married in a religious ceremony in a church or temple, but there are many variations. Nonreligious ceremonies can be performed by people licensed to do so, and people may get married in a garden, in a hot air balloon, under water, or dressed in the costumes of their favorite entertainers.

How cultures change

Cultures change over time. Sometimes the change occurs so slowly and gradually that it is hard to notice it happening. At other times it is rapid or sudden. A number of Western cultures, including that of the United States, experienced rapid cultural changes in the late 1960s, with the beginnings of a mass youth culture. The youth challenged many of the values of their parents in relation to sexual behavior, war, and materialism. This was expressed in radical changes in behavior, dress, and music.

Variation within a culture is one of the factors that leads to change in the culture over time. A difference in values and behaviors may take place in one subgroup. These different behaviors may then be gradually taken up by other groups. In the case of youth culture, the values of that generation may become dominant over time as the group grows older and takes power in the society.

A religious marriage ceremony in a church or temple is preferred by many people.

Some people choose unconventional ways to become husband and wife.

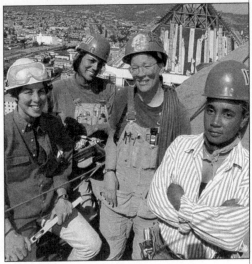

In the early twentieth century, sewing factories provided one of the few ways that women could earn a living. Modern cultural norms allow women to have more choices.

The introduction of new technologies is also a major factor in cultural change. You can probably imagine some of the possible changes in behavior that might happen when television or the telephone are introduced into a community for the first time. If we return to the distinction between material and nonmaterial culture, we can see that changes in the material aspects of a society can bring about changes in norms, behaviors, and values.

Cultural change also occurs when different cultures come into contact with one another, and then borrow from each other. They may exchange ideas, such as religious beliefs, or material artifacts, such as food or clothing. Often when these imported elements are added to the existing culture, they are altered in some way to fit in better with the local culture. For example, the popular Italian food, spaghetti, is said to have had its origins in Chinese noodles, which were brought back to Italy from China by the Italian adventurer, Marco Polo in the late twelfth century. Much later, in the early twentieth century, spaghetti made its way into the American diet with the arrival of Italian immigrants to the United States.

The values or norms of a culture may also change as a consequence of public debate and discussion, for example, in the media, at public meetings of various kinds, and as part of the process of political elections. These debates may strengthen or challenge existing values. Some of the issues that have been the subject of widespread public debate in most Western cultures over the past ten to twenty years include:

- men and women living together without being married
- career opportunities for women
- conservation of natural forests and undeveloped land
- smoking in public places
- teenagers having freedom to express their own values in music, dance, and dress

After you read

Task 1 SHARING YOUR CULTURAL PERSPECTIVE

> You can deepen your understanding of a topic by sharing your own cultural perspective and hearing the perspectives of people from other cultures.

As you read in the text, the material arti-facts of a culture reflect or symbolize the culture's nonmaterial customs, values, and beliefs. For example, in many cul-tures the sign on the right symbolizes concern for the environment.

1 Look at the following objects and decide what they symbolize in your culture. Make notes of your ideas.

2 Work in a small group and compare what you think these objects symbolize with the ideas of the other students in your group.

3 Add one or two more material artifacts and their meaning to the chart on page 194. Tell the students in your group what they are and what they symbolize in your culture.

Task 2 SUMMARIZING FROM TOPIC SENTENCES

> Topic sentences often provide a good starting point for writing a summary. You can sometimes build a summary of a text simply by combining paraphrases of the topic sentences.

1 Read the following topic sentences from the subsection, "Cultural variation."

- In all cultures, even those that appear from the outside to be very uniform or homogeneous, there is a great deal of variation in attitudes and values.
- Some cultures are more tolerant than others of differences in values and behaviors among their individual members and subgroups.

2 Now read an edited version that combines them into a summary. Notice the changes that were made.

All cultures, even those that appear to be very uniform, tolerate some variation in attitudes and values among their members and subgroups. Some cultures will, however, be more tolerant of diversity than others.

3 The topic sentences below are from the subsection, "How cultures change." Edit the sentences to make a cohesive summary paragraph. You could begin your summary paragraph like this:

All cultures change over time as a result of a number of factors...

- Cultures change over time.
- Variation within a culture is one of the factors that leads to change in the culture over time.
- The introduction of new technologies is also a major factor in cultural change.
- Cultural change also occurs when different cultures come into contact with one another, and then borrow from each other.
- The values or norms of a culture may also change as a consequence of public debate and discussion, for example in the media, at public meetings of various kinds, and as part of the process of political elections.

4 Exchange paragraphs with a partner. Give each other advice on how to improve your summary paragraphs.

Task 3 READING ACTIVELY

Remember that when you read actively, you think about what you are reading and how it relates to your own views or your own experiences.

Work in a group. Discuss one or more of the issues listed in the last paragraph of the text. Use the following questions as a guide.

- What are your own views on the issue(s)?
- Have there been changes in attitude on this issue within your culture? If so, what factors have contributed to these changes in attitude?

Preparing to read

THINKING ABOUT THE TOPIC

1 The text begins in the following way:

Culture is complex. We do not just belong to a single cultural group. Most of us belong to many. Just think for a moment of all the groups that you belong to.

Work in a small group and discuss the following questions:

1 What cultural groups do you belong to?
2 Do any of these groups use particular language, clothes, or behaviors as a sign of belonging to the group? If so, give examples.

2 Look at the picture on the right. Read the sentences below from the subsection of the text, "Subcultures."

A subculture is the culture of one group within a society. Subcultures are part of a larger culture but they differ from that larger culture in certain ways.

Write down examples of subcultures that come to mind. Compare your examples with a partner.

3 Look at the picture on the right. Read the sentence below from the subsection of the text, "Cults."

The word *cult* is used to describe a wide variety of groups, some of which have a religious or quasi-religious basis, and others of which are based more on a lifestyle or therapy of some kind.

Write down examples of cults that come to mind. Compare your examples with a partner.

Now read

Now read the text "Subcultures and Cults." When you have finished, turn to the tasks on page 201.

2 SUBCULTURES AND CULTS

Introduction

Culture is complex. We do not just belong to a single cultural group. Most of us belong to many. Just think for a moment of all the groups that you belong to. Each of these has its own values, beliefs, and behaviors. Sometimes the values, beliefs, and behaviors of one conflict with those of another. For example, you have probably experienced at some point in your life a conflict between the cultural values and expectations of your parents and those of your peer group. In the next section, we will look at the notion of *subcultures*, or cultures within cultures. We will also look at the phenomenon of cults.

Subcultures

A subculture is the culture of one group within a society. Subcultures are part of a larger culture but they differ from that larger culture in certain ways. For instance, they might differ in behaviors, language, religion, values, or norms. Subcultures include various racial, religious, age, and economic groups. Belonging to more than one subculture can create some of the personal conflicts we face daily. A common example for young people is when the values of the youth subculture conflict with the values of another (for example, racial, religious, or economic) subculture.

The youth subculture is one of the largest subcultures in the United States today, and while it is a recognizable subculture, it also represents many different influences. Within it we find distinct groups that are sometimes referred to as "tribes." Sociologists suggest that teenagers have always been attracted to tribes as a way of expressing identity. What is interesting about the current youth subculture and its tribes, is that it is the first generation of youth to belong to global tribes;

that is, the common features between members of these tribes have crossed national boundaries and have become global. A report ("Teen-mood," MojoPartners 1996) based on interviews with 10,000 teenagers around the world found that teenagers from countries as different as China, India, Canada, and Costa Rica share common subcultures, based on globally broadcast television shows, movies, international pop music stars, video games, and international sporting heroes. This generation of youth is the first to really experience the global village. They are growing up with technology that keeps them in touch with global influences, in terms of clothing, music, attitudes, and activities.

Examples of global youth subcultures include those based on African-American or Hispanic-American street culture, those related to sports such as surfing or skateboarding, some attached to particular styles of music, and others linked to a passion for computers. This latter group are sometimes called "nerds" or "net-heads" because they spend all their time on the Internet. Each tribe has evolved its own styles of talk, dress, and music, styles which keep changing so that they remain recognizably different from the mainstream.

Cults

cult

A cult is a subculture with a charismatic leader and a philosophy that offers members a totally new way of life.

The word **cult** is used to describe a wide variety of groups, some of which have a religious or quasi-religious basis, and others of which are based more on a lifestyle or therapy of some kind. According to sociologists, there are some common factors to all cults. They always have a charismatic leader, a mainly young and middle-class following, and a philosophy that offers members a totally new way of life. People who join cults are often going through a period when they feel dissatisfied with themselves or the world around them. Unlike in the past, they are less likely these days to join one of the established religions, in which memberships are declining, especially among young people.

Some cults have been accused of mind control and brainwashing techniques to attract and keep new members. One ex-cultist described the mind control techniques she experienced: "At first new recruits are showered with affection and compliments – this is known as 'love-bombing.' But then the love turns sour, and the newcomers may find themselves in a circle of people who are hurling abuse. It is a classic disorientation technique. It is real emotional hell, but when you are joining in the abuse, you think it is helping people"(Green 1995).

Some sociologists question the idea that cults keep their members through mind control and brainwashing techniques. They say this idea is popular because it removes the responsibility from the individual members. They accept that some cults put enormous pressure on individuals, but argue that the techniques can be resisted. Evidence of this is that eventually most people leave cults of their own free will.

After you read

Task 1 READING FOR DETAIL

Discuss in a small group:

1 How can belonging to a number of subcultures cause someone personal conflict?
2 How has a global youth culture come about?
3 What are some factors that are common to all cults?
4 Why do people stay in cults for as long as they do?

Task 2 WRITING EXPANDED DEFINITIONS

> Expanded definitions give the meaning of terms by providing longer explanations and/or examples. Such definitions are an important feature of academic texts. Review the examples in Chapter 2, on pages 32–33.

1 Write an expanded definition of *subculture* in two or three sentences. Include the following words:

groups   values   behaviors   conflict

2 Write an expanded definition of *youth subculture* in two or three sentences. Include the following words:

tribes   global   influence   technology

3 Write an expanded definition of *cult* in two or three sentences. Include the following words:

quasi-religious   charismatic leaders   middle class   brainwashing

4 Compare your definitions with a partner. See if you can help your partner improve his or her definitions and edit any grammar mistakes.

Task 3 PERSONALIZING THE TOPIC

Discuss with your class to what extent you belong to a global culture. Think about such things as:

- the clothes you wear
- the music you listen to
- the food you eat
- the products you use
- the movies and TV shows you watch
- the sports you enjoy

Preparing to read

PERSONALIZING THE TOPIC

1 How do you communicate with others? Complete the chart below by writing in answers such as the following: *every day, two or three times a week, once a month, never,* etc.

	How often do you use this form of communication with your friends?	How often do you use this form of communication for work or study?
e-mail		
ordinary mail		
the telephone		
a cell phone		
a fax machine		
face-to-face communication		

2 Compare your answers with others in the class.

THINKING ABOUT THE TOPIC

Look at the photographs below.

Discuss with a partner:

What are some ways in which communication has changed since these photographs were taken? How do you think communication might change in the future?

Now read

Now read the text "Changing Communication." When you finish, turn to the tasks on page 205.

Cell phones allow people to have great flexibility in communicating with each other.

3 CHANGING COMMUNICATION

"Times change and we change with them" is an old saying. One of the major ways in which the current times are changing is in how we communicate with each other. There have been rapid developments over the past few decades in technologies for communication. Advances in computing and **telecommunication** mean that information can now be exchanged and processed globally at amazing speeds. This has resulted in what has been called the "information revolution." Whereas the industrial revolution saw the rise of the power of machines, the information revolution is seeing the rise of information as a source of power.

All major technological advances, such as those we are experiencing in communications, are necessarily accompanied by other social and cultural changes. Think of your own personal communication patterns and the impact of the fax machine, the cell phone, e-mail and the Internet on how, when, where, and with whom you communicate. E-mail and the cell phone, for example, have enabled people to have more frequent and flexible contact with friends and family wherever they are. Much of this communication may seem trivial and mundane. You have probably overheard people on cell phones saying things such as:

- "I just left the office. Is there anything I should pick up on the way home?"
- "I'm in the video store. Have you seen *Terminator II*?"
- "I'm on the bus. Where are you?"

But psychologists say this kind of contact is important in counteracting the negative influence of city life that can leave us feeling isolated and alienated. Receiving a phone call or an e-mail can give us joy and pleasure and make us feel wanted, needed, and loved.

However, there are disadvantages too. When a cell phone is used for work, the easy access can mean that work never ends. It can follow us home and intrude on our home life. Then there is the intrusion into others' leisure space when a cell phone rings in a restaurant or theater. The French social theorist, Foucault, argued that citizens of modern urban societies have an increasing urge to keep track of one

telecommunication
communication systems, including telephone lines, radio, television, and satellites

another, and that we take part in this surveillance of each other because it gives us a sense of security. The cell phone enables, and perhaps encourages, this surveillance.

Education is another area of social life in which information technology is changing the way we communicate. Today's college students may not simply sit in a lecture or a library to learn about their field. Through their computers and the wonders of **virtual reality** they can participate in lifelike simulated experiences. They can visit virtual science laboratories, archaeological sites, or artists' studios.

Consider the following scenario of the future of education made possible through developments in information technology:

> For children over the age of 10, daily attendance at schools is not compulsory. Some of the older children attend school only once or twice weekly to get tutorial support or instruction from a teacher. For the most part, pupils are encouraged to work **on-line** from home. Students must complete a minimum number of study hours per year; however, they may make up these hours by studying at home at times that suit their family schedule. They can **log on** early or late in the day and even join live classes in other countries. In order to ensure that each student is learning adequately, computer software will automatically monitor the number of hours a week each student studies on-line as well as that student's learning materials and assessment activities. Reports will be available for parents and teachers. The software can then identify the best learning activities and conditions for each individual student and generate similar activities. It can also identify areas of weak achievement and produce special programs adjusted to the student's needs (Cummings 1999).

Some aspects of this scenario will seem attractive and others may frighten us. What would be the impact of such a scenario on the social development of children and young people? How would it affect the work of teachers? What would be the impact on family life? Who would benefit from such changes and who would not? What about those who do not have the financial resources to have access to the necessary technology? Would we want to be monitored by our computers in that way? Many people may wonder whether the benefits of on-line schooling can ever outweigh the disadvantages.

virtual reality

computer programs that allow the users to feel as though they are physically in other environments

on-line

connected to other computers through a telecommunication system

log on

to access a computer system

The equipment on this young man's head allows him to experience the *virtual reality* of the game he is playing.

After you read

Task 1 BUILDING VOCABULARY: DESCRIPTIVE WORDS

> When describing something, writers often use two or more descriptive words to describe the thing more accurately or fully.

Work with a partner.

1 Find and underline these pairs (or groups) of descriptive words in the second paragraph of the text. Find what each pair (or group) is referring to.

- frequent and flexible
- trivial and mundane
- isolated and alienated
- wanted, needed, and loved

2 Discuss the meaning of each word, using a dictionary if necessary.

3 Complete these sentences with suitable words from the following list.

motivating   convenient   unhelpful   inconsiderate   important   valuable

1 Fax machines provide an *easy* and _____ way to receive copies of documents.

2 If your cell phone rings when you are in a movie theater, others will think you are *rude* and _____ .

3 The Internet provides *interesting*, _____ , and _____ opportunities for children to learn.

Task 2 LANGUAGE FOCUS: WRITING ABOUT POSSIBILITIES

1 Discuss with a partner the differences in meaning between the sentences below.

If he had a TV, he <u>could</u> use it to practice his English.
If he had a TV, he <u>would</u> use it to practice his English.

2 Make sentences from the options in the grid, adding your own endings.

	a computer,		_____
If she had	access to the Internet,	she could/would	_____
	a cell phone,		_____

3 Work with a partner. Discuss the questions in the last paragraph of the text.

4 Write a paragraph that begins with the following sentence:

If children no longer had to go to school but could study on-line from home, there would be many social and cultural consequences. . . .

Preparing to read

PERSONALIZING THE TOPIC

1 Think about a job you have had (or have now). Read the statements below and decide whether each one is *true*, *somewhat true*, or *not true*, regarding that job. Place a check (✓) in the appropriate column in the chart.

	True	Somewhat true	Not true
I had the opportunity to interact with others.			
My opinion was asked for and valued.			
The tasks were challenging.			
I was paid well.			
My work was useful to society.			
All employees were treated with respect.			
I had the potential for advancement.			
My work tasks were varied.			
I had the opportunity to be creative.			
The work hours were flexible.			

2 Compare your answers with a partner.

3 Discuss in a small group:

1 What would an *ideal job* be like for you?

2 If you had to make a choice, which of the following jobs would you choose? Why?

a a job that offered personal satisfaction and opportunity for growth but didn't pay much

b a job that wasn't enjoyable or satisfying but paid an excellent salary

Now read

Now read the text "The Changing Workplace." When you finish, turn to the tasks on page 209.

Information technology makes it possible for more people to work at home today than in the past.

4 THE CHANGING WORKPLACE

Vince is a manager for a large electronics company. At least twice a week, he works from his Ohio home on a computer that is linked to his office. Through this computer, he can be in immediate, regular contact with his work team and with his company bosses. Vince is a part-time telecommuter. That is, he works from home for part of his week, avoiding the need to commute in the usual way – by car or public transportation. Vince is connected with his workplace through technology – computers, fax machines, and phone systems. There are many others like Vince in the United States today. Some are full-time telecommuters, working from home every day of the week. Vince and his team are typical of the workplace of today in other ways, too. Vince says, "We have to attend a lot of training sessions to keep up with new technology. We work in teams and manage our work activities ourselves rather than depend on a boss to tell us what to do."

The workplace of the United States and of other developed countries all over the world is changing. Technology has played a large part in this process, but there are also other factors at work. For one thing, there has been a change in the work ethic, or attitude toward work. Until recently, most people believed that a person who was supporting a family had a responsibility to choose a job that paid the most, rather than the one that was more satisfying for him or her. Many people worked hard to support their families, not thinking about how unpleasant or boring their work was. Today a majority reject this attitude. Most people are interested in jobs that allow for personal growth and that will give them some satisfaction or even enjoyment (Castro 1989; Schor 1991).

white-collar
| work that requires mental
| labor

blue-collar
| work that requires physical
| labor

How has this new work ethic come about? One reason is that the number of **white-collar** workers has increased substantially over the last few decades. Another is the increase in the average level of workers' education. In farming and manufacturing, new machines have dramatically decreased the number of people needed to produce things. Before 1945, there were far more **blue-collar** workers than white-collar workers, but since this time, the white-collar segment has grown rapidly. Now there are approximately three times as many white-collar workers (professionals, office workers, and salespeople) as blue-collar workers in most manufacturing companies. It is these white-collar and better-educated workers who value jobs that are satisfying and that give them the chance to develop themselves personally.

This change in attitude toward work has led, in turn, to changes in the workplace. Employers are increasingly offering their workers jobs and working conditions that will keep them happy: more interesting and varied tasks; more opportunities for self-direction; more flexible hours to make it easier to combine work and family life; increased participation in decision making; and, in some cases, a share in the profits of the company.

Other changes in work opportunities include changes in the types of industries where people are most likely to find work. While there has been a decrease in jobs in manufacturing and other industries that produce **goods,** there has been an increase in jobs in industries that provide **services** – for example, education, health care, banking, entertainment, and leisure.

goods
| items that are sold to the
| public

services
| things that people need
| that are not goods, for
| example, entertainment

So what changes can we expect in the future? In very recent years, some economic experts have been predicting a world where just 20 percent of the population will have jobs. They believe that this will be sufficient to keep the world economy going – to produce all the goods and services needed. Not surprisingly, they foresee very serious problems in the task of occupying the rest of the population (Martin & Schumann 1997). Whatever happens, it is clear that the world of work will continue to change at a fast pace, presenting huge challenges for individuals and societies alike.

What makes a good workplace?

A team of researchers (Levine et al. 1984) set out to identify the characteristics that individuals believe make for a good job. The characteristics mentioned by over 450 employees were:

1 My bosses treat me with respect and have confidence in my abilities.
2 There is variety in my daily work.
3 I find challenge in my work.
4 There is an opportunity for advancement.
5 The work I do contributes to society.

Notice that income is not on the list. Workers do want their work to give them an adequate income, but they also value respect, variety, challenge, and advancement.

After you read

Task 1 UNDERSTANDING THE FUNCTION OF DIFFERENT PARTS OF THE TEXT

> Remember that it is important when reading a text to be aware of the functions of different parts of the text and how these parts fit into the overall structure.

1 The following describe the functions of the different paragraphs in the text. Write the number of the appropriate paragraph next to its description.

_____ It describes the difference between present and past attitudes at work.

_____ It predicts how working conditions in the future will be different from the present.

_____ It explains why there is a different attitude to work today than in the past.

_____ It gives a personal example of one individual's modern working lifestyle.

_____ It gives some examples of how present-day workplace conditions are different from the past.

_____ It describes a change in the types of work available today.

2 Compare your answers with a partner. Discuss why you think the writer put the paragraphs in this order.

3 The sentences below could be placed at the end of one of the paragraphs in the text. Discuss with your partner where they could be placed and why.

There has also been an increase in the use of temporary, part-time, and contract workers. Temporary workers, for example, now compose one-third of the U.S. labor force, and their ranks are growing so fast that they are soon expected to outnumber full-time workers (Castro 1993).

Task 2 BUILDING VOCABULARY: USING CONTEXT CLUES

1 Find words in the text that mean the same as the words below:

1 travel to and from a workplace (par. 1) _____

2 do not accept (par. 2) _____

3 very much (par. 3) _____

4 able to be changed to suit the person or situation (par. 4) _____

5 money made by a business after taking out costs (par. 4) _____

6 free time (par. 5) _____

7 predict (par. 6) _____

8 difficulties (par. 6) _____

2 Compare your answers with a partner. Explain which parts of the text helped you to find the correct words.

Task 3 PUNCTUATION

> Punctuation is an important part of a text. It shows how ideas relate to each other. One way to become familiar with the purpose of different forms of punctuation is to study how writers use them. This will help you to be a more effective reader and also to use punctuation appropriately when you write.

1 Look back at the text and circle examples of these forms of punctuation:

- , (comma)
- ? (question mark)
- – (dash)
- ". . . ." (quotation marks)
- ( ) (parentheses)
- : (colon)
- ; (semi-colon)

2 Work with a partner. For each example that you circled in step 1, discuss why the writer used this punctuation mark.

At least twice a week, he works from his Ohio home on a computer that is linked to his office.

The writer uses a comma to separate a time phrase that occurs before the subject of the sentence from the main clause.

3 Read the paragraph below and punctuate it, using the ideas from your discussion above. Put in capital letters where necessary.

it may be extremely important to have a job but does it bring happiness in many studies over the last two decades workers have been asked whether they would continue to work if they inherited enough money to live comfortably without working more than 70 percent replied that they would asked how satisfied they were with their jobs even more 80 to 90 percent replied that they were very or moderately satisfied but asked whether they would choose the same line of work if they could begin all over again most said no only 43 percent of white-collar workers and 24 percent of blue-collar workers said yes and when asked do you enjoy your work so much that you have a hard time putting it aside only 34 percent of men and 32 percent of women said yes in short most people seem to like their jobs but are not too excited about them

CHAPTER 9 WRITING ASSIGNMENT

Choose one of the following topics as your chapter writing assignment.

1 Write an essay on cultural variation and change in one of the following areas:

- care for the elderly
- raising children
- youth culture

2 Describe youth subculture(s) in your own culture and explain where some of the influences on this youth culture come from.

3 What do you think has been the most important technological development of the past fifty years? Give your reasons.

4 Survey at least ten people about cell phone or computer use. Find out the following:

- How many own a cell phone/computer?
- If they own a cell phone/computer, how frequently do they use it?
- What are their main reasons for using it? (for example, personal, work, other)
- If they do not own a cell phone/computer, what are their reasons for not owning one?
- Do they think the cell phone/computer has changed the way people interact and relate to one another? If so how?

Write a short report describing:

- the focus of your survey
- how you conducted your survey (with whom, where, etc.)
- what your results showed

5 Describe your ideal job. What type of work would you do? What characteristics would be most important?

Preparing to read

READING AROUND THE TOPIC

Read the information below and discuss the questions that follow with a small group.

DID YOU KNOW?
- The population of the world grows by about 245,000 each day.
- About 94 million new babies are born every year – a number equal to the size of Mexico's population.
- Up until the year 1600, it took more than 500,000 years for the human population to reach about half a billion (500 million).
- Since 1600, it has taken only 400 years for the population to skyrocket to almost 6 billion.
- Today it takes only five or six years for the world to add 500 million people to the world's population.
- To keep world population at its present level, there needs to be a global fertility rate (average number of children a woman will have over a lifetime) of 2.1. At present, the rate is 2.71, but that rate is declining. The U.S. fertility rate is 2.03.
- Some countries – Italy and Spain for example – have very low fertility rates. Italy's is just under 1.2. This means that in a little over 100 years, Italy's current population of 55 million could drop to about 8 million.
- Other countries still have very high fertility rates. In Niger, for example, each woman averages 7.5 children.

---

1 What has been the pattern of human population growth?
2 Is the pattern likely to be the same in the future?
3 What is the approximate population of your country?
4 What population statistics of other countries do you know?
5 Is your country's fertility rate increasing or decreasing?

SKIMMING

1 Skim the text. Read the first paragraph, the first sentence of each of the other paragraphs, and look at the charts.

2 With a partner, answer the first two questions in "Reading Around the Topic" again. Notice how simply by skimming you can answer these questions more completely.

Now read

Now read the text "Population Change." When you finish, turn to the tasks on page 216.

Global Issues

1 POPULATION CHANGE

For the past million years the world's population has grown almost continuously, although not always at the same rate. Despite this, **demographers** are predicting that our population growth will slow down and then stabilize or stay steady.

There have been three great population surges in the life of humankind. Each followed a technological revolution that dramatically increased the number of people that the world could keep alive. The first revolution was the invention of tool making (using stone and animal parts to make hunting and cooking equipment) that occurred gradually around the world between a million and 100,000 years ago. The second was the invention of farming, which began at the end of the last ice age, about 10,000 years ago. Agriculture helped the world's population rise from less than 10 million to about 150 million at the time of Christ and 350 million one thousand years ago. Then, in the fourteenth century, the number of people dropped dramatically because of the Black Death – a terrible sickness that spread rapidly across Europe and Asia. In Europe it reduced the population by a third. But by the

1

2

demographers

scientists who study population patterns

industrial revolution

the time when work began to be done more by machines in factories than by hand at home

nineteenth century, the third technological revolution, the **industrial revolution,** had begun in Europe and its progress around the world continues today. This latest revolution has already raised the world's population to around 6 billion, six times what it was at the start of the nineteenth century. This is three times what it was in 1930, and almost twice what it was in 1960. The population may reach 10 billion before, as demographers predict, it stabilizes. At present, they think this will occur before the end of the twenty-first century.

Why do demographers predict that the world's population may begin to stabilize? The answer is that they believe that human populations go through different demographic stages (see Figure 10.1) and that these are linked to their societies' economic development. 3

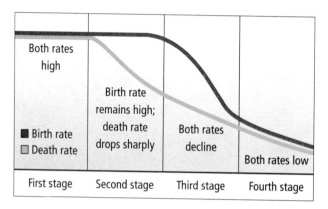

Figure 10.1 The demographic transition

In the first stage, birth and death rates are both high. This was the stage of the populations in Western Europe in the seventeenth century, before industrialization. In the second stage, there is a fall in death rates, because of improved health care and eating habits, but there is no change in birthrates. Populations in Western Europe entered the second stage after industrialization, but many countries in the developing world are still at this stage. In the third stage, social changes bring about a decline in the birthrate and the death rate, and the population begins to stabilize. Many Western countries reached this stage when they became highly industrialized. Today Taiwan, South Korea, and Argentina, for example, are in this stage. The fourth stage – with low birth and death rates – has been reached by a small number of highly industrialized countries today – for example, the United States, Japan, and some countries in Western Europe. These countries are moving close to **zero population growth** – a situation where birthrates are lower than death rates. 4

zero population growth

when birth rates are lower than death rates

What are the social changes that can bring about a decline in birthrates? Why do people in many countries of the world have fewer children now than in the past? In Europe, around the start of the twentieth century, population growth rates reached a high point and then began to fall, as people chose to have smaller families and use modern methods of birth control. This move to smaller families was linked to social changes. In poor rural or farming societies, children were needed to work in the fields and to take care of their parents in old 5 age. However, in richer urban societies typical of the twentieth century, they were not needed in this way. In fact, children were seen as costly to educate, clothe, and feed — in other words, it was better economics to have a small number of children. Another factor was that as child death rates fell, people became more confident that their children would survive to adulthood. They did not need to have a lot of children to make sure that one or two survived.

Now, although it varies from country to country, the fertility rate – the number of children per woman – is declining overall. The average world rate is now 2.9, but Table 10.1 perhaps gives a better picture of the situation. It shows that fertility rates are still very high in poor, developing nations, particularly in Africa. In fact, because of this, Africa's population, over the last few years, has become larger than Europe's.

6

Ten countries with highest fertility rates		Ten countries with lowest fertility rates	
Niger	7.5	Bulgaria	1.09
Oman	7.1	Latvia	1.11
Ethiopia	7.0	Spain	1.16
Gaza	7.0	Czech Republic	1.17
Uganda	6.9	Italy	1.19
Angola	6.8	Slovenia	1.22
Somalia	6.8	Estonia	1.24
Burkina Faso	6.7	Russia	1.24
Mali	6.7	Belarus	1.27
Yemen	6.7	Ukraine	1.28

Table 10.1
Countries with highest and lowest fertility rates

Source: 1999 World Population Data Sheet, Population Reference Bureau.

There are other theories about population growth, in particular the **doomsday theories** first developed by Malthus in the late eighteenth century, and taken up again by some environmentalists in the 1960s and 1970s. Malthus suggested that food production would not be able to keep up with population growth, and that this would result in the death of hundreds of millions of people. It is true that today nearly one billion people around the world do not have enough food, but opponents of the doomsday theories say that famine is mainly the result of other social and economic factors – for example, war, poverty, and politics. The problem is not that there is not enough food. It is that the food cannot get to the people who need it because of other problems.

7

doomsday theories
theories about disasters that might end life on Earth

After you read

Task 1 READING FOR DETAIL

Complete this chart using information from paragraph 2 of the text.

Year	Population
10,000 years ago	*less than 10 million*
1 AD	
1000 AD	
1800 AD	
1930 AD	
1960 AD	
2000 AD	
2100 AD	

Task 2 LANGUAGE FOCUS: REFERRING BACK TO IDEAS IN THE TEXT

Writers use many words to refer back to ideas mentioned earlier in a
text, for example, *it, they, he, this, that, those, each,* and *one.* To understand a text fully, you need to be able to identify which ideas these
small words refer back to.

1 Look back at the text to find the meaning of the word in italics.

1 *Each* followed a technological revolution that dramatically increased the number
of people that the world could keep alive. (par. 2) _____ *population surge* _____

2 *The second* was the invention of farming, which began at the end of the last ice
age, about 10,000 years ago. (par. 2) _____

3 . . . and *its* progress around the world continues today. (par. 2) _____

4 . . . but many countries in the developing world are still at *this* stage. (par. 4)

_____

5 Today Taiwan, South Korea, and Argentina, for example, are in *this* stage.
(par. 4) _____

6 . . . *they* were not needed in this way. (par. 5) _____

7 *It* is that the food cannot get to the people who need it because of other
problems. (par. 7) _____

2 Compare your answers with a partner.

Task 3 EXPLAINING THE TEXT IN YOUR OWN WORDS

A useful strategy to help you understand and remember a text containing complex ideas is to tell someone else about what you have read. (This is like the *Recite* part of the SQR3 approach – see page 89.) It will be easier for your listener if you use some of your own words, and if you give some interesting examples – from the text or from your own knowledge.

1 Re-read the parts of the text that answer the questions below.

1 What is the relationship between population and technological revolutions? (par. 2)
2 What is the relationship between population and social change? (par. 5)
3 What is the current situation with fertility rates around the world? (par. 6 and Table 10.1)
4 What do the doomsday theorists say and why? What do their opponents say? (par. 7)

2 Work with a small group. Choose one question each from step 1 and explain the answer to the group. As you listen to a member of your group answer his or her question, try to be an active listener. This means you should ask for clarification, try to restate what he or she is saying, or help by offering your own examples. Here are some phrases to help you be an active listener:

- Asking for clarification: "Could you explain a little more what you mean by . . . ?"
- Restating: "I see, so what you mean is . . ." or "I see, so you're saying that . . ."
- Offering examples: "So one example would be . . ."

Task 4 READING ACTIVELY

1 Look back through the text once more. Find information that supports the prediction that world population will stabilize within this century. Also find information that suggests it might not.

2 Discuss the following questions with a small group, using the information you found in step 1 and your own knowledge and ideas:

1 How confident are you that the world's population will stabilize over the next century?
2 If you were "president of the world," what would you do about population control?

Preparing to read

THINKING ABOUT THE TOPIC

1 | Make notes about a city that you are familiar with.

City: _____

Population (approximate): _____

Positive aspects of life in this city:

_____

_____

_____

Negative aspects of life in this city:

_____

_____

_____

_____

2 | Tell a partner about the city.

3 | Discuss with your partner whether you would rather live in an urban (city) area or a rural (country) area and why.

PREPARING FOR A SHORT-ANSWER TEST

Sometimes in college classes you are given the questions you will be asked about a text before you read the text. Thinking about these questions ahead of time will help you focus on the important ideas in your reading and note taking.

Read the six questions in Task 1, Writing Short-Answers to Test Questions, on page 222. Then skim the text quickly with these questions in mind. Do not try to answer them, but get an idea of where in the text you will find the answers.

Now read

Now read the text "Flight to the Cities." When you have finished, turn to the tasks on page 222.

2 FLIGHT TO THE CITIES

Picture these scenes:

- A group of mothers talk and laugh in a small neighborhood park as their children play close by.
- Angry commuters get stuck in early morning traffic and arrive at work up to two hours late.
- Two friends walk to the theater after work one evening and have coffee afterward in a cafe near the theater.
- A fight between two street gangs begins and the police are called by residents.
- An old woman lives alone in an apartment and talks to no one but her small pet cat most days of the week.
- People from a variety of social and racial backgrounds come together to sell their arts and crafts at a street market.
- A man grabs a woman's bag and knocks her to the ground as she does her shopping.

1

Each scene reflects an aspect of modern city life. Some are positive and some are negative, but all would be familiar to people who live in cities in many parts of the world. This mix of good and bad is one reason why social theorists cannot agree on the effect that city life has on its residents. Is the effect largely positive or is it largely negative?

2

Theories of city living

Some theorists believe that the conditions of urban life harm the people who live in cities. Louis Wirth, for example, argued in the 1930s that the huge numbers of people, population density, and great social diversity of cities led to alienation, impersonal relations, and stress. Many since then have agreed with him (for example, Sennett 1991). People live physically close to one another but are socially distant. They

3

make few friendships outside their own racial, social, or economic group. And they are constantly attacked on all sides by a variety of sights, sounds, and smells. They are frequently bumped by others on the street. They hear their neighbors' radios through thin apartment walls, and sirens wailing at all hours of the day and night.

However, not all theorists agree with Wirth's negative view of city living. Some say that the city does not make much difference in people's lives and that no matter how big a city is, people are involved in a small circle of friends and relatives. Palisi and Canning (1983), for example, found that city residents live their personal lives similarly to people in rural areas – visiting relatives at least once a week and so on. Gans (1982) found that people in ethnic neighborhoods of large cities had a strong sense of community. 4

Still other theorists (for example, Fischer 1984) say that the urban environment actually enriches people's lives by offering diverse opportunities and creating and strengthening various subcultures – college students, artists, etc. In general, city inhabitants also have access to better facilities and opportunities, in housing, entertainment, schools, and restaurants, for example. 5

Thio (1997) believes that none of these three theories presents the whole truth about city life or captures the love-hate relationship people have with cities. He cites a 1986 survey by Blundell, which indicates that most New Yorkers consider their city an urban hellhole, with its big city problems such as crime, homelessness, racial tension, heavy taxes, and high rents. Still, they very much like living in "the Big Apple." To them, the fast pace, the convenient, go-all-night action of the city, and its rich ethnic and cultural mix outweigh the negative aspects (Blundell 1986). 6

Increasing urbanization

Whatever the effects of living in the city may be, more and more people in countries all over the world are moving from rural to urban areas. This process is called **urbanization**. 7

urbanization

the process of more and more people moving from rural to urban areas

Many people are attracted to the varied cultural opportunities that cities offer.

In 1900, only one-tenth of the world's population lived in cities. **8** Today, for the first time in history, half the population lives in cities – and in 30 years' time it may rise to as much as three-quarters. The urban population is increasing at a rate of a quarter of a million people per day – the equivalent of a new London every month. (Rogers 1998).

Since the Industrial Revolution, people have been moving to the **9** cities because of the belief that there were more jobs and higher wages there than in rural areas. Some move because their jobs disappear. Some move because their rural homelands become less comfortable places to live due to environmental damage. All are attracted to the city for its work opportunities and for its support services – roads, schools, hospitals (Pearce 1998).

Megacities

This flight to the cities has led to the phenomenon of megacities – cities **10** with populations of more than 10 million. At present there are about twenty. Tokyo is the world's most populous city with almost 27 million people. It faces enormous problems including traffic and air pollution. Like most cities around the world, it also faces a huge problem getting rid of everyday household garbage. It is estimated that within five years, Tokyo will run out of space for the 2.5 million tons of household garbage it buries each year in landfill sites around the city (Hajari 1997).

A number of other megacities including Mexico City, New York, São **11** Paulo, Shanghai, and Bombay face similar problems. However, it is not all bad news for large cities. Many are learning to manage their problems. Tokyo, for example, has improved its air standards over the past two decades through increased use of public transportation and anti-pollution technology. New York has had massive clean-up campaigns of its streets and waterways. São Paulo is creating a 300-kilometer bicycle system to reduce traffic congestion. These are positive signs that large cities around the world may overcome their problems.

Table 10.2
The Top Ten Cities

City	Population (in millions)
Tokyo	26.5
São Paulo	18.3
Mexico City	18.3
New York City	16.8
Bombay	16.5
Los Angeles	13.3
Calcutta	13.3
Dhaka	13.2
Delhi	13.0
Shanghai	12.8

Source: "World Urbanization Prospects: The 2001 Revision," UN Population Division website, March 2002.

Traffic is one of the biggest problems in all large cities.

After you read

Task 1 WRITING SHORT ANSWERS TO TEST QUESTIONS

1 Look back at the text and highlight the words and sentences that answer the test questions below.

   1 Describe one of the theories about the effect of cities on their inhabitants.
   2 What does the study of New Yorkers show?
   3 Give three reasons that people move to the cities.
   4 What is a megacity?
   5 What are three problems of megacities?
   6 Give one example of how a megacity has begun to manage its problems.

2 Without looking back at your highlighted sections, write short answers to the questions.

Task 2 LANGUAGE FOCUS: NOMINALIZATIONS

Writers often need to use language that allows them to "pack" many meanings into a limited space. One language feature they use is *nominalization*. Nominalizations are nouns created from other words. They are usually long and they often end with a suffix like *-ion, -ence, -ship, -ness, -ity,* or *-ment*. College texts make heavy use of nominalizations. But while nominalizations make it easier for writers to express their ideas, they can make it harder for the reader to understand the text.

When you see an unfamiliar nominalization and have trouble understanding the sentence it occurs in, read the sentence carefully to "unpack" the meaning, and look for any part of the nominalized word that is familiar to you. Look at this sentence, for example:

> Increasing *migration* from country areas to city areas has led to *overdevelopment* of some urban areas.

Now look at an example of how you could unpack the sentence:

> With more and more people migrating from country areas to city areas, many urban areas have become overdeveloped.

Here are some strategies to help you "unpack" nominalizations:

- Look for any familiar words or word-parts in the nominalizations.
- Find the nominalizations in the text, and read the sentences in which they occur.
- Share your ideas about the meanings of the nominalizations and the sentences.

1 Work with a partner to understand the nominalizations listed below.

density (par. 3)
diversity (par. 3)
alienation (par. 3)
homelessness (par. 6)
tension (par. 6)
inhabitants (par. 5)
equivalent (par. 7)
revolution (par. 8)
pollution (par. 9)
transportation (par. 10)
technology (par. 10)
congestion (par. 10)

2 Find a nominalization from the list above to use in the sentences below.

1 The population ___*density*___ of some cities is greater than others.
Meaning: The number of people living per square mile is higher in some cities than others.

2 The bigger the city, the greater the _____.
Meaning: The bigger the city, the more people feel that others do not care about them.

3 _____ is a feature of city life.
Meaning: Every day, city residents are likely to see people who have nowhere to live.

4 There is great social _____ in most cities.
Meaning: There are people from many different social groups in most cities.

5 Attempts are being made to ease the traffic _____.
Meaning: City planners are trying to do something about the way that streets get blocked with too much traffic.

6 Racial _____ can be a feature of both urban and rural areas.
Meaning: Individuals can feel uncomfortable and nervous about living side by side with people from other races in both urban and rural areas.

Task 3 PERSONAL WRITING

Do some personal writing on the topic of city life. Don't worry about grammar and spelling too much. You could describe a city you like or dislike. You could describe a good or bad city experience. You could write about some urban problems or their solutions.

Preparing to read

THINKING ABOUT THE TOPIC

1 Complete the questionaire below about caring for our planet.

Are you a friend of planet Earth?	Yes	No
1 Do you turn off lights and power when they are not needed?		
2 Do you avoid wasting water?		
3 Do you re-use products as much as possible (for example, plastic containers)?		
4 Do you keep kitchen and garden waste to use on your plants (composting)?		
5 Do you recycle paper, cardboard, and glass?		
6 Do you bring your own bag to the supermarket?		
7 Do you try to buy products that do not have excessive packaging?		
8 Do you buy household cleaning products that do not have unnecessary chemicals?		
9 Do you always put your trash in the trash can?		
10 Do you use public transportation regularly?		
11 Do you avoid polluting water with oils or chemicals?		
12 If you have a yard, do you take care of your trees?		

2 Share your answers with the class and find out which classmate is the most planet-friendly.

3 Conduct the survey below in your class. Record the numbers of students for each response. Then discuss the reasons for your answers.

How is the quality of the environment?	Very good	Fairly good	Fairly bad	Very bad
Of your local area?				
Of the whole country?				
Of the whole planet?				

Now read

Now read the text "The Environment." When you finish, turn to the tasks on page 228.

3 THE ENVIRONMENT

Social change can be caused by changes in the physical environment. A flood, an earthquake, or a hurricane, for example, may change how people live and relate to one another. However, changes in society – the way we live and the way we behave – may also affect the environment.

Scientists believe that human beings are responsible for today's major environmental problems. They say we have ignored two important principles of nature. First, **natural resources** have a limit. There is only so much life that each **ecosystem** (for example, a forest, a river, or an ocean) can support. Second, all our actions have consequences. If we try to change one aspect of nature, we end up changing others as well. For example, farmers used to use DDT, a toxic chemical, on their crops to kill pests. However, DDT got into the soil and water, and from there into plankton (very small plants and animals on which fish feed), into the fish that ate the plankton, and into the birds that ate the fish. The chemical also found its way into our food.

We can blame some environmental damage on ignorance or poverty, but most damage has nothing to do with either. A major cause of environmental problems is the fact that clean air, clean rivers, and other natural resources are public, not private, possessions. And, in Aristotle's words, "What is common to the greatest number gets the least amount of care." Individually, we gain by using these resources and so, in our own interests, we keep doing so. Eventually, the resources are damaged or run out, and then society as a whole has to pay the cost.

What, then, are our main environmental problems? The major ones are a decrease in natural resources and an increase in environmental pollution.

natural resources

usable materials that are supplied by nature, for example, gas, minerals, and wood

ecosystem

a community of living things depending on each other and the environment for survival

Diminishing natural resources

Although they make up less than 6 percent of the world's population, each year people in the United States use about 30 percent of the world's energy and raw materials (such as oil, water, and basic food crops such as wheat). Other industrialized nations also take more than their fair share. If this continues, soon there will be no resources for anybody to use. According to some estimates, the global supply of oil will last only fifty years. We are also endangering supplies of good farming land and water. For example, we are losing topsoil–the good, rich top layer of soil that plants need to grow well – at an alarming rate. In the worst cases, an inch of topsoil, which nature takes 100 to 1,500 years to form, is being destroyed in ten to twenty years.

Not everyone agrees about the future dangers. Some argue that the future will be better. They say that we will know better how to control our environment and that technology will provide us with new resources. For example, solar energy will replace coal and oil, plastic will replace tin and other metals. In fact, this has been happening for some time. However, producing some of these new resources may contribute to the second major environmental problem – pollution.

Environmental pollution

For a long time now, we have been producing more waste than nature can deal with. We have also created new toxic substances that cannot be recycled safely. The result is pollution. Air pollution, in particular, is a problem for us all.

There are many sources of air pollution but the greatest is the automobile. It accounts for at least 80 percent of air pollution. The pollutants – the gases and other materials that do the damage – get into our eyes, noses, and throats and can cause serious illnesses such as bronchitis and lung cancer. Industry is another major cause of air pollution. Burning coal, oil, and wood release carbon dioxide and other gases into the atmosphere. A thick blanket of these gases forms and traps heat within our atmosphere. This is called the *greenhouse effect*. The result of the greenhouse effect is **global warming.** Many scientists believe that global warming will cause worldwide flooding due to rising sea levels, serious climatic change, and social disruption (Stevens 1995; Lemonick 1995). Small low-lying island communities in the Pacific, for example, may lose their homes as ocean levels rise higher and higher.

Another problem relates to the **ozone layer** that surrounds our planet and protects us from the harmful rays of the sun. Now, because of the use of certain gases such as chlorofluorocarbons (used in refrigeration and air conditioners) there is a hole in the ozone layer. At present the hole is largest over the Antarctic.

global warming

increasing temperatures on the planet as a result of the greenhouse effect

ozone layer

the layer of gas that protects us from the sun

Saving the environment

Today, there is considerable awareness of the need to "save the environment." There are many "good news" stories about communities, governments, and industries that have worked together to protect our environment. In many countries around the globe "green" political parties are now having a strong influence, and environmental organizations such as Greenpeace are often asked for advice by governments and private organizations that are planning major developments (roads, bridges, mines, dams, etc.).

One of the most important achievements over the last decade has been progress toward the Kyoto Protocol, an international agreement to fight global warming. This treaty would require each participating country to reduce its level of greenhouse gas emissions. Another achievement has been the fact that many countries have banned the use of the kinds of gases that can destroy the ozone layer. In fact, there are signs that the ozone hole may be beginning to repair itself.

At a national level, there is the example of Suriname, in South America, which, in 1998, set aside 1.6 million hectares of its rain forests – about 10 percent of the entire country – as a reserve. The reserve is now protected from development and destruction.

Of course, individuals all over the world are trying to live in a way that is friendly to the environment – saving energy around the home and workplace, recycling paper and glass, using public transportation, and planting trees.

Greenpeace blocks the entry of an oil tanker into Long Beach Harbor off the California coast.

It is not uncommon today to see people picking up and recycling trash left in public recreation areas.

After you read

Task 1 READING FOR THE MAIN IDEA

1 | All of the sentences below express main ideas in the text. Which best sums up the main idea of the whole text?

   a We must recognize two important principles: natural resources are limited and all our actions have environmental consequences.

   b Changes in society may affect the environment.

   c A major cause of environmental problems is the fact that we tend to take less care of public natural resources, such as air and water, than of our private possessions.

   d The major environmental problems are a decrease in natural resources and an increase in environmental pollution.

   e Today, there is considerable awareness of the need to "save the environment."

2 | Which main idea from step 1 does the paragraph below illustrate?

A group of farmers uses a piece of public grassland for grazing* sheep. To make more money, one farmer increases the number of sheep he grazes on this piece of land. While he has the full benefit of the additional sheep, he may be damaging the land by overgrazing. Soon each farmer sees how the first farmer is making more money by having more sheep on the land and does the same. Eventually, the overgrazing destroys the land completely and no one can use it at all.

*grazing: putting animals on land where they can eat the grass

Task 2 THINKING ABOUT THE TOPIC

1 | In the chart below, list all the "good news" and all the "bad news" about the environment that you can find in the text.

Good News	Bad News

2 | Compare your chart with a small group and discuss:

   1 Do you think the news about the environment is mostly bad? mostly good? getting worse? getting better?

   2 Think back to the survey you did in "Thinking About the Topic," on page 224. What do you think now about the environment of your local area, the country, and the planet?

Task 3 UNDERSTANDING LINKING OF IDEAS

Writers often use linking words such as *in other words, for example*, or *as a result* to tell the reader what the relationship is between one sentence and the next. However, when there are no linking words, readers must figure out for themselves what relationship exists.

The five pairs of sentences below, from "The Environment," do not have linking words. For each pair, decide how the second sentence is related to the first. Select an answer from the following choices:

a It gives a consequence or effect of something described in the first sentence.
b It explains or clarifies the idea in the first sentence using different words.
c It gives an example or fact to support the statement in the first sentence.

  _b_   **1** First, natural resources have a limit. There is only so much life that each ecosystem (for example, a forest, a river, or an ocean) can support.

       2 If this continues, soon there will be no resources for anybody to use. According to some estimates, the global supply of oil will last only fifty years.

       3 Some argue that the future will be better. They say that we will know better how to control our environment and that technology will provide us with new resources.

       4 There are many sources of air pollution but the greatest is the automobile. It accounts for at least 80 percent of air pollution.

       5 Burning coal, oil, and wood release carbon dioxide and other gases into the atmosphere. A thick blanket of these gases forms and traps heat within our atmosphere.

Task 4 WRITING A PROBLEM-SOLUTION TEXT

Writing about problems and proposing solutions is a common academic writing task. In a problem-solution text, you should describe the problem and its causes and then offer several solutions, indicating which one you think is best and why.

1 Work with a small group. Tell your group about an environmental problem in your town, city, or region.

2 Write about the environmental problem you presented in step 1. Use the questions below to organize your writing.

  1 What is the problem?
  2 What is the cause of the problem?
  3 What is being done about it?
  4 What do you think can be done about the problem – by government, by community groups, by individuals?

Preparing to read

THINKING ABOUT THE TOPIC

1 | Read these predictions for the future. Which do you think will happen within the next 100 years?

   1 The average life expectancy in industrialized countries will be about 100 years.
   2 There will be computerized robots that look, act, and think like humans.
   3 Many parents will have babies by cloning (genetically copying) themselves.
   4 It will take about one hour to complete an air journey that now takes twenty hours.
   5 We will program our cars to find their way to where we want to go.
   6 Nobody will work full-time (approximately forty hours a week).
   7 We will do all our shopping from home by computer.
   8 Books will not exist.
   9 The world will be governed by a single organization.
  10 There will be no wars.
  11 People will travel to the moon and other planets for vacations.
  12 We will discover life on other planets.

2 | Discuss your opinions with the class.

SKIMMING

Read the first and last paragraphs of the text, the first sentence of each paragraph, and the title of the boxed text. Now you should be able to complete this short summary of the text.

The future will definitely bring change to our lives. We can look for signs in the

1_____ (par. 1) to help us predict what the future might be like. These signs

include **2**_____ changes (par. 2), **3**_____ trends (par. 3), and advances

in **4**_____ (par. 4) and **5**_____ (par. 5). However, we can never be

6_____ about the future (par. 6). One area of activity that humans are likely to

continue is the search for life on other **7**_____ (boxed text).

Now read

Now read the text "Into the Future." When you finish, turn to the tasks on page 233.

4 INTO THE FUTURE

No matter which generation or which society we belong to, we can all expect to see great changes during our lives, and we can all expect our children and grandchildren to live in a different world from the one we know. Change is inevitable, but it is not random. There are patterns of change and there are signs in the present of what the future will bring. **1**

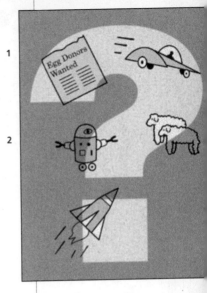

Demography, the science of population composition and change, can help us to predict what our world will be like. One prediction for the United States is based on the fact that working adults and the elderly will make up a larger part of the population and the young will be a smaller part. Some (such as Thio 1997) predict that this is likely to mean less crime and more employment opportunities because of fewer youth. It could also mean that, with more employed and elderly adults, society will be more conservative. A conservative society may encourage unsympathetic attitudes to criminals, to the poor, or to other disadvantaged groups in the community. Other results of conservatism might be resistance to the efforts of women and minorities to gain social and economic equality. **2**

What changes will the future bring?

Today's social trends are a signpost to tomorrow's world. Thio (1997) comments on the increasing focus on "rights" and gives a long list of examples including criminal rights, animal rights, the right to privacy, and the right to own a gun. He sees this as a consequence of a more individualistic focus in society. He suggests that with an increase in demands for individual rights, there will be less concern for the good of the society as a whole, and thus an increase in conflict between different groups. Others predict more religious activity as people try to make sense of their lives. This is based on the huge increase in church attendance in the 1990s and an increasing interest in nontraditional religions and cults. **3**

Popular discussions of the future very often focus on the way technology will affect our lives – cars that drive themselves, computerized robots that think like humans, and vacations on the moon. Some of these predictions may sound like absolute fantasy. However, if the developments of recent years are any indication, they are probably not. Only ten years ago, most of us thought electronic shopping, computerized body parts, and virtual reality games were science fiction. Now these things are here. **4**

Science is a very important indicator of the future. Every scientific advance or discovery gives us a clue about what the future will hold for society. Perhaps the most amazing scientific discovery in recent times was the birth of Dolly the sheep. Dolly was the first successful cloned animal – that is, she was the first animal ever to be created from a single adult cell. She is an exact copy of her biological mother. Since Dolly's birth, there has been debate about what this means for society in the future – because if we can clone sheep, we can surely clone humans. Some think that there are already signs that such things will eventually happen. For example, couples in the United States who can't or don't want to have children by natural methods can now select the **5** human egg and sperm they want through catalogues, audiotapes, or even computer order systems. One journalist has commented, "Ordering a frozen embryo is a little more emotionally complicated than ordering a pizza home delivered – but not so different logistically" (Hewitt 1998).

Thinking about the future is part of being human. It is endlessly fascinating. Part of the fascination is that nothing is ever certain. Even predictions based on sciences such as demographics may turn out to be wrong because of other factors such as technological or political developments. The only sure thing is that, in the future, for the individual in society, things will be different.

6

Life on other planets

Will the future bring the answer to the question "Is anyone else out there?" Surveys over the last decade show that roughly half the population in the United States believes in the existence of life on other planets. Since 1960 there have been more than sixty Search for Extra-Terrestrial Intelligence (SETI) projects. The most recent, Project Phoenix, used the most advanced equipment to date – 100 trillion times more sensitive than that used in the first SETI project. Unfortunately, however, the project found nothing.

How would society cope if we discovered extraterrestrial life? Ray Norris (1996), one of the Project Phoenix scientists warns, "If there really is a civilization out there that is millions of years more advanced than we are, will our science and arts suffer if we find out that all our brightest ideas have already been thought of? How will culture survive if we find that we're a primitive Palaeolithic tribe compared with our neighbors . . . ? This might sound far-fetched, but we should be aware of these risks, however remote, and be prepared to pull the plug on our search if necessary."

Despite this risk, it seems certain that we will continue to be fascinated by the possibility of life on other planets and that the search will continue.

"Is anyone else out there?"

After you read

Task 1 READING FOR DETAIL

1 The text mentions predictions for the future about the following features of society. Check (✔) if the prediction is for an *increase* or a *decrease*.

	Increase	Decrease
1 numbers of young people in the population	....	....
2 crime	....	....
3 job opportunities	....	....
4 conservative attitudes	....	....
5 negative attitude to disadvantaged groups	....	....
6 demand for individual rights	....	....
7 concern for the good of the whole society	....	....
8 interest in religion	....	....

2 Mark these statements true (T) or false (F), based on the text.

_____ **1** Predictions about technology are usually wrong.

_____ **2** Cloning of human beings seems quite possible.

_____ **3** It is not yet possible to order a particular type of child.

_____ **4** One reason that we like to predict the future is that we can never be sure if our predictions will be right or wrong.

_____ **5** The most recent project that searched for life on other planets found nothing.

_____ **6** Ray Norris is worried that we might find primitive, uncivilized cultures on other planets.

_____ **7** Norris warns that we should be ready to stop searching for life on other planets if it seems dangerous to us as a society.

3 Work with a partner. Compare and discuss your answers. Go back to the text to justify your answers.

Task 2 LANGUAGE FOCUS: VERBS TO USE INSTEAD OF "SAY" AND "WRITE"

> In writing assignments, you will often have to refer to what people have written, either exactly or in your own words (for example, *X says that* . . . or *X writes that* . . .). Note that the verb is usually in the present tense, unless a specific time is referred to (for example, *In 1995, Smith said that* . . . or *In 1995, Smith wrote that* . . .).
>
> You can add interest to your writing by sometimes using other verbs instead of *say* and *write*, for example:
>
> | | | | |
> |---|---|---|---|
> | agree | argue | assert | believe |
> | comment | disagree | discuss | estimate |
> | explain | identify | list | point to |
> | predict | question | report | state |
> | suggest | think | warn | |

1 Look back at the text and underline the verbs used instead of *say* or *write*.

2 Use the correct form of one of the verbs in the box above to complete these sentences. (There may be more than one possible answer.)

  1 In 1997, the World Health Organization _____ that there would be an increase in heart disease and other "lifestyle" illnesses.

  2 The writers _____ how many past predictions have been wrong.

  3 In 1977, a well-known computer executive _____ that there would be no use for home computers.

  4 A number of scientists _____ that machines are beginning to control the human race. Others _____, and say that humans will always be in control.

  5 Some medical experts _____ that the practice of cloning raises many disturbing issues.

  6 The study _____ a number of important factors to consider when discussing the future of computerized technology.

  7 The researchers _____ how they came to their conclusions about the impossibility of life on other planets.

  8 Communication experts _____ that artificial intelligence will change every aspect of our lives.

  9 The writer _____ that we will need to think very carefully as a species about the consequences of our scientific achievements.

  10 The demographers _____ that it will take about eighty years for the world population to stop increasing and begin to stabilize.

Task 3 CONDUCTING A SURVEY

The boxed text at the end of "Into the Future" tells us, "Surveys over the last decade reveal that roughly half the population in the United States believes in the existence of life on other planets."

1| Find out how many of your classmates believe there is life on other planets.

2| Conduct a survey outside the classroom to find out what other people believe. Work as a class to prepare the survey:

- Decide the wording of the questions.
- Decide who you will ask.
- Decide how many people you will ask. (If each person in the class agrees to ask ten people, you will have a good size sample.)
- Decide if you want to analyze your results by age, gender, or other factors, and if so, work out how you will do this.
- Decide how you will record the results gathered by the class.

3| Write up the findings.

4| Discuss how your results compare with the results reported in the boxed text.

CHAPTER 10 WRITING ASSIGNMENT

Choose one of the following topics as your chapter writing assignment.

1 Compare and contrast urban and rural life. Focus on three or four aspects – for example, entertainment, employment, friendships, social life, and so on.

2 Create a small brochure to encourage people to protect your local environment. Tell them why it is important, and include a list of things they could do at home, at work, at school, and in the community.

3 Write about what you think life will be like in the next fifty years. Use evidence from texts in this book to support your view. Choose *one* of these areas of activity:

- travel
- environment
- work
- home and family
- population
- relationships
- gender issues
- crime
- entertainment
- mass media

TEXT CREDITS

Chapter 1

5   From pp. 214, 225, Alex Thio, *Sociology: A Brief Introduction, 3e,* © 1997. Reprinted/adapted by permission by Allyn & Bacon.

6   Ibid., 226–227.

9   From p. 225, Alex Thio, *Sociology: A Brief Introduction, 3e,* © 1997. Reprinted/adapted by permission by Allyn & Bacon.

11   From U.S. Census Bureau, 1999 www.census.gov/population/socdemo/ms-la/tabad-2.txt.

From p. 228, Alex Thio, *Sociology: A Brief Introduction, 3e,* © 1997. Reprinted/adapted by permission by Allyn & Bacon.

17   From *Living Sociology, 1st edition,* by D. Knox © 1990. Reprinted with permission of Wadsworth, an imprint of the Wadsworth Group, a division of Thomson Learning. Fax 800 730-2215, pp. 108, 120.

18   Ibid., 120, 129–130.

24   From pp. 59–60, Alex Thio, *Sociology: A Brief Introduction, 3e,* © 1997. Reprinted/adapted by permission by Allyn & Bacon.

Chapter 2

30   From *Living Sociology, 1st edition,* by D. Knox © 1990. Reprinted with permission of Wadsworth, an imprint of the Wadsworth Group, a division of Thomson Learning. Fax 800 730-2215, p. 64.

31   Ibid., 69–70.

From "A Guide to European Kissing Etiquette" Blistex® website http://www.blistex.com/global_lips.htm. Reprinted/adapted with permission.

35   From pp. 69–70, Alex Thio, *Sociology: A Brief Introduction, 3e,* © 1997. Reprinted/adapted by permission by Allyn & Bacon.

39   Ibid., 330.

40   Ibid., 334–335.

42   From *Living Sociology, 1st edition,* by D. Knox © 1990. Reprinted with permission of Wadsworth, an imprint of the Wadsworth Group, a division of Thomson Learning. Fax 800 730-2215, pp. 419, 421–422.

46   From pp. 330, 332–333, Alex Thio, *Sociology: A Brief Introduction, 3e,* © 1997. Reprinted/adapted by permission by Allyn & Bacon.

Chapter 3

56   From pp. 193–194, Alex Thio, *Sociology: A Brief Introduction, 3e,* © 1997. Reprinted/adapted by permission by Allyn & Bacon.

From *Living Sociology, 1st edition,* by D. Knox © 1990. Reprinted with permission of Wadsworth, an imprint of the Wadsworth Group, a division of Thomson Learning. Fax 800 730-2215, p. 215.

59   From p. 194, Alex Thio, *Sociology: A Brief Introduction, 3e,* © 1997. Reprinted/adapted by permission by Allyn & Bacon.

61 From *Living Sociology, 1st edition*, by D. Knox © 1990. Reprinted with permission of Wadsworth, an imprint of the Wadsworth Group, a division of Thomson Learning. Fax 800 730-2215, p. 221.

62 Ibid.

63 Ibid.

67 From pp. 194, 197, Alex Thio, *Sociology: A Brief Introduction, 3e*, © 1997. Reprinted/adapted by permission by Allyn & Bacon.

68 Ibid., 194.

71 Ibid., 195.

72 Ibid.

75 From "Disappearing Dads" by Zuel, Bernard © 1999 *Sydney Morning Herald*, The Guide, May 31–June 6, p. 4. Reprinted/adapted with permission.

Chapter 4

77 From "I Want It So I Got It, But It's No Fun" by Julianne Greenfield © 1991 *Sydney Morning Herald*, June 8, p. 14.

79 From *Living Sociology, 1st edition*, by D. Knox © 1990. Reprinted with permission of Wadsworth, an imprint of the Wadsworth Group, a division of Thomson Learning. Fax 800 730-2215, pp. 218, 220.

84 Ibid., 221–223.

85 From "Doting Dad is a Busy Mr. Mum" by Debbie Cramsie, *Daily Mirror*, Sydney, Australia, 1989 July 21, p. 5. Reprinted/adapted with permission by the author.

87 From p. 196, Alex Thio, *Sociology: A Brief Introduction, 3e*, © 1997. Reprinted/adapted by permission by Allyn & Bacon.

88 From *Living Sociology, 1st edition*, by D. Knox © 1990. Reprinted with permission of Wadsworth, an imprint of the Wadsworth Group, a division of Thomson Learning. Fax 800 730-2215, pp. 212–213.

From pp. 196, 198–199, Alex Thio, *Sociology: A Brief Introduction, 3e*, © 1997. Reprinted/adapted by permission by Allyn & Bacon.

92 From *Living Sociology, 1st edition*, by D. Knox © 1990. Reprinted with permission of Wadsworth, an imprint of the Wadsworth Group, a division of Thomson Learning. Fax 800 730-2215, pp. 227.

Chapter 5

101 From *Living Sociology, 1st edition*, by D. Knox © 1990. Reprinted with permission of Wadsworth, an imprint of the Wadsworth Group, a division of Thomson Learning. Fax 800 730-2215, pp. 440–441.

From "Nation's Largest Radio Broadcasters Invest in USA Digital Radio," www.ibiquity.com/news/usadr_archive/news_invest.html Jan. 7, 1999. Sources: Arbitron, Inc. and According to Euromonitor International the world's leading provider of global Strategic market information. Reprinted/adapted with permission.

From "Time Spent Viewing — Households, and Time Spent Viewing — Persons" www.tvb.org/tvfacts/tvbasics. Source: Television Bureau of Advertising, Nielsen Media Research, NTI Annual Averages. Reprinted/adapted with permission.

From San Antonio Business Journal, www.bizjournals.com/sanantonio.

102 From *Living Sociology, 1st edition*, by D. Knox © 1990. Reprinted with permission of Wadsworth, an imprint of the Wadsworth Group, a division of Thomson Learning. Fax 800 730-2215, p. 442.

103 Ibid., 442–444, 449–450.

107 From *The Language of News Media* pp. 156–158 by Allan Bell. © 1991. Oxford: Blackwell Publishers Ltd. Reprinted/adapted with permission by the author.

108 Ibid.

111 Ibid.

112 From "Al Gore v. the Media" by Robert Parry © 2000, http://consortiumnews.com/2000/020100a.html. Reprinted with permission.

From *The Language of News Media* pp. 220–222 by Allan Bell. © 1991. Oxford: Blackwell Publishers Ltd. Reprinted/adapted with permission by the author.

Chapter 6

123   From *Living Sociology, 1st edition*, by D. Knox © 1990. Reprinted with permission of Wadsworth, an imprint of the Wadsworth Group, a division of Thomson Learning. Fax 800 730-2215, p. 454.

124   Ibid., 456.

      From "Hey, Wanna Buy Some Pix?" by R. Zoglin *Time* magazine, © 1997 Time Inc. reprinted by permission. Sept. 15, pp. 56–57.

125   Ibid.

      From *Living Sociology, 1st edition*, by D. Knox © 1990. Reprinted with permission of Wadsworth, an imprint of the Wadsworth Group, a division of Thomson Learning. Fax 800 730-2215, p. 456.

129   From "Wired Child" by Dr. Brent Waters, Consultant Child Psychiatrist, Sydney, Australia *Sydney Morning Herald* Section: Computers, 1998 Feb. 14, p. 14. Reprinted/adapted with permission of the author.

130   From "Dealing with Internet Misuse in the Workplace" www.netaddiction.com/workplace.htm. Reprinted/adapted with permission of Dr. Kimberly S. Young, Executive Director of Center for Online Addiction www.netaddiction.com.

133   Ibid.

135   From p. 337, Alex Thio, *Sociology: A Brief Introduction, 3e*, © 1997. Reprinted/adapted by permission by Allyn & Bacon.

136   Ibid., 337, 338.

138   From "Tied to the TV" by Catherine Armitage © 1991 Australia *Sydney Morning Herald*, Feb. 25, p. 12. Reprinted/adapted with permision by the author.

      From "Children Glued to the Tube, and Junk Food" by Andrew Darby 1998 Australia *The Age*, June 19, p. 5. Reprinted/adapted with permission of the author.

139   From *Living Sociology, 1st edition*, by D. Knox © 1990. Reprinted with permission of Wadsworth, an imprint of the Wadsworth Group, a division of Thomson Learning. Fax 800 730-2215, pp. 445–446.

      From "Time Spent Viewing — Households, and Time Spent Viewing — Persons" www.tvb.org/tvfacts/tvbasics. Source: Television Bureau of Advertising, Nielsen Media Research, NTI Annual Averages. Reprinted/adapted with permission.

      From San Antonio Business Journal, www.bizjournals.com/sanantonio.

      From The Henry J. Kaiser Family Foundation, "Kids & Media @ The New Millennium," November 1999. Reprinted/adapted with permission.

      From pp. 449–451, Anthony Giddens, *Sociology*, 1993. Cambridge, England: Polity Press in association with Blackwell Publishers Ltd. Reprinted by permission of the publisher.

      From "Children & Television: Frequently Asked Questions" http://www.cme.org/children/kids_tv/c_and_t.html. Reprinted with permission by Center for Media Education (www.cme.org).

      From *Living Sociology, 1st edition*, by D. Knox © 1990. Reprinted with permission of Wadsworth, an imprint of the Wadsworth Group, a division of Thomson Learning. Fax 800 730-2215, pp. 445–446, 456.

140   Ibid., 445–446.

      From "The Young Ones Take Aim at the Media" by Julie Delvecchio © 1995 *Sydney Morning Herald*, Section: News and Features, Sept. 24, p. 3.

Chapter 7

149   From *Living Sociology, 1st edition*, by D. Knox © 1990. Reprinted with permission of Wadsworth, an imprint of the Wadsworth Group, a division of Thomson Learning. Fax 800 730-2215, pp. 158–159.

From pp. 123, Alex Thio, *Sociology: A Brief Introduction, 3e*, © 1997. Reprinted/adapted by permission by Allyn & Bacon.

150 Ibid., 123–124.

From *Living Sociology, 1st edition*, by D. Knox © 1990. Reprinted with permission of Wadsworth, an imprint of the Wadsworth Group, a division of Thomson Learning. Fax 800 730-2215, pp. 160–161.

From "United States Crime Rates 1960–2000" by Christopher Effgen © 1997–2001 The Disaster Center, http://www.disastercenter.com/crime/uscrime.htm. Source: FBI, Uniform Crime Reports. Reprinted with permission by Christopher Effgen, owner, The Disaster Center.

153 From pp. 123–124, Alex Thio, *Sociology: A Brief Introduction, 3e*, © 1997. Reprinted/adapted by permission by Allyn & Bacon.

From "What Made This Boy A Killer?" by Simon Beck 1989 *South China Morning Post*, March 28, p. 17. Reprinted/adapted with permission by the author.

From Crime in the United States, 1999. Press Release, Oct. 15, 2000, http://www.fbi.gov/pressrel/pressrel00/cius99.htm.

From *Living Sociology, 1st edition*, by D. Knox © 1990. Reprinted with permission of Wadsworth, an imprint of the Wadsworth Group, a division of Thomson Learning. Fax 800 730-2215, pp. 161.

154 Ibid., pp. 161–162.

From pp. 133–134, Alex Thio, *Sociology: A Brief Introduction, 3e*, © 1997. Reprinted/adapted by permission by Allyn & Bacon.

155 From *Living Sociology, 1st edition*, by D. Knox © 1990. Reprinted with permission of Wadsworth, an imprint of the Wadsworth Group, a division of Thomson Learning. Fax 800 730-2215, p. 162.

From p. 127, Alex Thio, *Sociology: A Brief Introduction, 3e*, © 1997. Reprinted/adapted by permission by Allyn & Bacon.

159 From "Business: Your Money Fighting On-line Fraud" 1999 http://news.bbc.co.uk, April 7. Courtesy BBC News Online.

160 From "Computer Cops" by Jeff Lancaster 1998 *The Weekend Australian*, Aug. 8–9, p. IT 12. Jeff Lancaster is the Director of Jeff Lancaster Incorporated Threat Management and Writer. Reprinted/adapted with permission of the author.

From "The Technology Ethics Gap: New Rules Aren't Yet Clear" by Judith Harkham Semas. Reprinted with permission, High Technology Careers Magazine © 1998, Oct/Nov edition and Judith Harkham Semas, a business and technology writer based in San Jose, California.

163 From "Fingerprints and Other Impressions — The Techniques" by Katherine Ramsland, http://www.crimelibrary.com/forensics/fingerprints/4.htm. Copyright 2001, Courtroom Television Network LLC. Used by permission of the publisher.

164 From "Quietly, DNA Testing Transforms Sleuth's Job; But Practice Alarms Civil Libertarians" by David Rohde, *New York Times*, Late Edition (East Coast), March 9, pp. B1, B5. Copyright © 1999 The New York Times Co. Reprinted by permission.

Chapter 8

170 From *Living Sociology, 1st edition*, by D. Knox © 1990. Reprinted with permission of Wadsworth, an imprint of the Wadsworth Group, a division of Thomson Learning. Fax 800 730-2215, pp. 171–172.

174 From Ibraheem, Abdullah, "The Black Peoples' Prison Survival Guide," self-published on the Internet at http://www.cs.oberlin.edu/~pjaques/etext/prison-guide.html 1995. Reprinted/adapted with permission.

From pp. 120–121, 138–139, Anthony Giddens, *Sociology*, 1989. Cambridge, England: Polity Press in association with Blackwell Publishers Ltd. Reprinted by permission of the publisher.

From *Living Sociology, 1st edition,* by D. Knox © 1990. Reprinted with permission of Wadsworth, an imprint of the Wadsworth Group, a division of Thomson Learning. Fax 800 730-2215, pp. 174–175.

179   From "The Death Penalty" by Alex Thio (*Sociology Online 3rd edition*) © 1998. Reprinted/adapted with permission by the author.

184   From p. 139, Alex Thio, *Sociology: A Brief Introduction, 3e,* © 1997. Reprinted/adapted by permission by Allyn & Bacon.

Chapter 9

190   From Population Connection: www.populationconnection.org.

193   From pp. 40–41, Alex Thio, *Sociology: A Brief Introduction, 3e,* © 1997. Reprinted/adapted by permission by Allyn & Bacon.

194   From *Living Sociology, 1st edition,* by D. Knox © 1990. Reprinted with permission of Wadsworth, an imprint of the Wadsworth Group, a division of Thomson Learning. Fax 800 730-2215, p. 64.

195   From *Understanding Ways: Communicating Between Cultures* by K. O'Sullivan © 1994 Sydney: Hale and Ironmonger, pp 12–14, 18. Reprinted/adapted with permission.

From *Living Sociology, 1st edition,* by D. Knox © 1990. Reprinted with permission of Wadsworth, an imprint of the Wadsworth Group, a division of Thomson Learning. Fax 800 730-2215, p. 80.

199   From *Living Sociology, 1st edition,* by D. Knox © 1990. Reprinted with permission of Wadsworth, an imprint of the Wadsworth Group, a division of Thomson Learning. Fax 800 730-2215, p. 75.

200   From "Teens of '96: Alienated and Cynical." by A. Hornery © 1996 *Sydney Morning Herald*, Aug. 7, p. 3.

From "The Far-Out World of Cults" by Caroline Green 1995 *Focus*, Feb., pp. 34–38. Reprinted with permission on courtesy of Focus Magazine © National Magazine Company.

203   From *Living Sociology, 1st edition,* by D. Knox © 1990. Reprinted with permission of Wadsworth, an imprint of the Wadsworth Group, a division of Thomson Learning. Fax 800 730-2215, p. 400.

204   From "Fasten Your Seat Belts" by R. Neville © 2000 *Sydney Morning Herald, Good Weekend* magazine, Jan. 1, pp. 16–20. Reprinted/adapted with permission.

207   From "The Future is Now" by Jennifer Hewett © 1998 *Sydney Morning Herald*, Spectrum, Jan. 24, pp. S1, S6. Reprinted/adapted with permission by the author.

208   From pp. 267–269, Alex Thio, *Sociology: A Brief Introduction, 3e,* © 1997. Reprinted/adapted by permission by Allyn & Bacon.

From *Living Sociology, 1st edition,* by D. Knox © 1990. Reprinted with permission of Wadsworth, an imprint of the Wadsworth Group, a division of Thomson Learning. Fax 800 730-2215, p. 376.

209   From pp. 267–268, Alex Thio, *Sociology: A Brief Introduction, 3e,* © 1997. Reprinted/adapted by permission by Allyn & Bacon.

210   Ibid., 268.

Chapter 10

212   From Population Connection: www.populationconnection.org.

From p. 296, Alex Thio, *Sociology: A Brief Introduction, 3e,* © 1997. Reprinted/adapted by permission by Allyn & Bacon.

From "Population Paradox" by Francis G. Castles © 2000 *Sydney Morning Herald*, Jan. 12, p. 13. Reprinted/adapted with permission by the author.

From "1999 World Population Data Sheet." Copyright © 1999 Population Reference Bureau, May 1999, ISSN 0085–8315. Data prepared by demographers Carl Haub and Diana Cornelius. Reprinted with permission by Population Reference Bureau.

213 From "Population Bombshell" by Fred Pearce 1998 *New Scientist*, No 112, July 11, pp. 1–4. Reproduced with permission from New Scientist magazine, the global authority on science and technology news © RBI 2000 www.NewScientist.com.

214 Ibid.

From pp. 299–300, Alex Thio, *Sociology: A Brief Introduction*, 3e, © 1997. Reprinted/adapted by permission by Allyn & Bacon.

215 From "Population Bombshell" by Fred Pearce 1998 *New Scientist*, No. 112, July 11, pp. 1–4. Reproduced with permission from New Scientist magazine, the global authority on science and technology news © RBI 2000 www.NewScientist.com.

220 From p. 320, Alex Thio, *Sociology: A Brief Introduction*, 3e, © 1997. Reprinted/adapted by permission by Allyn & Bacon.

225 From *Living Sociology, 1st edition*, by D. Knox © 1990. Reprinted with permission of Wadsworth, an imprint of the Wadsworth Group, a division of Thomson Learning. Fax 800 730-2215, p. 395.

From p. 310, Alex Thio, *Sociology: A Brief Introduction*, 3e, © 1997. Reprinted/adapted by permission by Allyn & Bacon.

226 Ibid., pp. 308–311.

227 From "The Best of the Environment in 1998" *Time Asia*, Dec. 21, p. 63. © 1998 Time Inc. reprinted by permission.

228 From p. 310, Alex Thio, *Sociology: A Brief Introduction*, 3e, © 1997. Reprinted/adapted by permission by Allyn & Bacon.

232 From "Is Anyone Else Out There Listening?" by Professors Ray Norris and Gary Trompf © 1996 *Sydney Morning Herald*, April 7, p. 13. Reprinted/adapted with permission by Norris.

ART AND PHOTO CREDITS

Chapter 1

1, 3 © Gary Buss/Getty Images/FPG

2 © David R. Frazier Photolibrary (l), © Michael Newman/PhotoEdit (m), © Stewart Hughs/Getty Images/Stone (r)

4 © Peter Cade/Getty Images/Stone

5 © Ryan McVay/Getty Images/Photodisc (t), From Alex Thio, *Sociology: A Brief Introduction, 4th edition*, © 2000. Reprinted/adapted by permission by Allyn & Bacon. (b)

6 From www.census.gov/population/socdemo/hh-fam/FM-2.txt (t), From Alex Thio, *Sociology: A Brief Introduction, 3rd edition*, © 1997. Reprinted/adapted by permission by Allyn & Bacon. (b)

11 © CORBIS Stock Market (t), © Deborah Davis/PhotoEdit (b)

12 © Frank Pedrick/The Image Works (t), © Getty Images (b)

17 © Michael Newman/PhotoEdit (l, r)

23 © Lwa-Dann Tardif/CORBIS Stock Market

Chapter 2

29 © Tom Prettyman/PhotoEdit

31 © Chase Swift/CORBIS (l), © RB Studio/CORBIS Stock Market (r)

35 © Ed Bock/CORBIS Stock Market (t), © Syracuse Newspapers/Jim Commentucci/The Image Works (m), © Lawrence Manning/CORBIS (b)

38 © Jan Butchofsky-Houser/CORBIS (l), © Paul Conklin/PhotoEdit (m), © AFP/CORBIS (r)

39 © Joseph Sohm; ChromoSohm Inc./CORBIS

40 © James Leynse/CORBIS Saba (t), © Don Spiro/Getty Images/Stone (b)

45 © Myrleen F. Cate/PhotoEdit

Chapter 3

51, 53 © Scott Speakes/CORBIS

54 Courtesy of American Plastic Toys, Inc. (l), MONOPOLY ® © 2002 Hasbro, Inc. Used with permission. (m), SuperSoaker ® is a registered Trademark of Hasbro, All Rights Reserved; Courtesy of Larami Limited, A subsidiary of Hasbro. (r)

55 © Mug Shots/CORBIS Stock Market (t), © Gerhard Steiner/CORBIS Stock Market (m), © Rob Lewine/CORBIS Stock Market (b)

56 © Michael Newman/PhotoEdit (l), © Mark Richards/PhotoEdit (r)

60 Illustration from *The Fairy Tales of the Brothers Grimm*, p. 131, New York: Derrydale Books, distributed by Crown Publishers, Inc., © 1987.

62 THE POWERPUFF GIRLS and all related characters and elements are trademarks of Cartoon Network © 2001. An AOL Time Warner Company. All Rights Reserved.

64 Illustrations from *The Red Fairy Book* by Andrew Lang, edited by Brian Alderson, illustrated by Faith Jaques. Kestrel Books, 1976. Pages 274 and 277. Illustrations © Faith Jacques 1976. Reproduced by permission of Penguin Books Ltd.

67 © Michael Newman/PhotoEdit (t), From Alex Thio, *Sociology: A Brief Introduction, 4th edition,* © 2000. Reprinted/adapted by permission by Allyn & Bacon. (b)

68 © Michael Newman/PhotoEdit (t), © Giles Keyte/Universal/MPTV.net (b)

71 © The New Yorker Collection 1992 Robert Weber. From cartoonbank.com. All Rights Reserved.

72 © The New Yorker Collection 1986 Eldon Dedini. From cartoonbank.com. All Rights Reserved.

Chapter 4

77 © Michael Goldman/Getty Images/FPG (l), © Mug Shots/CORBIS Stock Market (r)

78 © Tony May/Getty Images/Stone

83 © Tony Freeman/PhotoEdit

84 © R.B. Studio/CORBIS Stock Market

85 © Chuck Savage/CORBIS Stock Market

87 © FPG International/Getty Images (l), © AFP/CORBIS (r), From Alex Thio, *Sociology: A Brief Introduction, 3rd edition,* © 1997. Reprinted/adapted by permission by Allyn & Bacon. (b)

88 From Alex Thio, *Sociology: A Brief Introduction, 4th edition,* © 2000. Reprinted/adapted by permission by Allyn & Bacon.

91 © Ed Taylor Studio/Getty Images/FPG

93 © Romilly Lockyer/Getty Images/Image Bank

Chapter 5

101 © Eric Fowke/PhotoEdit

102 © Reuters NewMedia Inc./CORBIS

107 © AP/Wide World Photos (t), © Sam Mircovich/Reuters/Getty Images (b)

108 © AP/Wide World Photos

111 © Jonathan Nourok/PhotoEdit

117 © Randy Faris/CORBIS

118 © Bill Aron/PhotoEdit (t), Courtesy of Toyota Motor North America (b)

119 © 1999 National Fluid Milk Processor Promotion Board

Chapter 6

122 © David Burnett/Contact Press Images (l), © Tim Graham/CORBIS Sygma (r)

123 © AP/Wide World Photos

124 © Chung Sung-Jun/Newsmakers/Liaison/Getty Images

125 © Mitchell Gerber/CORBIS

129 © Ephraim Ben-Shimon/CORBIS

130 © Robin L. Sachs/PhotoEdit

131 © David Young-Wolff/PhotoEdit

135 © Reuters NewMedia Inc./CORBIS

136 © AFP/CORBIS

139 © Rob Lewine/CORBIS Stock Market

140 © Bud Gray/MPTV.net (t), © Tri Star/MPTV.net (l), © S.S.Archives/Shooting Star (r)

144 © The New Yorker Collection 1991 Michael Crawford. From cartoonbank.com. All Rights Reserved.

Chapter 7

145, 147 © Dante Burn-Forti/Getty Images/Stone

146 © Bettman/CORBIS. Sherlock Holmes © 1932 Twentieth Century Fox. All rights reserved.

148 From *Living Sociology, 1st edition,* by D. Knox © 1990. Reprinted with permission of Wadsworth, an imprint of the Wadsworth Group, a division of Thomson Learning. Fax 800 730-2215, p. 159.

149 © Bill Aron/Photo Edit

150 © Ken Light/CORBIS Saba

153 © AP/Wide World Photos

154, 155 © David Young-Wolff/Getty Images/Stone

159 © Deborah Schwartz/Getty Images/Stone

160 © Getty Images (t), © Joel Gordon Photography 1996 (b)

162 © Tribune Media Services, Inc. All Rights Reserved. Reprinted with permission. (l), © Michael Newman/PhotoEdit (m), © Charles Thatcher/Getty Images/Stone (r)

163 © Telegraph Colour Library/Getty Images/FPG

164 From "Quietly, DNA Testing Transforms Sleuth's Job; But Practice Alarms Civil Libertarians" by David Rohde, *New York Times*, Late Edition (East Coast), March 9, pp. B1, B5. Copyright © 1999 The New York Times Co. Reprinted by permission.

167 From *Sourcebook of Criminal Justice Statistics 1997*. US Department of Justice, Bureau of Justice Statistics. Washington, DC.

Chapter 8

169 © Bonnie Kamin/PhotoEdit

170 © Dennis MacDonald/PhotoEdit

172 From www.bop.gov/inmate

173 © Joel Gordon Photography 1996

174 © A. Ramey/PhotoEdit

177 © Reuters NewMedia Inc./CORBIS

178 © Peter Silva/Reuters/Getty Images

179 From USA Executions by Year and State, http://web.cis.smu.edu/~deathpen/execyrst1.html. Reprinted with permission of Dr. Rick Halperin, History Professor – SMU and: PRESIDENT, TEXAS COALITION TO ABOLISH the DEATH PENALTY and FORMER CHAIR OF THE BOARD OF DIRECTORS, AMNESTY INTERNATIONAL USA.

183 © Susan Van Etten/PhotoEdit

184 © CORBIS

188 From Alex Thio, *Sociology: A Brief Introduction, 4th edition*, © 2000. Reprinted/adapted by permission by Allyn & Bacon.

Chapter 9

189, 191 Hulton/Archive by Getty Images (l), © Barbara Stitzer/PhotoEdit (r)

190 © Peter Turnley/CORBIS (l), © Tony Freeman/PhotoEdit (r)

193 © AP/Wide World Photos (t), © Ronnie Kaufman/CORBIS Stock Market (m), © Phil Borden/PhotoEdit (l), © Bob Krist/CORBIS (r),

194 © Michael Newman/PhotoEdit (t), © AP/Wide World Photos (b)

195 © Arthur Montes De Oca (l), © AP/Wide World Photos (r)

196 © Spencer Grant/PhotoEdit (t), © William Whitehurst/CORBIS Stock Market (fl), © Philip Bailey/CORBIS Stock Market (l), © Telegraph Colour Library/Getty Images/FPG (r), © James A. Sugar/CORBIS (fr)

198 © FPG International/Getty Images (t), © Paul Conklin/PhotoEdit (b)

199 © Ken Reid/Getty Images/FPG (l), © John Henley/CORBIS Stock Market (r)

202 © David Young-Wolff/PhotoEdit (l), © Archive Photos/Getty Images (m), © Tony Freeman/PhotoEdit (r)

203 © AJA Productions/Getty Images/The Image Bank

204 © AFP/CORBIS

207 © Don Mason/CORBIS Stock Market

Chapter 10

213 © Ken Fisher/Getty Images/Stone

214 From Alex Thio, *Sociology: A Brief Introduction, 5th edition*. Boston: Allyn & Bacon, © 2003.

215 From "1999 World Population Data Sheet." Copyright © 1999 Population Reference Bureau, May 1999, ISSN 0085–8315. Data prepared by demographers Carl Haub and Diana Cornelius. Reprinted with permission by Population Reference Bureau.

219 © Dennie Cody/Getty Images/FPG (l), © Yves Marcoux/Getty Images/Stone (r), © John M. Roberts/CORBIS Stock Market (m), © Jerry Driendl/Getty Images/FPG (b)

220 © Lee Snider/Photo Images

221 From "The Top Ten Cities" from "World Urbanization Prospects: the 2001 Revision, Data Tables and Highlights, ESA/P/WP.173." United Nations, Population Division website, March 2002, www.unpopulation.org. Reprinted with permission by the United Nations. (t), © Telegraph Colour Library/Getty Images/FPG (b)

225 © Paul Steel/CORBIS Stock Market (l), © Josef Beck/Getty Images/FPG (r)

227 © AP/Wide World Photos (t), © David Young-Wolff/PhotoEdit (b)

232 © Telegraph Colour Library/Getty Images/FPG

TASK INDEX

Page numbers in boldface indicate tasks that are headed by commentary boxes.